PENGUIN (●) CLASSICS

THE EPIC OF GILGAMESH

'Humankind's first literary achievement ... *Gilgamesh* should compel us as the well-spring of which we are inheritors ... Andrew George provides an excellent critical and historical introduction' Paul Binding, *Independent on Sunday*

'This volume will endure as one of the milestone markers ... [Andrew George] expertly and easily conducts his readers on a delightful and moving epic journey' Samuel A. Meier, *The Times Literary Supplement*

'Appealingly presented and very readably translated ... it still comes as an exhilarating surprise to find the actions and emotions of the Sumerian superhero coming to us with absolute immediacy over 30-odd centuries' *Scotsman*

'Andrew George has formed an English text from the best of the tablets, differentiating his complex sources but allowing the general reader a clear run at one of the first enduring stories ever told' Peter Stothard, *The Times*

'An exemplary combination of scholarship and lucidity ... very impressive ... invaluable as a convenient guide to all the different strands which came together to produce the work we now call *Gilgamesh*' Alan Wall, *Literary Review*

WINNER OF THE BRITISH-KUWAIT FRIENDSHIP SOCIETY PRIZE IN MIDDLE EASTERN STUDIES

The Epic of Gilgamesh is best known from a version called 'He who saw the Deep', which circulated in Babylonia and Assyria in the first millennium BC. The Babylonians believed this poem to have been the responsibility of a man called Sîn-liqe-unninni, a learned scholar of Uruk whom modern scholars consider to have lived some time between 1300-1000 BC. However, we now know that 'He who saw the Deep' is a revision of one or more earlier versions of the epic. The oldest surviving fragments of the epic are the work of an anonymous Babylonian poet writing more than 3700 years ago. The Babylonian epic was composed in Akkadian, but its literary origins lie in five Sumerian poems of even greater antiquity. The Sumerian texts gained their final form probably as court entertainments sung for King Shulgi of Ur of the Chaldees, who reigned in the 21st century BC.

ANDREW GEORGE was born in 1955 in Haslemere, Surrey. He was educated at Christ's Hospital, Horsham, and the University of Birmingham, where he studied Assyriology. For a while he kept a public house in Darlaston. He began teaching Akkadian and Sumerian language in 1983 at the University of London's School of Oriental and African Studies, where he is now Professor of Babylonian. He is also an Honorary Lecturer at the university's Institute of Archaeology.

His research has taken him many times to Iraq to visit Babylon and other ancient sites, and to museums in Baghdad, Europe and North America to read the original clay tablets on which the scribes of ancient Iraq wrote. He has published extensively on Babylonian literature and religion.

THE EPIC OF
GILGAMESH

*The Babylonian Epic Poem and Other Texts
in Akkadian and Sumerian*

TRANSLATED and with an introduction by
ANDREW GEORGE

PENGUIN BOOKS

PENGUIN BOOKS

Published by the Penguin Group
Penguin Books Ltd, 80 Strand, London WC2R 0RL, England
Penguin Putnam Inc., 375 Hudson Street, New York, New York 10014, USA
Penguin Books Australia Ltd, 250 Camberwell Road, Camberwell, Victoria 3124, Australia
Penguin Books Canada Ltd, 10 Alcorn Avenue, Toronto, Ontario, Canada M4V 3B2
Penguin Books India (P) Ltd, 11 Community Centre, Panchsheel Park, New Delhi – 110 017, India
Penguin Books (NZ) Ltd, Cnr Rosedale and Airborne Roads, Albany, Auckland, New Zealand
Penguin Books (South Africa) (Pty) Ltd, 24 Sturdee Avenue, Rosebank 2196, South Africa

Penguin Books Ltd, Registered Offices: 80 Strand, London WC2R 0RL, England

www.penguin.com

First published in Great Britain by Allen Lane The Penguin Press 1999
Published in Penguin Books 2000

8

Copyright © Andrew George, 1999
All rights reserved

Map on pp. lviii–lix by Nigel Andrews

Illustrations on pp. iii, 26, 45, 53, 60, 72, 92, 103, 110, 117, 121, 125, 130,
146, 160, 175, 185 and 200 by Joanna Richards

Illustrations on pp. 26, 117 and 160 after drawings by Tessa Rickards from *Gods,
Demons and Symbols of Ancient Mesopotamia* by Jeremy Black and Anthony Green
© the British Museum, British Museum Press

Illustrations on pp. xxix, 3, 13, 31, 64, 87, 128, 134, 213 and 216
by Andrew George

The moral right of the author has been asserted

Printed in England by Clays Ltd, St Ives plc

Contents

List of Figures

24 Detail from a mosaic panel known as the 'Royal Standard', twenty-seventh century BC, Ur. British Museum, WA 121201. Line drawing by Joanna Richards.
25 Limestone plaque depicting wrestlers, middle of third millennium BC, Tutub. Iraq Museum, Baghdad. Line drawing by Joanna Richards.

Appendix

26 British Museum tablet fragments WA K 3423+Sm 2097+Rm 579, K 8589+Sm 1681 and Rm 751+34853+35546. Photograph copyright the British Museum.
27 Cuneiform text, fourth century BC, Uruk. Iraq Museum, Baghdad, IM 76873. Line drawing by the author.
28 Details of British Museum tablet fragments WA K 3423+Sm 2097+Rm 579, K 8589+Sm 1681 and Rm 751+34853+35546. Line drawings by the author.

Preface

My first encounter with the magic of Gilgamesh came as a boy when I read this book's predecessor in the Penguin Classics series, Nancy Sandars's prose synthesis of the ancient poems (*The Epic of Gilgamesh*, 1960). At university I was given the happy opportunity of reading some of the cuneiform text of the epic under the guidance of the foremost expert in Babylonian literature, W. G. Lambert. The work of recovering the text of Gilgamesh from the original clay tablets and preparing what will be only the third scholarly edition of the Babylonian epic has been my principal object of research for the past dozen years. During this time I am lucky to have benefited from the advice and encouragement of many of Gilgamesh's latter-day devotees. Among them I single out for special mention David Hawkins, my colleague at the School of Oriental and African Studies, who has also contributed the translation of a Hittite fragment on p. 55, and Aage Westenholz of the University of Copenhagen, who in the course of making an independent translation of the epic into Danish travelled with me the long and arduous road to Uta-napishti and back. To Antoine Cavigneaux of the University of Geneva and Farouk N. H. Al-Rawi of the University of Baghdad I am indebted for the use of their unpublished book on the Sumerian composition we know as the Death of Bilgames. Douglas Frayne of the University of Toronto has shared with me his work in progress on the Sumerian Gilgamesh poems. On several obscure points of Sumerian Mark Geller of University College London and Steve Tinney of the University of Pennsylvania have come to my aid.

The modern translator of Gilgamesh has the advantage of standing on the shoulders of those editors and translators who have gone before him. The list of scholars who during the last century and a half have contributed materially to the recovery of the ancient sources is long indeed, but among them one should not fail to honour George Smith, who was the first to decipher much of the Babylonian epic and whose pioneering translations of 1875 and 1876 gave the world a first glimpse of its majesty; Paul Haupt, who in 1891 first collected the cuneiform text of the epic; Peter Jensen, whose transliterations of 1900 were the first comprehensive modern edition; R. Campbell Thompson, who in 1930 brought up to date the work of both Haupt and Jensen; and Samuel Noah Kramer, who in the 1930s and '40s first pieced together the Sumerian poems of Gilgamesh. In the often unsung task of adding to our knowledge of the text of the epic no contemporary Assyriologists can match the achievements of Irving Finkel of the British Museum, Egbert von Weiher of the University of Cologne and, especially, W. G. Lambert of the University of Birmingham.

New pieces of Gilgamesh continue to appear. This paperback edition differs from its hardback predecessor in being able to use on p. 90 a fragment of Tablet XI that came to light only in June 1999. My thanks go to its discoverer, Stefan M. Maul of the University of Heidelberg, and to the Vorderasiatisches Museum, Berlin, and the Deutsche Orient-Gesellschaft for permission to quote it.

A.R.G.

London,
June 1999

Introduction

Ever since the first modern translations were published more than one hundred years ago, the Gilgamesh epic has been recognized as one of the great masterpieces of world literature. One of the early translations, by the German Assyriologist Arthur Ungnad, so inspired the poet Rainer Maria Rilke in 1916 that he became almost intoxicated with pleasure and wonder, and repeated the story to all he met. 'Gilgamesh,' he declared, 'is stupendous!' For him the epic was first and foremost 'das Epos der Todesfurcht', the epic about the fear of death. This universal theme does indeed unite the poem, for in examining the human longing for life eternal, it tells of one man's heroic struggle against death – first for immortal renown through glorious deeds, then for eternal life itself; of his despair when confronted with inevitable failure, and of his eventual realization that the only immortality he may expect is the enduring name afforded by leaving behind some lasting achievement.

The fear of death may be one of the epic's principal themes but the poem deals with so much more. As a story of one man's 'path to wisdom', of how he is formed by his successes and failures, it offers many profound insights into the human condition, into life and death and the truths that touch us all. The subject that most held the attention of the royal courts of Babylonia and Assyria was perhaps another topic that underlies much of the poem: the debate on the proper duties of kingship, what a good king should do and should not do. The epic's didactic side is also evident in the exposition of a man's responsibilities to his family. The eternal conflict of nurture and nature – articulated as the benefits of civilization over savagery – is also examined, as too are the rewards of friendship, the nobility of heroic enterprise and the immortality of fame. Artfully woven into Gilgamesh's own story are the traditional tale of the Deluge, the great flood by which early in human history the gods sought to destroy mankind, and a long description of the gloomy realm of the dead. From all this Gilgamesh emerges as a kind of cultural hero. The wisdom he received at the ends of the earth from the survivor of the Deluge, Uta-napishti, enabled him to restore the temples of the land and their rituals to their ideal state of antediluvian perfection. In the course of his heroic adventures it seems Gilgamesh was the first to dig oases in the desert, the first to fell cedars on Mount Lebanon, the first to discover the techniques of killing wild bulls, of sailing ocean-going craft and of diving for coral.

Amid the momentous themes, the epic is full of absorbing moments, often just minor, incidental details which serve every so often to catch the imagination or to lighten the mood. The text explains in passing why temples take in orphans, how there came to be two New Year's Days in the Babylonian calendar, how the Levantine Rift Valley was riven, how dwarfs came about, why nomads live in tents, why some prostitutes eke out a living on the cruel fringes of society and others enjoy a life of attentive luxury, how it is that doves and swallows cleave to human company but ravens do not, why snakes shed their skins, and so on.

The spell of Gilgamesh has captured many since Rilke, so that over the years the story has been variously reworked into plays, novels and at least two operas. Translations have now appeared in at least sixteen languages and more appear year by year, so that the last decade has added ten to the dozens already published. Among the ten are two in English. Why so many, and why another? There are two replies that answer both these questions. First, a great masterpiece will always attract new renditions and will go on doing so while its worth is still recognized. This goes for Homer and Euripides, Virgil and Horace, Voltaire and Goethe – indeed any classic text, ancient or modern – as well as for Gilgamesh. But the difference with Gilgamesh, as also with the other works of ancient Mesopotamian literature, is that we keep finding more of it. Seventy years ago we possessed fewer than forty manuscripts from which to reconstruct the text and there were large gaps in the story. Now we have more than twice that number of manuscripts and fewer gaps. As the years pass the number of available sources will assuredly go on rising. Slowly our knowledge of the text will become better and better, so that one day the epic will again be complete, as it last was more than two thousand years ago.

Sooner or later, as new manuscripts are discovered, this translation, like all others, will be superseded. For the moment, based as it is on first-hand study of very nearly all the available sources, unpublished as well as published, the present rendering offers the epic in its most complete form yet. However, gaps still remain and many preserved lines are still fragmentary; the epic is indeed riddled with holes. In many places the reader must set aside any comparison with the more complete masterpieces of Greek and Latin literature and accept those parts of text that are still incomplete and incoherent as skeletal remains that one day will live again.

The manuscripts of Gilgamesh are cuneiform tablets – smooth, cushion-shaped rectangles of clay inscribed on both sides with wedge-shaped cuneiform writing – and they come from the ancient cities of Mesopotamia, the Levant and Anatolia. Especially in the land that is now Iraq, there are few ancient sites that have not yielded clay tablets. Cuneiform writing was invented in the city-states of lower Mesopotamia in about 3000 BC, when the administration of the great urban institutions, the palace and the temple, became too complex for the human memory to cope with. It developed, with painful slowness, from an accountant's *aide-mémoire* into a system of writing which could express not just simple words and numbers, but all the creativity of the literate mind. And because clay does not easily perish when thrown away or when buried in the ruins of buildings, archaeologists provide us with enormous quantities of clay tablets inscribed with cuneiform characters. These documents range in date across three thousand years of history and in content from the merest chit to the most sophisticated works of science and literature.

Literary compositions that tell the story of Gilgamesh come down to us from several different periods and in several different languages. Some modern renderings disregard the enormous diversity of the material, so that the reader forms a mistaken impression of the epic's contents and state of preservation. In the translations given in this book the texts are segregated according to time, place and language, allowing the reader to appreciate each body of material for itself. The texts fall into five different chapters. To summarize, Chapter 1 presents the version of the epic in the Akkadian language that was standard in the first-millennium Babylonia and Assyria, with some of its gaps filled with older material. This, if you like, is the classical Epic of Gilgamesh. It was known to the Babylonians and Assyrians as 'He who saw the Deep'. In this book it is referred to as the standard version. Chapters 2–4 give the full text of older material in Akkadian, including earlier, more fragmentary versions of the epic, such as that known in antiquity as 'Surpassing all other kings', and isolated extracts of text on school practice tablets. Chapter 2 presents texts from the first half of the second millennium (the Old Babylonian period), Chapter 3 material from Babylonia of the second half of the second millennium (the Middle Babylonian period) and Chapter 4 texts of the same period from the ancient West – the Levant and Anatolia. Chapter 5 contains the five narrative poems in the Sumerian language, best known from copies made by Babylonian apprentice scribes in the eighteenth century BC, but certainly older. In order to understand how the different texts and fragments of Gilgamesh relate to each other it may help to place them in the context of the long history of ancient Mesopotamian literature.

Gilgamesh and ancient Mesopotamian literature

Literature was already being written down in Mesopotamia by 2600 BC, though because the script did not yet express language fully, these early tablets remain extremely difficult to read. From at least this time, and probably much earlier, lower Mesopotamia was inhabited by people who spoke two very different languages. One was Sumerian, a language without affinities with any known tongue, and this appears to be the medium of the earliest writing. The other was Akkadian, which is a member of the Semitic family of languages and thus related to Hebrew and Arabic. The two languages, Sumerian and Akkadian, had long been used side by side by the people of lower Mesopotamia, though Sumerian predominated in the urban south and Akkadian in the more provincial north. This geographical division was enshrined in the terminology of later tradition, according to which the homeland of 'the black-headed ones', as these people called themselves, comprised two regions, Sumer, the southern part of lower Mesopotamia, and Akkad, the northern part. The bilingualism of the urban civilization of lower Mesopotamia in the third millennium BC perhaps resembled the division between French and Flemish in modern-day Belgium.

Texts in Akkadian appear in quantity from about 2300 BC, when the language became an administrative tool in the service of the first great Mesopotamian empire. This empire stretched at its height from the Gulf to Levantine Syria. It was built by Sargon and his successors, the kings of Akkade, a northern city which soon lent its name to the region round about and to the language spoken at the court of its kings. A legend describes how Sargon was a foundling like the infant Moses:

My mother, a priestess, conceived me and bore me in secret,
she put me in a basket of reeds, sealed its lid with pitch;
she cast me adrift on the river from which I could not arise,
the river bore me up and brought me to Aqqi, a drawer of water.[1]

According to tradition, Sargon rose to power by winning the favour of the goddess Ishtar. For nearly a hundred years his dynasty exercised dominion over the city-states of lower Mesopotamia and much of northern Mesopotamia too. The early texts in Akkadian dating from this period include a very small body of literature. Much more, no doubt, was passed down in an oral tradition and was never written down, or only much later. Sumerian seems to have been losing ground to Akkadian as a spoken language from at least this time, but its function as the primary language of writing was bolstered by a Sumerian renaissance in the last century of the third millennium. For a short period much of Mesopotamia was again united, this time under the kings of the celebrated Third Dynasty of the southern city of Ur, most famously Shulgi (2094–2047 BC in the conventional chronology). The perfect prince was an intellectual as well as a warrior and an athlete, and among his many achievements King Shulgi was particularly proud of his literacy and cultural accomplishments. He had rosy memories of his days at the scribal school, where he boasted that he was the most skilled student in his class. In later life he was an enthusiastic patron of the arts and claims to have founded special libraries at Ur and at Nippur, further north in central Babylonia, in which scribes and minstrels could consult master copies of, as it were, the Sumerian songbook. Thus he envisaged that hymns to his glory and other literature of his day would be preserved for posterity:

For all eternity the Tablet House is never to change,
for all eternity the House of Learning is never to cease functioning.[2]

In this enlightened atmosphere the courts of the kings of Ur and the succeeding dynasty of Isin were witness to the composition of much literature in Sumerian. This literature we know best not from tablets written at the time, though some survive (including a fragment of a Gilgamesh poem), but from the scribal curriculum of the Babylonians.

After the rise to power of the city of Babylon in the eighteenth century, under its most famous ruler, King Hammurapi (1792–1750 BC), the land of Sumer and Akkad was ruled by Babylon. Though the people of Sumer and Akkad did not themselves refer to their homeland as Babylonia, which is a Greek term, it is customary to call them Babylonians from this time onwards. Sumerian had by then died out among the people as a spoken language, but it was still much in use as a written language. Mesopotamian culture was nothing if not conservative and since Sumerian had been the language of the first writing, more than a thousand years before, it remained the principal language of writing in the early second millennium. Much more was written in the Babylonian dialect of Akkadian, but Sumerian retained a particular prestige. Its primacy as the language of learning was enshrined in the curriculum that had to be mastered by the student scribe. In order to learn how to use the cuneiform script, even to write Akkadian, the student had to learn Sumerian, for, as the proverb said, 'A scribe who knows no Sumerian, what sort of scribe is he?'[3] None at all, for in this period the language of tuition was, at least in part, Sumerian. Falling foul of every regulation, one young student lamented,

> The door monitor said, 'Why did you go out without my say-so?' and he
>   beat me.
> The water monitor said, 'Why did you help yourself to water without my
>   say-so?' and he beat me.
> The Sumerian monitor said, 'You spoke in Akkadian!' and he beat me.
> My teacher said, 'Your handwriting is not at all good!' and he beat me.[4]

To prove he could write, the would-be scribe copied out, on dictation and from memory, texts in Sumerian. The most advanced Sumerian texts that he had to master were a prescribed corpus of traditional Sumerian literary compositions.

Nearly all the literature that we have in Sumerian derives from the tablets written by these young Babylonian scribal apprentices, many of which were found in the remains of the houses of their teachers. The two largest such discoveries were made at Nippur, where the scribal quarter was abandoned at the end of the eighteenth century, and at Ur, where the houses in question are slightly older. More recently significant bodies of Sumerian literature from the same era have been discovered at Isin, a city just south of Nippur, and at Tell Haddad (ancient Mê-Turan) by the river Diyala on the periphery of north-east Babylonia, but most of these tablets remain unpublished. The private dwelling-houses of Nippur and Ur were not the royal Tablet Houses inaugurated by King Shulgi but they amply fulfilled the purpose he envisaged, the preservation of Sumerian literature for future generations. That now we are reading the songs of Shulgi again, four thousand years later, would probably have exceeded even his expectations, and it would have surprised him too that his libraries of Sumerian lived anew, as it were, in the tablet collections of Philadelphia, London, and other strange and far-away places.

The work of reconstructing the Sumerian literary corpus began before the Second World War and still continues. The pioneering task of identifying, joining and reading the thousands of fragments of clay tablets from Nippur, many of them tiny, was largely the work of the late Samuel Noah Kramer and his students at the University Museum in Philadelphia. His life was summed up by a teasing colleague as 'all work and no play', but there is nothing dull about being the first to read a tablet for nearly four millennia and Kramer certainly found much to be excited about. This was a completely new literature, the oldest large body of literature in human history, and its existence came as a total surprise to all but a tiny band of professional scholars. Many of these Sumerian literary texts are difficult and imperfectly understood, but it remains a serious failure of modern scholarship that their riches are not known more widely.

Among those Sumerian literary texts which have achieved some degree of publicity are the five poems of Gilgamesh (or Bilgames as he is known in older texts), translated in Chapter 5. These are not the same as the Babylonian Gilgamesh epic, which was written in Akkadian, but separate and individual tales without common themes. They were probably first committed to writing under the Third Dynasty of Ur, whose kings felt a special bond with Bilgames as a legendary hero whom they considered their predecessor and ancestor. It seems likely that much of the traditional Sumerian literary corpus goes back to lays sung by minstrels for the entertainment of the royal court of the Third Dynasty. The Sumerian poems of Bilgames are well suited for such amusement. The texts that we have, although known almost entirely from eighteenth-century copies, are very probably directly descended from master copies placed by King Shulgi in his Tablet Houses. Even so, it is entirely possible that the poems stem ultimately from an older, oral tradition. To some extent these Sumerian poems were source material for the Babylonian epic, but they can be enjoyed for their own sake too. Reading them takes us back four millennia to the courtly life of the Sumerian 'renaissance'.

Alongside the great mass of Sumerian literary tablets from the schools of eighteenth-century Babylonia, we have also recovered a little contemporaneous literature in Akkadian. This we call Old Babylonian literature. A few Old Babylonian literary tablets derive from the same schools as the literary tablets in Sumerian and also appear to be the work of apprentice scribes. These include a few scraps of Akkadian Gilgamesh, which are among the texts translated in Chapter 2. But though it seems that some literature in Akkadian was studied in the schools of this period, literary tablets in this language are so rare among the huge quantities of Sumerian tablets that it is clear they were not part of the prescribed curriculum. What narrative poems in Akkadian that we do have from the schools may instead have been copied down by students for fun, or even composed by them *ad lib*.

Other tablets of Akkadian literary works have been recovered from this period which are of less certain provenance than the school tablets. Some of them are finely written and were evidently kept, perhaps by individual scholars, as permanent library-copies. Among these are three Old Babylonian tablets of Gilgamesh which contribute significantly to our knowledge of the story: the Pennsylvania and Yale tablets and the fragment reportedly from Sippar. These are also translated in Chapter 2. Another masterpiece of Babylonian literature known from late in the Old Babylonian period is the great poem of Atramhasis, 'When the gods were man', which recounts the history of mankind from the Creation to the Flood.[5] It was this text's account of the Flood that the poet of Gilgamesh used as a source for his own version of the Deluge myth. It also provided a striking model for the story of Noah's Flood in the Bible. Other Akkadian literature begins to appear at this time, such as texts expounding the Babylonian sciences, divination by extispicy, astrology and mathematics, and incantations in both Sumerian and Akkadian whose purpose was to ward off evil by magic means. So the Old Babylonian period was an era of great literary creativity in Akkadian, but the school curriculum, at least in the centres we know best, was evidently too hidebound to reflect this development.

The Old Babylonian Gilgamesh tablets reveal that there was already, at this time, an integrated Gilgamesh epic, which, as the Pennsylvania tablet reports, bore the title *Shūtur eli sharrī*, 'Surpassing all other kings'. Works of ancient Mesopotamian literature were rarely created out of nothing and the origins of this epic probably also go back to an oral tradition. Certainly the Old Babylonian Gilgamesh tablets are far from being translations of the individual Sumerian poems of the scribal curriculum, though the two traditions hold in common several episodes and themes. The Old Babylonian texts bear witness to a wholesale revision of Gilgamesh material to form a connected story composed around the principal themes of kingship, fame and the fear of death. For this reason one suspects that the Old Babylonian epic was essentially the masterpiece of a single, anonymous poet. This epic, 'Surpassing all other kings', is only a fragment as it is now preserved, but many find the simple poetry and spare narrative of this poem and of the other Old Babylonian material more attractive than the more wordy standard version. Some stanzas of the Pennsylvania and Sippar tablets, especially, are unforgettable. To explain what is meant by the standard version of the Gilgamesh epic it is necessary to continue the story of Mesopotamian literature.

Some time after the eighteenth century BC the contents of scribal curriculum changed radically. We next have large numbers of school tablets at our disposal from the sixth century on, but the best witnesses to the nature and contents of the late scribal tradition are the several first-millennium libraries that have been excavated in Babylonia, especially at Babylon, Uruk and Sippar, and in Assyria. Assyria is the Greek name for the Land of Ashur, a small country to the north of Babylonia on the middle reaches of the river Tigris that was home in the early first millennium BC to the greatest empire the Near East had yet seen. Foremost among these late libraries is the collection of clay tablets amassed at Nineveh by the last great king of Assyria, Ashurbanipal (668–627 BC).

Like Shulgi before him, King Ashurbanipal claimed to have been trained in the scribal tradition and to have had a special talent for reading and writing. His education had been all-round, however, and had encouraged intellectual development and martial pursuits equally, as this summary reveals:

The god Nabû, scribe of all the universe, bestowed on me as a gift the knowledge of his wisdom. The gods (of war and the hunt) Ninurta and Nergal endowed my physique with manly hardness and matchless strength.[6]

This is clearly a statement of the ideal schooling for a royal prince, the same then as in Shulgi's day and as now. Though we do not certainly possess any tablet actually written by Ashurbanipal, it is clear that he was an avid collector and, by good fortune, much of his collection is still extant today. The royal libraries, housed in at least two separate buildings on the citadel of Nineveh, had at their core a small nucleus of tablets that had been written more than four hundred years earlier in the reign of King Tiglath-pileser I (1115–1077 BC). To these were added the collections of at least one distinguished Assyrian scholar and, in due course, the libraries of many Babylonian scholars that were apparently appropriated as part of the reparations that followed the bitter hostilities of the great Babylonian revolt (652–648 BC). By royal command scholars in such cities as Babylon and nearby Borsippa were set to work copying out texts from their own collections and from the libraries of the great temples. They did not risk incurring Ashurbanipal's wrath: 'We shall not neglect the king's command,' they told him. 'Day and night we shall strain and toil to execute the instruction of our lord the king!'[7] This they did on wooden writing-boards surfaced with wax, as well as on clay tablets. The scriptorium of Nineveh was also engaged on the task of copying out texts. Some of the copyists were prisoners-of-war or political hostages and worked in chains.

Among the texts that were copied out by Ashurbanipal's scribes was the Gilgamesh epic, of which the library may have possessed as many as four complete copies on clay tablets. Whatever was inscribed on wax has perished, of course. After the sack of Nineveh by the Median and Babylonian alliance in 612 BC, Ashurbanipal's copies of the epic, like his other tablets, lay in pieces on the floors of the royal palaces, not to be disturbed for nearly 2,500 years. The royal libraries of Nineveh were the first great find of cuneiform tablets to be discovered, in 1850 and 1853, and are the nucleus of the collection of clay tablets amassed in the British Museum. They are also the foundation stone upon which the discipline of Assyriology was built and for much research they remain the most important source of primary material. The first to find these tablets were the young Austen Henry Layard and his assistant, an Assyrian Christian called Hormuzd Rassam, as they tunnelled in search of Assyrian sculpture through the remains of the 'Palace without Rival', a royal residence built by Sennacherib, Ashurbanipal's grandfather. Three years later Rassam returned on behalf of the British Museum and uncovered a second trove in Ashurbanipal's own North Palace. Rassam is something of an unsung hero in Assyriology. Much later, in 1879–82, his efforts provided the British Museum with tens of thousands of Babylonian tablets from such southern sites as Babylon and Sippar. Neither Layard nor Rassam was able to read the tablets they sent back from Assyria, but of the find he made in what he called the Chamber of Records Layard wrote, 'We cannot overrate their value.' His words remain true to this day, not least for the Gilgamesh epic.

The huge importance of the royal libraries found at Nineveh by Layard and Rassam first became widely known in 1872 when, sorting through the Assyrian tablets in the British Museum, the brilliant George Smith came across what remains the most famous of Gilgamesh tablets, the best-preserved manuscript of the story of the Deluge. His reaction is described by E. A. Wallis Budge in his history of cuneiform studies, *The Rise and Progress of Assyriology*: 'Smith took the tablet and began to read over the lines which Ready [the conservator who had cleaned the tablet] had brought to light; and when he saw that they contained the portion of the legend he had hoped to find there, he said, "I am the first man to read that after two thousand years of oblivion." Setting the tablet on the table, he jumped up and rushed about the room in a great state of excitement, and, to the astonishment of those present, began to undress himself!' One hopes the George Smith who made his discovery public was a figure more composed and fully clad, since the occasion was a formal paper delivered to the Society of Biblical Archaeology in the presence of Mr Gladstone and other notables. This must be the only occasion on which a British Prime Minister in office has attended a lecture on Babylonian literature. Assyriology had arrived, and so had Gilgamesh.

While other libraries of clay tablets from ancient Mesopotamia

seem to belong to individual scholars and often comprise the work of
the scholar's family and students as part of their scribal apprenticeship,
King Ashurbanipal's library, which was far bigger than any other,
was the result of a deliberate programme of acquisition and copying.
The purpose of this labour was to provide Ashurbanipal with the best
possible expertise to govern in the manner that would please the gods.
'Send me,' he commanded, 'tablets that are beneficial for my royal
administration!'[8] With its advice for proper government the Gilgamesh
epic certainly came into this category, but it is clear from the contents
of the libraries of Nineveh that the phrase summed up the entire
scribal tradition current at the time.

The scribal tradition then current comprised a very different body
of texts from that copied by the apprentices of the Old Babylonian
period. Much of the Sumerian corpus was no longer extant. Almost
without exception, those few texts that survived from it had been
supplied with line-by-line Akkadian translations. The Akkadian liter-
ary texts known from Old Babylonian copies had been considerably
reworked and many new texts in Akkadian had been added. The
written traditions of the great professions had been incorporated.
Many of the treatises on divination had been enormously expanded
and the incantations of the exorcists had been organized and placed
in series. This work of revision, organization and expansion is known
to have taken place at the hands of many different scholars between
seven and four hundred years earlier, in the last centuries of the
second millennium. The labour of these individual Middle Babylonian
scholars resulted in the creation of standard editions of most texts,
editions which remained essentially unaltered until the death of cunei-
form writing a thousand years later.

The Babylonian Gilgamesh epic did not escape the attentions of a
redactor. This by tradition was a learned scholar by the name of
Sîn-liqe-unninni, which means 'O Moon God, Accept my Prayer!' By
profession he was an exorcist, which is to say that he was trained in
the art of the expulsion of evil by prayer, incantation and magic ritual.
This was a very important skill, whose principal applications were
treating the sick, absolving sin, averting bad portents and consecrating
holy ground. We know nothing else about Sîn-liqe-unninni, except
that he was considered their ancestor by several well-known scribal
families of Uruk, in southern Babylonia, that flourished in the late
first millennium. Current opinion supposes that he lived some time

in the thirteenth to eleventh centuries. He could not have been the original composer of the Babylonian epic, for a version of it already existed in the Old Babylonian period, but probably he gave it its final form and was thus responsible for the edition current in first-millennium libraries, the text that here we call the standard version. Even so, we cannot rule out the possibility that, between Sîn-liqe-unninni's lifetime and the seventh century, minor changes were made in the text he established.

The long epic poem that the ancients attributed to Sîn-liqe-unninni was called in antiquity *Sha naqba īmuru*, 'He who saw the Deep', a title taken from its first line. A glimpse of the nature of Sîn-liqe-unninni's revision can be obtained by comparing the standard version of the epic and the older material, which is of course only possible where a particular episode is extant in both. The later epic often follows the Old Babylonian epic, 'Surpassing all other kings', line-for-line, sometimes with almost no changes in vocabulary and word order, sometimes with minor alterations in one or the other. Elsewhere one finds that the late text is much expanded, whether by repetition or by invention, and even that passages present in the Old Babylonian epic have been dropped and new episodes inserted.

Something of the intermediate stages in this development from 'Surpassing all other kings' to 'He who saw the Deep' can be learnt from the scraps of Babylonian Gilgamesh that survive from the era in which Sîn-liqe-unninni lived. This material falls into two groups: texts that come from within Babylonia and texts that come from outside it. The first group comprises only two tablets, from Nippur and Ur, translated in Chapter 3. They closely resemble the standard version of the epic attributed to Sîn-liqe-unninni, but there are differences. On grounds of content and style it is hard to say whether these tablets are witness to the text as it was immediately before Sîn-liqe-unninni's editorship, or immediately after it.

The existence of the second group of tablets, from outside Babylonia, needs some explanation. In the fourteenth century, at the height of the Late Bronze Age when the eastern Mediterranean was dominated by the great powers of the Egyptian New Kingdom and the Hittite Empire, the *lingua franca* of international communications in the Near East was the Akkadian language. Kings of Assyria and Babylonia naturally wrote to Pharaoh in Akkadian, but Pharaoh replied in Akkadian too. The Hittite king and Pharaoh likewise corresponded in Akkadian, and, when writing to their overlords, the minor rulers of the Levantine coast and Syria used the same language, though often shot through with local Canaanite and Hurrian idioms. This Akkadian was written in the traditional manner, in cuneiform script on clay tablets. In order to learn to compose their lords' letters, treaties and other documents in Akkadian, local scribes were trained in cuneiform writing, and they were trained in the time-honoured way, by rote-learning of the lists, vocabularies and literature of the Babylonian scribal tradition.

This was not the first time that the cuneiform script had made the journey to the West. The first known occasion was in the mid-third millennium, when cuneiform was exported to Ebla and elsewhere in Syria and texts in both Sumerian and Akkadian went with it as part of the skills that trainee scribes had to master in order to acquire the new technology. In the nineteenth century Akkadian had been written at Kanesh and other Assyrian trading posts in Cappadocia. In the eighteenth century it was widely used in Syria, not only in Mesopotamian Syria but also close by the Mediterranean Sea, and it even appears at Hazor in Palestine. But in the later second millennium the spread of cuneiform schooling and scholarship was wider still.

The result was that tablets inscribed with Akkadian scholarly and literary texts were copied out at Hattusa (modern Boğazköy), the Hittite capital in Anatolia, at Akhetaten (el-Amarna), the royal city of Pharaoh Akhenaten in Upper Egypt, at Ugarit (Ras Shamra), a principality on the Syrian coast, and at Emar (Tell Meskene), a provincial town on the great bend of the Euphrates – just to list the principal sites. Except for Amarna, all these sites have produced tablets of Gilgamesh, as too has Megiddo in Palestine. These texts are translated in Chapter 4. Some of the material from Hattusa, which is the oldest in this group, is very similar to the Old Babylonian epic that we know from the Pennsylvania and Yale tablets and clearly predates Sîn-liqe-unninni. The texts from Emar, which are several centuries younger, are much more like his text, though again, it is impossible at present to determine whether they precede his work or not.

Other Gilgamesh texts from the West are abridgements of the Babylonian epic, or reworkings of it, and are probably local developments. Indeed, the epic fired the imagination then as it does now and adaptations of it were composed in local languages. So far a Hittite version and a Hurrian version have come to light, both found in the archives of the Hittite capital. Though Hittite is pretty well understood, Hurrian is still barely comprehensible and our understanding of both versions of the Gilgamesh story is badly hampered by their fragmentary state of preservation. Therefore no rendering of them is given here. Not so long ago it seemed that a Gilgamesh text had also been composed in Elamite, the language of a people who occupied what became Susiana and is now Khuzistan. The tablet, discovered in Armenia, far from Elam, was published promptly and in due course translations followed. However, further study revealed that the text was, in fact, a private letter with no connection to Gilgamesh at all. This development elicited from one scholar the wry comment that the document was 'a good illustration of the fact that Elamite remains the worst-known language of the ancient Near East'. With the Akkadian language we are fortunately on much firmer ground.

The standard version of the Babylonian epic is known from a total of 73 manuscripts extant: the 35 that have survived from the libraries of King Ashurbanipal at Nineveh, 8 more tablets and fragments from three other Assyrian cities (Ashur, Kalah and Huzirina), and 30 from Babylonia, especially the cities of Babylon and Uruk. Ashurbanipal's tablets are the oldest. The latest manuscript discovered so far was written in about 130 BC by one Bel-ahhe-uṣur ('O Lord, Protect the Brothers!'), a trainee temple-astrologer of Babylon. By that time this once mighty city was much diminished in power and population but, in a country whose inhabitants had long spoken not Akkadian but Aramaic and Greek, its ancient temple was the last surviving bastion of cuneiform scholarship. From the 73 surviving manuscripts it is possible to reconstruct much of Sîn-liqe-unninni's epic but there are still considerable gaps. To fill these lacunae it is sometimes possible to fall back on the older material in Akkadian and for one episode it is even necessary to utilize the Hittite version. The result of this reconstruction is the text given in Chapter 1. There, in order clearly to distinguish between text of different periods, old material used to bridge lacunae in the standard version is explicitly identified in editorial notes.

The standard version of the epic is divided by Babylonian tradition into sections. The definition of a section is that it is the text customarily contained on an individual clay tablet, and so the sections are called, in accordance with Babylonian custom, 'tablets'. The epic is told over eleven such sections, Tablets I–XI. The organizing of Babylonian literature in the latter part of the second millennium resulted in much of it being arranged in standard sequences of tablets, sequences that were known as 'series'. The 'series of Gilgamesh', in fact, comprises twelve tablets, not just the eleven of the epic. Tablet XII, the last, is a line-by-line translation of the latter half of one of the Sumerian Gilgamesh poems. Somehow this partial translation survived into the first millennium while the original Sumerian text, like the other Sumerian poems of Gilgamesh, did not. Though some have tried to show that Tablet XII had a real place in the epic, most scholars would agree that it does not belong to that text but was attached to it because it was plainly related material. The principle of bringing together related material was one of the criteria by which the scholars of Babylonia organized different texts into the same series.

The eleven tablets of the epic vary in length from 183 to 326 lines of poetry, so that the whole composition would originally have been about 3,000 lines long. As the text now stands, only Tablets I, VI, X and XI are more or less complete. Leaving aside lines that are lost but can be restored from parallel passages, overall about 575 lines are still completely missing, that is, they are not represented by so much as a single word. Many more are too badly damaged to be useful, so that considerably less than the four-fifths of the epic that is extant yields a consecutive text. In the translation offered here the damaged state of the text is all too evident, pock-marked as it is by the clutter of brackets and ellipses.

While there is a temptation for a modern editor to ignore the gaps, to gloss them over or to join up disconnected fragments of text, I believe that no adult reader is well served by such a procedure. The gaps are themselves important in number and size, for they remind us how much is still to be learned of the text. They prevent us from assuming that we have Gilgamesh entire. Whatever we say about the epic is provisional, for new discoveries of text may change our interpretation of whole passages. Nevertheless, the epic we have now is considerably fuller than that which fired the imagination of Rilke. Approach what lies ahead not as you might the poems of Homer but

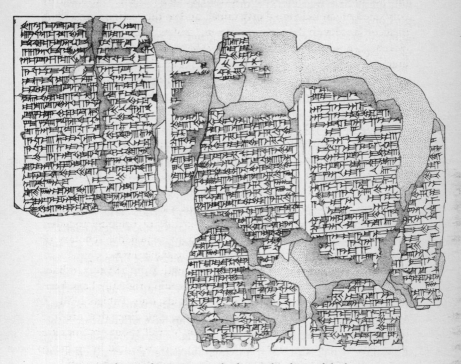

1 *A damaged masterpiece: the front side of one of the better
preserved tablets of the Gilgamesh epic*

as a book part-eaten by termites or a scroll half-consumed by fire.
Accept it for what it is, a damaged masterpiece.

In time, the holes that pepper the standard version of the epic
will undoubtedly be filled by further discoveries of tablets in the
ruin-mounds of Mesopotamia and in the museums of the world – for
such is the lack of professional Assyriologists everywhere that we
have yet to study properly many thousands of tablets that have long
been in museum collections. The correct identification and accurate
placement of what are often only small fragments make for difficult
and painstaking work. Not even a genius like George Smith always
came up with the right identification. The *Daily Telegraph* was so
impressed with his famous lecture on the Deluge story from the

Gilgamesh epic that in 1873, in the hope of recovering the missing portions of text, they provided the splendid sum of one thousand guineas (£1,050) to enable him to reopen for the British Museum the old excavations at Nineveh. In comparison with those who had dug there before him, Smith brought home only a very small number of tablets – the 'DT' collection – from this, his first expedition, but there among them was indeed a fragment of the Flood, one that even filled an important gap in the narrative. This was a most impressive fulfilment of the *Daily Telegraph*'s expectations, but the expedition was a victim of its own success. The desired fragment so exactly met the newspaper's requirements that the news of its discovery led to the expedition's early recall.

In fact, we now know that this particular fragment of the Deluge story is part of a late version of the poem of Atram-hasis and not a piece of Gilgamesh at all. Smith had no way of knowing that at the time. His identification was the best that could then be expected, and went unchallenged for many years. Employed by the British Museum in 1867 to assist Sir Henry Creswicke Rawlinson, one of the grand pioneers of cuneiform decipherment, George Smith was more than the discoverer of Gilgamesh and the epic's first translator. He was among the first in a long line of scholars who have sifted through the libraries of Ashurbanipal and, by sorting, joining and identifying thousands of pieces of Assyrian clay tablets, have over a period of 130 years steadily increased our knowledge of the literature of the Babylonians. It is in this continuing work of discovery and identification of manuscripts, from Nineveh and elsewhere, in the field as well as in museums, that the Gilgamesh epic (along with most other literary texts written in cuneiform on clay tablets) differs from fragmentary texts in Greek and Latin. The eventual recovery of this literature is assured by the durability of the writing medium. It is only a matter of time – providing, of course, that the society in which we live continues to place value on such things and to support the scholars who study them.

The setting of the epic

The central setting of the epic is the ancient city-state of Uruk in the land of Sumer. Uruk, the greatest city of its day, was ruled by the tyrannical Gilgamesh, semi-divine by virtue of his mother, the goddess Ninsun, but none the less mortal. He was one of the great figures of legend. His enduring achievement was to rebuild the wall of Uruk on its antediluvian foundations, and his military prowess ended the hegemony of the northern city-state of Kish. He appears as a god in early lists of deities and in the later third millennium he benefited from a cult. Later tradition made it his function, as explained in one of the Sumerian poems, to govern the shades of the dead in the Netherworld. Because we have actual records from kings whom the ancients held to be his contemporaries, it is possible that, as perhaps there was once a real King Arthur, so there was once an actual King Gilgamesh. Certainly the native historical tradition held this to be the case, for Gilgamesh appears in the list of Sumerian kings as the fifth ruler of the First Dynasty of Uruk. He would thus have flourished about 2750 BC, though some would place him a century or so earlier. His reign, which the list of kings holds to have lasted a mythical 126 years, falls in the shadowy period at the edge of Mesopotamian history, when, as in the Homeric epics, the gods took a personal interest in the affairs of men and often communicated with them directly.

Foremost among the gods was the supreme triad, which comprised the Sky God Anu, remote in his celestial palace, the more important Enlil, who presided over the affairs of gods and men from his temple on earth, and the clever Ea, who lived in his freshwater ocean beneath the earth (the Ocean Below) and sent the Seven Sages to civilize mankind. Then there were the kindly Mother Goddess, Lady of the Gods, who first created men with Ea's help, the violent Adad, god of the storm, and the Moon God, Sîn, the majestic son of Enlil. The Moon's children were Shamash, the Sun God, the patron of travellers and Gilgamesh's special protector, and the Babylonian Venus, the impetuous Ishtar, whose responsibilities were sexual love and war, and whose appetite for both was inexhaustible. Beneath Ea's watery domain, deep in the Netherworld, the gloomy realm of the dead, lived its queen, the bitter Ereshkigal. There she lay prostrate in perpetual mourning, attended by her minister, the gruesome Namtar, and the rest of her fell household.

Men lived in cities and cultivated the land. Where irrigation could not reach, the farmland gave way to rougher country in which shepherds grazed their flocks, ever on the look-out for wolves and lions. And further off still was the 'wild', the empty country prowled by hunters, outlaws and bandits, where legend had it there once roamed a strange wild man whom the gazelles brought up as their own. Enkidu was his name. Several months' journey across this wilderness, over many ranges of mountains, there was a sacred Forest of Cedar, where some said the gods dwelt. It was guarded for the gods by a fearsome ogre, the terrible Humbaba, cloaked for his protection in seven numinous auras, radiant and deadly. Somewhere at the edge of the world, patrolled by monstrous sentries who were half man and half scorpion, were the twin mountains of Mashu where the sun rose and set. Further still, at the other end of the Path of the Sun, was a fabulous Garden of Jewels, and nearby, in a tavern by the great impassable ocean that surrounded the earth, lived the mysterious goddess Shiduri, who dispensed wisdom from behind her veils. Across the ocean were the lethal Waters of Death, and beyond them, on a remote island where the rivers Euphrates and Tigris welled up again from the deep, far outside the ken of men and visited only by his ferryman Ur-shanabi, dwelt Uta-napishti the Distant, a primeval king who survived the great Deluge sent by Enlil early in human history and as a consequence was spared the doom of mortals. Many other powers populated the Babylonian cosmos – deities, demons and demi-gods of legend – but these are the principal characters of the Babylonian Gilgamesh epic.

The epic in its context: myth, religion and wisdom

The Gilgamesh epic is one of the very few works of Babylonian literature which can be read and enjoyed without special knowledge of the civilization from which it sprang. The names of the characters may be unfamiliar and the places strange, but some of the poet's themes are so universal in human experience that the reader has no difficulty in understanding what drives the epic's hero and can easily identify with his aspirations, his grief and his despair. The Assyriologist William L. Moran has recently expounded Gilgamesh's story as a tale of the human world, characterized by an 'insistence on human values'

and an 'acceptance of human limitations'. This observation led him
to describe the epic as 'a document of ancient humanism',[9] and indeed,
even for the ancients, the story of Gilgamesh was more about what
it is to be a man than what it is to serve the gods. As the beginning
and end of the epic make clear, Gilgamesh is celebrated more for his
human achievement than for his relationship with the divine.

Though the story of Gilgamesh is certainly fiction, Moran's diag-
nosis is also a warning not to read the epic as myth. There is little
consensus as to what myth is and what it is not, and ancient Meso-
potamian mythological texts show considerable variety. Some of them,
particularly the older ones, contain just one myth. Others put together
two or more myths. Two features are particularly characteristic of
these mythological compositions: on the one hand, the story centres
on the deeds of a god or gods, and, on the other, its purpose is to
explain the origin of some feature of the natural or social world.

More of the characters of the Epic of Gilgamesh are divine than
not, but set beside the protagonist they are insignificant. The gods
even attract unfavourable similes: in Tablet XI the poet compares
them to dogs and flies, as if the rulers of the universe were parasitical
scavengers. In the main the function of the poem is not to explain
origins. It is more interested in examining the human condition as it
is. On these grounds the epic is not myth. It certainly contains myths
– the myth of the snake which shed its skin in Tablet XI being the
purest example, the Flood story the most famous – and it makes many
allusions to the mythology of the day, particularly in the episode of
Gilgamesh's repudiation of the goddess Ishtar in Tablet VI. But most
such myths are incidental to the story and the epic is certainly much
more than the sum of its mythological parts – unlike, for example,
Ovid's *Metamorphoses*. Nevertheless, the text of Gilgamesh is often
studied alongside compositions which are truly mythological. Indeed,
no book on the mythology of ancient Mesopotamia can resist it. The
reason for this can best be explained by quoting the words of G. S.
Kirk, who dealt at length with Gilgamesh in his important study of
myth: 'Above all [the epic] retains, in spite of its long and literate
history, an unmistakable aura of the mythical – of that kind of
emotional exploration of the permanent meaning of life, by the release
of fantasy about the distant past, that Greek myths, at least as we
experience them, so often fail to exemplify in their own right.'[10]

If not truly mythological, in the sense defined above, what is this poem? Moran's phrase, 'a document of ancient humanism', is again a useful one, for it highlights the fact that the epic is not a religious poem either, at least not in the same way as, for example, John Henry Newman's 'Dream of Gerontius'. Both poems wrestle with the fear of death and comparing them is instructive. Sensing on his deathbed the dreadful approach of the Angel of Death, Gerontius laments,

> A visitant
> Is knocking his dire summons at my door,
> The like of whom, to scare me and to daunt,
> Has never, never come to me before.

These are words that could also have been placed in Gilgamesh's mouth. Gerontius in his anguish puts himself in the hands of his God, and in religious poetry this is the proper recourse of the pious afflicted. There is plenty of Babylonian poetry in which a sufferer, often sick and feeling himself near to death, throws himself on the mercy of one or other of the inscrutable gods and asks for forgiveness and reconciliation. Gilgamesh, however, in his terror and misery spurns the help of his gods – specifically rejecting the good advice of Shamash, the god who protects him – and, even at the last, turns for solace to his own achievements rather than to his creator. The poem concludes with Gilgamesh proudly showing his companion the monument for which he became famous:

> O Ur-shanabi, climb Uruk's wall and walk back and forth!
> Survey its foundations, examine the brickwork!
> Were its bricks not fired in an oven?
> Did the Seven Sages not lay its foundations?

For it was Gilgamesh who in Babylonian tradition rebuilt his city's wall on its primordial foundations, and it was the fame won him by this enduring monument that would be his comfort.

The late Thorkild Jacobsen, a renowned Sumerologist who wrote on ancient Mesopotamian religion with considerable vision, once described the epic as a 'story of learning to face reality, a story of "growing up"'.[11] Gilgamesh begins as an immature youth, capable of anything and accepting no check; eventually he comes to accept the power and reality of Death, and thus he reaches reflective maturity.

But there is more to the epic than that. In charting the hero's progress, the poet reflects profoundly on youth and age, on triumph and despair, on men and gods, on life and death. It is significant that his concern is not just Gilgamesh's glorious deeds but also the suffering and misery that beset his hero as he pursues his hopeless quest. 'Read out', the poet enjoins us in the prologue, 'the travails of Gilgamesh, all that he went through!' As a poem which explores the truth of the human condition the epic bears a message for future generations, then as now. Maturity is gained as much through failure as success. Life, of necessity, is hard, but one is the wiser for it.

There is in fact a formal indication that the epic is a work from which one is expected to learn. In the prologue the poet asks the reader to believe that his poem was set down on stone by Gilgamesh himself for all to read. In other words, we are to imagine that the epic is an autobiography of the great hero himself, written in the third person. These are the words of King Gilgamesh for the benefit of future generations! The epic accordingly bears some relation to the well-established literary genre of 'royal counsel'. Kings, by virtue of their many counsellors and the special trappings and rituals of kingship, were expected to be wise and sagacious. Many ancient Near Eastern collections of proverbial sayings purport to be the teachings of a king or other notable to his son or successor. The biblical Proverbs are the 'wisdom of King Solomon' addressed to his son, and the wise author of the book of Ecclesiastes introduces himself as 'the son of David, king over Israel in Jerusalem'. Several such compositions survive from ancient Egypt, the best known perhaps being the 'Instructions of Amen-em-Opet'. In ancient Mesopotamia the genre is represented by the 'Instructions of Shuruppak', a Sumerian composition that is among the very oldest extant works of literature, appearing first in copies from about the twenty-sixth century BC. In this text the wise old Shuruppak, son of Ubar-Tutu, counsels his son Ziusudra. It is this same Ziusudra who was known to the Babylonians by the twin names of Atram-hasis and Uta-napishti, and who survived the Deluge and dispensed sage counsel to Gilgamesh at the ends of the earth.

More particularly the epic can be compared with a small group of Babylonian texts that have been described as 'fictional royal autobiography'. Another example of such a text is the composition we know as the 'Cuthean Legend of Naram-Sîn', in which an Old Babylonian

poet adopts the identity of this famous third-millennium king of
Akkade and warns future rulers of the dire consequences that attend
failure to rule in the manner prescribed by the gods. Naram-Sîn's
lapse was to go into battle without their consent. The following
injunction from his 'autobiography' bears close comparison with the
prologue of Gilgamesh:

Whoever you may be, governor, prince or anyone else,
   whom the gods may choose to exercise kingship,
I have made you a tablet-box and written a stone tablet.
I have deposited them for you in Cutha,
   in the cella of Nergal in the temple E-meslam.
Behold this stone tablet,
   give ear to what this stone tablet says![12]

The lesson for the future rulers who were the target of the text about
Naram-Sîn is one of patience: wait for the gods, do nothing without
their say-so. The message of the Gilgamesh epic is the vanity of the
hero's quest: pursuit of immortality is folly, the proper duty of man
is to accept the mortal life that is his lot and enjoy it to the full.
'Do your duty in the embrace of your woman!' enjoins the poet of
Naram-Sîn's 'autobiography', just as in the Old Babylonian Gilgamesh
epic Shiduri famously tells the hero:

But you, Gilgamesh, let your belly be full,
   enjoy yourself always by day and by night!
Make merry each day,
   dance and play day and night!

Let your clothes be clean,
   let your head be washed, may you bathe in water!
Gaze on the child who holds your hand,
   let your wife enjoy your repeated embrace!

So too advises the author of Ecclesiastes: 'Go thy way, eat thy bread
with joy, and drink thy wine with a merry heart . . . Let thy garments
be always white; and let not thy head lack ointment. Live joyfully
with the wife whom thou lovest all the days of thy life.' The themes
of the vanity of human endeavour and of taking one's pleasure in

one's family are typical of 'wisdom' literature of the kind found elsewhere in the ancient Near East.

In the ancient world religion permeated intellectual activity in a way that it does not now. Read as 'wisdom', ultimately the epic bears a message of serious religious content. Its views on the proper duties of men and kings are strictly in line with the gods' requirements and conform to the religious ideology of ancient Mesopotamia: do the will of the gods, fulfil your function as they intended. So while the epic can be enjoyed for its own sake without further inquiry, some knowledge of the mythology which expressed the relationship between gods, kings and men, of how the Babylonians understood their universe, and of their religion and how their beliefs conditioned the Babylonians' approach to the divine, will give us greater insight into this masterpiece.

We know from many ancient Mesopotamian sources, in Sumerian and in Akkadian, that the Babylonians believed the purpose of the human race to be the service of the gods. Before mankind's creation, the myth tells us, the cities of lower Mesopotamia were inhabited by the gods alone and they had to feed and clothe themselves by their own efforts. Under the supervision of Enlil, the lord of the earth, the lesser deities grew and harvested the gods' food, tilled the soil and, most exhaustingly, dug the rivers and waterways that irrigated the fields.[13] Even the rivers Tigris and Euphrates were their work. Eventually the labour became too much for them and they mutinied. The resourceful god Ea (called Enki in the poem of Atram-hasis) devised first the technology to produce a substitute worker from raw clay and then the means by which this new being could reproduce itself. The first humans were duly born from the womb of the Mother Goddess and allotted their destiny, 'to carry the yoke, the task imposed by Enlil, to bear the soil-basket of the gods'. This act of creation could be repeated as necessary. So when, as related in Tablet I of the Gilgamesh epic, the need arises to make a match for Gilgamesh, which plainly could not be done by human reproduction,

The goddess Aruru, she washed her hands,
    took a pinch of clay, threw it down in the wild.
In the wild she created Enkidu, the hero,
    offspring of silence, knit strong by Ninurta.

Enkidu is thus a replica of the first man, born without a mother's cries of pain.

In the poem of Atram-hasis the yoke and soil-basket, the means of carrying earth from the diggings, symbolize the burden imposed on mankind by the god Enlil. This burden was much more than earth-moving, however; it was all the work that went into looking after the gods in their temples on earth, from irrigating their fields, raising their crops and pasturing their livestock to baking their bread, butchering their meat and clothing their statues. And so it was in reality. The principal deities of the Babylonian pantheon lived, embodied in anthropomorphic statues, in palatial houses, surrounded by their divine families, courtiers and servants. The ideology was that soon after the sundering of heaven from earth the rulers of gods had divided up the land between the major deities of the pantheon, allocating to each a city and its surrounding territory. Though many cities possessed more than one temple – Babylon traditionally had forty-three – the notion remained that the city and its hinterland belonged in principle to its patron deity, the god to whom they had been given in the original partition of the land, and that they were his to exploit.

Accordingly, the patron deity occupied a large complex in the centre of town. This, the chief temple of the city, functioned as his house or, better, his palace, for the domestic arrangements of the great gods were in all essentials modelled on those of the king. Here in his palace the god (or goddess) was looked after by means of elaborate rituals. He was seated on a throne, fed regular meals, clothed in expensive garments woven with gems, and entertained with music, dance and song. In the case of a god, his wife occupied a suite of rooms close by his own, where a suitably outsize marriage bed was ready for their conjugal bliss. Other members of the family, especially the first-born son, might also be provided with a suite of rooms. The god also needed on hand his court, especially his vizier or minister, the lesser deity who did his bidding, and his domestic servants, who likewise were minor gods and goddesses.

All these deities, from the greatest to the smallest, were resident in the temple and received some kind of cult there: ritual offerings of incense, ritual worship with prayer and song. The larger temples contained several different cult-chambers and a number of small shrines – more than a hundred in the case of temple at Babylon – which were settings for carefully prescribed ritual activity. The ideology was that the god was served by his divine court. The reality was that his needs were cared for by a body of human personnel specially inducted into temple service. We call these men priests, but not all of them are properly so described. For the great temples were centres of economic activity, too. In line with the belief that the land was divided among the gods in remotest history, many of these temples possessed huge holdings of arable land let out to tenant farmers. They also owned vast herds of cattle and flocks of sheep and goats. Some temples were also involved in manufacturing, scribal training and other social and commercial activities. Such temples employed a considerable workforce, comprising more or less independent persons, as it were sub-contractors, and dependent persons such as those dedicated to temple service. Among the latter were those who had no other means of support, widows, orphans and foundlings, who wore a symbol of some kind that disclosed their status. As Gilgamesh's mother declares when she adopts Enkidu for her son, orphans brought up by the temples were considered the latter-day counterparts of Enkidu, the foundling *par excellence*:

'O mighty Enkidu, you are not sprung from my womb,
    but henceforth your brood will belong with the votaries of Gilgamesh,
the priestesses, the hierodules and the women of the temple.'
    She put the symbols on Enkidu's neck.

The administration of the temple's estates, workshops and personnel was in the hands of the temple managers, just as they had responsibility for servicing the cult. This was right and proper, for the purpose of all mankind, as Ea created him, was to till the land, tend the flocks and engage in every other activity that was conducive to the comfort, satisfaction and best advantage of his divine lords. The long life of this ideology, from at least the third millennium BC until the coming of Islam, long after the demise of Babylonian civilization, is confirmed by Sura 51 of the Koran, which makes a particular point of rejecting the old belief: 'I have not created genii (jinn) and men for any other end than that they should serve me. I require not sustenance from them; neither will I that they feed me.'

There was a flaw built into Ea's creation of man, a flaw that explains how it was that something made by the gods for their own purposes was nevertheless a very imperfect tool. The clay that Ea

gave to the Mother Goddess as the raw material from which she bore
mankind was animated – given spirit – by mixing it with the blood
of a god:

Let one god be slaughtered
   and the gods be thereby cleansed.
With his flesh and his blood
   let the Lady of the Gods mix some clay,
so that god and man
   are mixed together in the clay.
In future time let us hear the drumming of the heartbeat,
   from the flesh of a god let the spirit be produced.[14]

The divine element in mankind's creation explains why, in obvious
distinction from the animals, the human race has selfconsciousness
and reason. It also explains why, in Babylonian belief, men live on
after death as spirits or shades in the Netherworld – as famously
reported in Enkidu's dream of the Netherworld in Tablet VII and in
the Sumerian poem of Bilgames and the Netherworld. But the trouble
was that the god who was executed to provide the blood was not the
best material. In one tradition, at least, he was the leader of the rebels,
who had instigated a mutiny. Small wonder, then, that mankind could
be wayward. Uta-napishti tells his wife in Tablet XI, 'Man is deceitful,
he will deceive you', and Gilgamesh duly confirms this unpalatable
aspect of human nature by lying to him.

   The innately rebellious and unruly nature of man encapsulated in
this myth of his creation also informs one tradition about early human
history, first found in several Sumerian literary compositions, that in
the beginning the human race roamed the land like the beasts of the
field, naked but hairy, and for sustenance grazing on grass. According
to Berossus, a Babylonian scholar of the fourth century BC who wrote
in Greek, at this stage men 'lived without laws just as wild animals',[15]
that is, without government, cities or social institutions. The creation
of Enkidu in Tablet I of the Gilgamesh epic also alludes to this
tradition:

   He knows not a people, nor even a country.
Coated in hair like the god of the animals,
   with the gazelles he grazes on grasses.

The myth of man's early barbarism is at odds with the tradition in which the human race is created to take up the tools of the city-dwelling gods; but the mythology of many civilizations is oral and diverse in origin, so that different traditions of how things came to be tend to coexist without difficulty. As is well known, the first two chapters of Genesis preserve two quite different accounts of God's creation of man. The civilization of mankind, according to Babylonian mythology, was the work of the gods, who sent kingship from heaven, and especially of the god Ea, who despatched the Seven Sages to Eridu and other early cities, and with them all the arts and crafts of city life. These were the beings who, according to the epic's prologue, founded Uruk with its wall: 'Did the Seven Sages not lay its foundations?' Foremost among these Sages was the fish-man Oannes-Adapa, who rose from the sea. Government, society and work were thus imposed on men.

The tradition that the first men roamed free and lawless and were not subject to kings helped to give rise to a myth that kings were created as distinct beings, significantly different from other mortals in appearance, capabilities and duties. The text that tells us most in this regard is known from a single tablet from Babylon written in the middle or late first millennium BC, but coronation prayers from seventh-century Assyria quote part of it and the text itself may be older. In it, the god Ea and the Mother Goddess between them create man from clay, as in the poem of Atram-hasis and other mythological texts. Then they create a superior being and give him the tools for ruling:

Ea opened his mouth to speak, saying a word to the Lady of the Gods:
   'You are Belet-ili, the sister of the great gods,
you have created man the human,
   fashion now the king, the counsellor-man!
Gird the whole of his figure sweet,
   make perfect his countenance and well formed his body!'
The Lady of the Gods fashioned the king, the counsellor-man!
   They gave to the king the task of doing battle for the [great] gods.
Anu gave him his crown, Enlil gave him his throne,
   Nergal gave him his weapons, Ninurta gave him his corona of
      splendour;
The Lady of the Gods gave him his features (of majesty),
   Nuska commissioned counsellors, stood them before him.[16]

This image, of the king as a man of perfect beauty, ready for battle but guided by divinely inspired counsel, is one that informs the Gilgamesh epic. The hero is shaped by the gods, of perfect looks and majestic stature, as the poet tells us in Tablet I:

It was the Lady of the Gods drew the form of his figure,
   while his build was perfected by divine Nudimmud . . .
When he grew tall his beauty was consummate,
   by earthly standards he was most handsome.

Not only this, but as king he exhibits an instinctive longing for trustworthy counsel, and at the end of the same tablet he looks forward with enthusiasm to the predicted arrival of Enkidu:

Let me acquire a friend to counsel me,
   a friend to counsel me I will acquire!

Aside from fighting the gods' battles for them – maintaining law and order in the land by repelling the advance of the enemy and subduing internal revolt – the principal duty of the Babylonian king was to oversee the repair and maintenance of the gods' cult-centres and to ensure that they were stocked with foodstuffs and treasure. In another myth, which forms the prologue of a prayer to be said during the elaborate rituals that attended the building and rebuilding of Babylonian temples, the god Ea organizes the world to ensure the gods' comfort in their houses. In doing so, 'he created the king for the task of provisioning, he created men to be the workforce'.[17] It is with this in mind that one should understand the second part of Uta-napishti's counsel to Gilgamesh in Tablet X (ll. 28off.). This passage is much broken, but the gist of it seems to be that, just as the moon and constellations ('the gods of the night') mark out the regular progression of month and year, so the king must ensure the delivery of the regular offerings required by the gods' temples.

In the epic Uta-napishti fills the role of the quintessential wise man who knows the secrets of the cosmos – as it were, the meaning of life. He and his knowledge, ancient and unique among men, are the end of Gilgamesh's long and arduous quest. Uta-napishti's counsel and story form the climax of the epic and it is here, in Tablets X and XI, that we should expect the poet's message to come through most strongly. Apart from the observation on the duties of kings regarding the provisioning of temples, what does the old sage say?

First Uta-napishti contrasts the lot of kings with the lot of fools. By fools are meant simpletons, halfwits and village idiots, those who occupied the position in human society furthest from kings. Kings are enthroned in splendour, clad in finery, nourished with the best-quality foodstuffs. Fools make do with the opposite. One implication seems to be that Gilgamesh, who has been wandering alone clad in ragged skins and eating raw meat, is behaving not as a king but as a fool. His quest is the quest of an idiot. This is a matter of reproach, for one born to be king should act as one. Another implication is that it was the duty of kings to help those who could not help themselves. The second part of Uta-napishti's counsel, as already explained, outlines the gods' expectations of the king. This is what Gilgamesh should have been doing instead of wandering the wild: looking after the gods, his masters, and the people, his subjects. The third part of Uta-Napishti's counsel – and certainly the most important – is his discourse on life and death and on the futility of Gilgamesh's search for immortality. In the Old Babylonian epic Gilgamesh received a similar, but much shorter, lecture from Shiduri:

The life that you seek you never will find:
   when the gods created mankind,
death they dispensed to mankind,
   life they kept for themselves.

These lines, and the advice that follows, do not appear in the episode of the late epic where Gilgamesh talks with Shiduri. It seems that the poet of the standard version wanted to keep the wisdom for the climax and intentionally held it in reserve for Uta-napishti. The dispensing of death and life took place, as Uta-napishti tells us, in an assembly of the gods. This is another reference to the mythology of early human history. Newly created man, as we have seen, was flawed by virtue of his innate rebelliousness. Being innate this flaw could not be corrected. But the human race had another defect: it bred with great ease and rapidly became too numerous. As the poem of Atram-hasis relates, three times, at intervals of 1,200 years, the god Enlil tired of the relentless hubbub of the new creation, which kept him awake in his chamber. Each time he resolved to reduce the human population,

first by plague, then by drought and finally by famine. Each time he
was successful at first, so that the numbers of man were considerably
diminished. But inevitably he was thwarted by the god Ea, who each
time communicated the method of man's salvation to Atram-hasis
(another name for Uta-napishti), king of the city Shuruppak. Eventu-
ally the exasperated Enlil came up with the final solution, which all
the gods, including Ea, swore to keep secret: he would send the Deluge
to wipe out mankind. By subterfuge, however, Ea managed to warn
Atram-hasis in advance, and Atram-hasis built his curious ark, ostens-
ibly so that he could sail down to Ea's cosmic domain, the Ocean
Below. The Deluge came but Atram-hasis survived, safe aboard the
ark with his family, his treasure and representatives of each craft and
species of animal. But the gods were stricken with hunger and thirst.
Their temples were flooded. The human servants who fed and watered
them were dead. Enlil's final solution was exposed as fatally flawed.
The gods were about to die of want.

In the meantime the flood had abated and the ark had grounded on
a high mountain peak. Then, as incense rose from where Atram-hasis
offered thanks for his survival, the sweet smell of food wafted up to
heaven and the gods all rushed down to feed. Enlil remonstrated with
the gods for the failure of his plan and fingers were pointed at Ea. Ea,
clever as always, responded by exposing the unwisdom of the Deluge.
In the story as adapted for the Gilgamesh epic, Ea then asks the gods
in assembly to determine what to do with the survivor. Enlil gives
Uta-napishti and his wife life 'like the gods' – they will live for ever
– and removes them to the ends of the earth. In the poem of Atram-hasis
a bigger task is undertaken, in line with the theme of that composition.
The problem of human noise has not been resolved. Ea's solution to
it constitutes the climax of the poem. He has the Mother Goddess
redesign man slightly so that the human race does not reproduce so
effectively. Women are to be barren as well as fertile. Stillbirth and
infant mortality are introduced. Certain classes of women are to be
chaste as a religious requirement, like nuns. In this way fewer babies
will be conceived, not all will be born alive and not all will survive
to adulthood. But the biggest change, one that will have the greatest
effect on the numbers of men, is that the gods establish an end to the
natural lifespan. This development is not yet found in the text itself,
which is broken at the crucial point, but it is suspected by force of

argument. What must happen is that Enki commands the Mother Goddess to make death an inevitable fact of life:

[You,] O mother goddess, maker of destiny,
  [assign death] to the people![18]

The implication is that before this reform men could die, as indeed gods could, from acts of violence, from disease and otherwise at the will of the gods, but not naturally from old age. From the time of the Deluge onwards, death is to follow life as a matter of course. This crucial moment in human history is the mythological background to the conclusion of Uta-napishti's discourse on life and death in the epic of Gilgamesh:

The Anunnaki, the great gods, held an assembly,
  Mammitum, maker of destiny, fixed fates with them:
both Death and Life they have established,
  but the day of Death they do not disclose.

In fact, the context of this momentous change in man's destiny is now confirmed by the newly available text of the Death of Bilgames, in the words of the god Enki to his partners, An and Enlil:

After the assembly had made the Deluge sweep over . . .
Ziusudra, one of mankind, still lived! . . .
From that time we swore that mankind should not have life eternal.

The sole exception to the new doom of mankind is the survivor of the Flood, who is made immortal. And how this came about, the story of the Deluge, is the subject of the continuation of Uta-napishti's teaching to Gilgamesh. But, as he himself explains, Uta-napishti's elevation to immortal status was an isolated event born of a particular set of circumstances never to be repeated. Gilgamesh may acquire the 'secret of the gods', the knowledge of how Uta-napishti 'found life' in the company of the gods, but he cannot follow in his footsteps. To underline his message of the futility of Gilgamesh's quest Uta-napishti challenges his visitor to defeat Sleep, the younger brother of Death, knowing that he will fail. Then he arranges that Gilgamesh should find the 'plant of rejuvenation', knowing that he will lose it by his own hand. Only the snake is destined to benefit from it. 'Had I only turned back, and left the boat by the shore!' With these words Gilgamesh laments that he would have been better off had he not made the journey to Uta-napishti at all, when all it has brought him is the cruel realization of his own mortal inadequacy. And aware at last of his own capabilities he becomes reconciled to his lot, and wise. In the words of the prologue, to which we return: 'He came a far road, was weary, found peace.' The story of Gilgamesh's 'growing up' is, in fact, the story of a hero who grows wise, wise in the sense of learning his place in the divinely ordained scheme of things. In fact, it is the tale of one whose extraordinary experiences make him extraordinarily wise. The poet makes it clear right at the beginning that we should expect this:

He who saw the Deep, the country's foundation,
    [who] knew . . . , was wise in all matters . . .
and [*learnt*] of everything the sum of wisdom.

The change wrought in Gilgamesh occurs only after a long history of heroic misdemeanours. At first he does everything wrong. He is king but he does not behave like a king. In Babylonian ideology, as throughout the ancient Near East, the king should be to his people as a shepherd to his sheep, guiding them, protecting them and ruling them with a just and equitable hand. Far from that, Gilgamesh is a cruel tyrant, whose brutality calls forth the complaint of his people. The contrast between the ideal and the actual is implicit in their lament:

Yet he is the shepherd of Uruk-the-Sheepfold,
    Gilgamesh, [*the guide of the*] teeming [*people.*]
. . . he is their shepherd and *their* [*protector,*]
    powerful, pre-eminent, expert [and *mighty.*]

The nature of Gilgamesh's tyranny is not explained by the poet, for it is not necessary to know more than that he is a tyrant. All that is certain is that his demands mean that filial and conjugal duties are displaced. Daughters have no time to help their mothers nor sons their fathers, and wives are unable to tend the needs of their husbands. Some commentators have inferred that Gilgamesh's abuse is sexual. It is certainly true that in the Old Babylonian version of the epic the

Babylonian audience, like Enkidu, would have reacted with horror to the 'the right of first night' (*ius primae noctis*) which the wedding-guest reports as customary in Gilgamesh's Uruk:

Gilgamesh will couple with the wife-to-be,
   he first of all, the bridegroom after.

Such things did not happen in Babylonia in the historical period. However, according to the text this activity was divinely sanctioned, and therefore could not have been an abuse in the context:

By divine consent it is so ordained;
   when his navel-cord was cut, for him she was destined.

Others suppose that Gilgamesh's tyranny is related to his reputation as the builder of Uruk's wall. Like new irrigation projects and other grand municipal building works, city walls in ancient Mesopotamia were constructed by public labour. The workforce was conscripted from the citizenry. From the references that we have to mutinies of labour-gangs – as in the myth of the gods' revolt in the poem of Atram-hasis – it seems that the regime of such organized labour could be harsh to the point of brutality.

A third suggestion turns for inspiration to the Sumerian poem of Bilgames and the Netherworld, in which the young men of Uruk are required to share Bilgames's inexhaustible appetite for what appears to be a game of great physical demands, and the city's women spend all day attending to the needs of their exhausted menfolk. This is probably nearest the mark. In the Babylonian epic the line, 'He has no equal when his weapons are brandished,' suggests that in the Akkadian tradition the games, if that is what they were, have become more martial than they are in the Sumerian. At all events, in contrast to his splendidly regal appearance Gilgamesh's behaviour, here at the beginning of the epic, is far from the royal ideal.

The arrival of Enkidu brings relief to the people of Uruk but does nothing to make Gilgamesh wise. Full of youthful bravado he turns down sage counsel and makes the perilous journey to the Cedar Forest. There he and Enkidu kill the ogre Humbaba, in the full knowledge that the god Enlil, the greatest power on earth, had given Humbaba the job of guarding the cedar. There, too, Gilgamesh does not hold

back from desecrating the sacred groves of the gods. A similar disregard
for the divine powers characterizes the next episode, in which Gilgam-
esh repudiates the goddess Ishtar with gratuitous insults and then
fights and kills the celestial bull she hopes will avenge her. The gods,
driven to act by the repeated violation of their order, doom Enkidu
to die young and without a family, in fulfilment of Humbaba's dying
curse. At this point Gilgamesh abandons all the responsibilities of his
position for personal ends. He takes to the wild. Still unwise, he
continues to reject sound advice wherever he meets it. Still he acts
before he thinks. When, at the edge of the ocean that surrounds the
world, he encounters the wise Shiduri in her tavern, he threatens her
with violence so that she tells him how to continue on his road.
Following her instructions to seek out Ur-shanabi, the ferryman of
Uta-napishti, he comes across Ur-shanabi's crew, the mysterious Stone
Ones, and smashes them. In doing so he only makes his journey more
perilous. It is only when he reaches the realm of the Flood hero beyond
the cosmic ocean that Gilgamesh begins to lose his unthinking instinct
for violence. Even then, he admits that his intention had been to win
Uta-napishti's secret by force of arms:

I was fully intent on making you fight,
    but now in your presence my hand is stayed.

Uta-napishti's realm is in some ways an enchanted place, a kind of
Prospero's isle, for it seems that on arriving there Gilgamesh begins
to mend his ways. At the old man's feet he learns the lessons that
make him wise. As a sign of the change wrought in Gilgamesh Uta-
napishti sends him home in a magic garment that cannot become
dirty. The new raiment symbolizes his new state of mind. 'Let your
clothes be clean!' counselled Shiduri. 'Let thy garments be always
white!' enjoins Ecclesiastes.

In the epic the explicit wisdom that Gilgamesh gained at the end
of the world is knowledge of himself and the story of the Deluge. In
Babylonian tradition he also gained another kind of wisdom. The
prologue of the epic fêtes the hero as one

who reached through sheer force Uta-napishti the Distant;
who restored the cult-centres destroyed by the Deluge,
    and set in place for the people the rites of the cosmos.

There is mythology to be explained here too, relating to the post-diluvian history of mankind. The ancient historical tradition, as reported in the king lists, is that after the Deluge human kingship had to be re-established by the gods: 'after the Flood had swept over, then, kingship being sent down from heaven, kingship was in the city of Kish'.[19] The dynasty of Kish was followed by that of Uruk, of which Gilgamesh (or Bilgames) was the fifth king. The implication is that, when kings began to reign again, the antediluvian civilization was restored, that is, the order ordained by the gods came back into operation. This was important, for the traditional belief was that the gods had supplied all that was needed for human beings to flourish – cities, agriculture, the arts of civilization – at the outset of human history, in the antediluvian age. Nothing more was to be discovered; the antediluvian model was how human society should be run.

According to one ancient view, most fully reported by Berossus in his *Babyloniaca*, civilization was restored by those who had accompanied Ziusudra (the Sumerian name of Uta-napishti) on board the ark and thus survived the Deluge. This tradition is implicit in the Flood story preserved in Tablet XI of Gilgamesh and in the poem of Atram-hasis, where the mention of the craftsmen and animals taken aboard the ark explains how it was that the skills of artisans and herdsmen (and the animal kingdom in general) survived the catastrophe. But there was also a tradition, local to the town of Lagash in the early second millennium, that the gods withheld kingship for a time. During this time they did not require mankind to look after their needs by irrigating and tilling the land, and no agriculture took place:

After the Flood had swept over . . .
when the gods An and Enlil . . .
had not sent down from heaven (once more)
kingship, crown and even city,
and for all the overthrown people had not established (once more)
mattock, spade, earth-basket and plough,
the things which ensure the life of the land,
then a man spent one hundred years as a boy, free of duties,
another hundred years he spent, after he grew up,
(but still) he performed no task of work.[20]

In this feckless, idle state the human race went hungry and failed to
flourish. The tablet is broken at this point but there must have followed
a description of the re-establishment of kingship and ordered life, for
when the text is again legible the gods are re-introducing the people
to the arts of agriculture.

The implication of the prologue of the epic is that Gilgamesh
played a key role in restoring the antediluvian order after the Flood,
particularly in restoring the cults of the gods to their proper glory.
The new discovery of text of the Sumerian poem we know as the
Death of Bilgames confirms this inference. On his deathbed Bilgames
has a dream, in which the gods relate to him his heroic achievements:

You reached Ziusudra in his abode!
The rites of Sumer, forgotten there since distant days of old . . .
[*after* the] Deluge *it was you* made known all the *tasks* of the land.

Here also is a connection between Gilgamesh's journey to the survivor
of the Flood and the restoration of cultic life. So the wisdom he
brought back from his journey was more than personal knowledge.
It did not suit the poet's needs to include more than allusions to it,
but evidently Gilgamesh was responsible for re-civilizing his country.
In this he was the tool of the god Ea, like the Seven Sages, for as
Ninsun predicted in Tablet III, Gilgamesh grew 'wise with Ea of the
Ocean Below'. The epic's opening words make the same connection:
he 'saw the Deep, the country's foundation'. The Deep signifies Ea's
cosmic domain, especially as the fount of wisdom. From this source
Gilgamesh learnt the profound truths that underpinned human society
and government.

In a poem whose hero becomes obsessed with the avoidance of
death, it is to be expected that the poet will be much interested in the
Netherworld. Conditions there are the subject of a large section of
Tablet VII, in which Enkidu on his deathbed dreams of being dragged
down to the Netherworld by the Angel of Death. The funeral and
wake of Enkidu, described in the latter part of Tablet VIII, can be
understood as the ideal model for the mortuary rites that preceded
the burial of a Babylonian noble. The appended Tablet XII tells more
of the fate of the shades. The relevance of this is more than a question
of theme, however. The ultimate destiny of Gilgamesh would be
known to every Babylonian: after death he became the deified ruler

and judge of the shades of the dead. In the Sumerian poem of the
Death of Bilgames this position is given to him by the gods on account
of his mother's divinity:

Bilgames, in the form of his ghost, dead in the underworld,
shall be [the governor of the Netherworld,] chief of the shades!
[He will pass judgement,] he will render verdicts,
[what he says will be as weighty as the word of] Ningishzida and
    Dumuzi.

Gilgamesh's fate as one of the gods of the Netherworld is a matter
which is understood in the epic. His posthumous place in the pantheon
is not revealed to him, but his mother has foreknowledge of it, as she
reminds Shamash in Tablet III:

  Will he not rule with Irnina the black-headed people?
Will he not dwell with Ningishzida in the Land-of-No-Return?

  It is a neat irony, surely appreciated by every educated Babylonian,
that the hero who failed to become a god in life became one in death.

Notes

1. For the full text of the composition from which these lines are quoted see
   Benjamin R. Foster, *From Distant Days: Myths, Tales and Poetry of Ancient
   Mesopotamia* (Bethesda, Md.: CDL Press, 1995), pp. 165–6: Birth Legend of
   Sargon. This quotation and other passages from Sumerian and Akkadian
   literature given in this Introduction are my own translations.
2. Shulgi Hymn B 314–15. For the whole composition see G. R. Castellino, *Two
   Šulgi Hymns (bc)*. Studi semitici 42 (Rome: Istituto di Studi del Vicino Oriente,
   1972).
3. Proverb Collection 2, no. 49; see Edmund I. Gordon, *Sumerian Proverbs:
   Glimpses of Everyday Life in Ancient Mesopotamia* (Philadelphia: University
   Museum, 1959), p. 206.
4. Schooldays, ll. 38–41. The composition was last edited by Samuel N. Kramer,
   Schooldays: A Sumerian Composition Relating to the Education of a Scribe
   (Philadelphia: University Museum, 1949), but it is now better understood.
   For the passage quoted see Konrad Volk, 'Methoden altmesopotamischer
   Erziehung nach Quellen der altbabylonischen Zeit', *Saeculum* 47 (Freiburg
   and Munich: Verlag Karl Alber, 1996), p. 200.

5. For this composition see Foster, *From Distant Days*, pp. 52–77: Story of the Flood.

6. Ashurbanipal Tablet L⁴, ll. 11–12. For the whole text see Daniel David Luckenbill, *Ancient Records of Assyria and Babylonia* 2 (Chicago: University of Chicago Press, 1927), pp. 378–82.

7. The tablet from which these words are quoted is still unpublished. See for the moment A. R. George, 'Assyria and the Western World', in S. Parpola and R. M. Whiting (eds.), *Assyria 1995. Proceedings of the Tenth Anniversary Symposium* (Helsinki: Neo-Assyrian Text Corpus Project, 1997), pp. 71–2.

8. There is no modern English translation of the famous document that contains this instruction, R. Campbell Thompson, *Late Babylonian Letters* (London: Luzac, 1906), no. 1.

9. William L. Moran, 'The Epic of Gilgamesh: a document of ancient humanism', *Bulletin, Canadian Society for Mesopotamian Studies* 22 (Toronto, 1991), pp. 15–22.

10. G. S. Kirk, *Myth: its Meaning and Function in Ancient and Other Cultures* (Cambridge: Cambridge University Press and Berkeley: University of California Press, 1970), Chapter IV.

11. Thorkild Jacobsen, 'The Gilgamesh epic: romantic and tragic vision', in Tzvi Abusch, John Huehnergard and Piotr Steinkeller (eds.), *Lingering over Words. Studies in Ancient Near Eastern Literature in Honor of William L. Moran*, Harvard Semitic Studies 37 (Atlanta: Scholars Press, 1990), pp. 231–49.

12. Cuthean Legend, ll. 147–53. For a translation of the whole text see Foster, *From Distant Days*, pp. 171–7.

13. This myth is most fully retold in the first part of the poem of Atram-hasis, 'When the gods were man': this is the text referred to in note 5 above.

14. Atram-hasis, I, 208–17.

15. Stanley Mayer Burstein, *The Babyloniaca of Berossus* (Malibu: Undena Publications, 1978).

16. The only edition of this recently discovered text is by Werner R. Mayer, 'Ein Mythos von der Erschaffung des Menschen und des Königs', *Orientalia* 56 (Rome: Pontificio Istituto Biblico, 1987), pp. 55–68.

17. The most recent English translation of this text is by A. Sachs in James B. Pritchard (ed.), *Ancient Near Eastern Texts Relating to the Old Testament* (3rd edition, Princeton: Princeton University Press, 1969), pp. 341–2.

18. Atram-hasis, III, vi, 47–8, as restored by W. G. Lambert, 'The theology of death', in B. Alster (ed.), *Death in Mesopotamia*. Mesopotamia 8 (Copenhagen: Akademisk Forlag, 1980), pp. 53–66.

19. The Sumerian King List, known in antiquity as 'Kingship being sent down from heaven', edited by T. Jacobsen, *The Sumerian King List*. Assyriological Studies 11 (Chicago: University of Chicago Press, 1939).

20. The Sumerian text which tells this myth was edited by E. Sollberger, 'The rulers of Lagaš', *Journal of Cuneiform Studies* 21 (Cambridge, Mass.: American Schools of Oriental Research, 1969), pp. 279–91.

A Note on the Translation

The essential unit of poetry in Akkadian is the poetic line or verse, which usually forms a unit of sense complete in itself. There is therefore a pause at the end of each line. The verse is easily identified, for on cuneiform tablets the beginning and end of a verse coincide with the beginning and end of a line on the tablet (though not in Syria and elsewhere in the ancient West). In older poetry a single verse may occupy two or even three lines on the tablet. In the first millennium one verse usually occupies one line, though sometimes two verses are doubled up on to a single line of tablet. Extra-long lines occur occasionally; sometimes these have been arranged as two lines in the translation. (One or other of these points explains those occasions in the translation where the line-count in the margin seems to disagree with the numbers of lines of text.) In Gilgamesh the verse is the only poetic unit explicitly identifiable on the ancient manuscripts. However, more complex patterns can be detected. Usually two verses are complementary, parallel or otherwise paired by meaning or by the development of the narrative, and form a distich or couplet. A couplet is followed by a longer pause, more often than not one that in modern punctuation would be marked by a full stop (there was no punctuation in cuneiform writing). In some Babylonian poetry the division into couplets is rigorous. This is generally true of the earlier Gilgamesh poems, especially the old version of the epic represented by the Pennsylvania and Yale tablets. In the later, standard version the couplet system is not so strictly applied and one can often detect three-line combinations, or triplets. In the older texts, especially, one may also observe that two couplets usually hold together and that the poetry therefore progresses in a sequence of four-line stanzas, or quatrains.

In contrast with other renderings of the epic, some of which, it is true, do manage to observe the division into couplets, the present translation attempts to highlight the existence of longer poetic units. To this end the second line of a couplet is indented and the stanzas are separated in the conventional modern way, by introducing space between them. Where the stanzas are consistently of two couplets, the division into quatrains is confirmed by the regularity of the poetry. In the standard version of the epic, where the system of couplets was not so consistently applied, the division into stanzas is more arbitrary and the punctuation less secure. As a working hypothesis I have assumed that in the standard version stanzas will normally comprise four lines but may on occasion consist of two, three, five or even six lines. Other translators will have other ideas.

The plot summaries that in this translation introduce each Tablet of the standard version, the line-numbers, the editorial notes which link disconnected fragments of text, and other material in small type are, like the punctuation, modern additions.

Some explanation is needed of the conventions that mark damaged text:

[Gilgamesh]	Square brackets enclose words that are restored in passages where the tablet is broken. Small breaks can often be restored with certainty from context and longer breaks can sometimes be filled securely from parallel passages.
Gilgamesh	Italics are used to indicate insecure decipherments and uncertain renderings of words in the extant text.
[*Gilgamesh*]	Within square brackets, italics signal restorations that are not certain or material that is simply conjectural, i.e. supplied by the translator to fill in the context.
. . .	An ellipsis marks a small gap that occurs where writing is missing through damage or where the signs are present but cannot be deciphered. Each ellipsis represents up to one quarter of a verse.
. . . .	Where a full line is missing or undeciphered the lacuna is marked by a sequence of four ellipses.
* * *	Where a lacuna of more than one line is not signalled by an editorial note it is marked by a succession of three asterisks.

Note in addition the following convention:

*Humbaba   In old material that has been interpolated into the standard version of the epic some proper nouns are preceded by an asterisk. This is to signify that for consistency's sake the name in question (e.g. Huwawa) has been altered to its later form.

Further Reading

A number of useful introductions to various aspects of ancient Meso-potamian civilization are now available in paperback as well as hard-back. A good anthology of Babylonian literature is Benjamin R. Foster, *From Distant Days: Myths, Tales and Poetry of Ancient Mesopotamia* (Bethesda, Md.: CDL Press, 1995). There is also Stephanie Dalley, *Myths from Mesopotamia* (Oxford: OUP, 1989). For the religion of Sumer and Akkad, as well as of Babylonia and Assyria, see Thorkild Jacobsen, *The Treasures of Darkness* (New Haven, Conn.: Yale University Press, 1976). An encyclopedic approach is Jeremy Black and Anthony Green, *Gods, Demons and Symbols of Ancient Mesopotamia* (London: British Museum Press, 1992). See also Gwendolyn Leick, *A Dictionary of Ancient Near Eastern Mythology* (London and New York: Routledge, 1998). The intellectual background of Babylonian scholarship and religion is examined by Jean Bottéro, *Mesopotamia: Writing, Reasoning and the Gods* (Chicago: University of Chicago Press, 1992). A useful survey of the history of ancient Mesopotamia is Georges Roux, *Ancient Iraq* (Harmondsworth: Penguin, 3rd edition 1992). For a wider perspective see Amélie Kuhrt, *The Ancient Near East c. 3000–300 BC* (London and New York: Routledge, 1995). The economic and social life of ancient Mesopotamia in the late third and early second millennia BC is examined by J. N. Postgate, *Early Mesopotamia: Society and Economy at the Dawn of History* (London and New York: Routledge, 1992). See also Daniel C. Snell, *Life in the Ancient Near East* (New Haven, Conn.: Yale University Press, 1997). A collection of recent essays on Gilgamesh, with a full bibliography to 1994, is edited in hardback by John Maier, *Gilgamesh: A Reader* (Wauconda, Ill.: Bolchazy-Carducci, 1997).

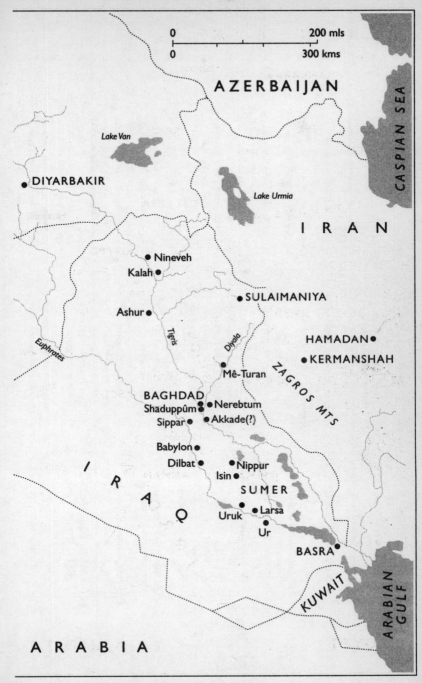

Map of the Ancient Near East

Time Chart

	POLITICAL HISTORY	INTELLECTUAL LIFE	GILGAMESH	
3000	Early city states of Sumer	Invention of writing. Earliest Sumerian tablets →		3000
2800	Gilgamesh, king of Uruk →		Gilgamesh, king of Uruk	2800
2600	Early city states of Sumer	Early Sumerian literature	Gilgamesh deified in god lists →	2600
2400			Gilgamesh worshipped in cult	2400
2300	Old Akkadian Empire / Sargon of Akkade → / Naram-Sin →	Akkadian as language of empire →		2300
2200			Oral Gilgamesh poems in Sumerian and Akkadian?	2200
2100	Third Dynasty of Ur / Shulgi →	Sumerian renaissance / Royal Tablet Houses / Sumerian court literature		2100
2000	Fall of Ur	Spoken Sumerian dying out	Oldest copy of a Sumerian Gilgamesh poem	2000
1900	Isin Dynasty → Larsa Dynasty →	Scribal schools at Ur and Nippur		1900
1800	Old Babylonian Kingdom / Hammurapi of Babylon →		Many copies of Sumerian Gilgamesh poems	1800
1750	Decline of southern Babylonia			1750
1700		Literary creativity in Akkadian	Akkadian fragments 'Surpassing all other kings' / Old Babylonian Gilgamesh epic	1700
1600	Sack of Babylon by the Hittites / Kassite Dynasty →	Very few tablets extant from this period		1600
1500				1500
1400	Amarna Age	Akkadian as *lingua franca* / Spread of Babylonian texts to the West	Middle Babylonian versions of the Gilgamesh epic copied in Anatolia, Palestine, Syria and Babylonia.	1400
1300				1300

Date	Political events	Babylonian literature / language	Gilgamesh epic	Date
1200		Organization and editing of Babylonian literature →	Sin-liqe-uninni edits the Babylonian epic into the standard version 'He who saw the Deep' →	1200
1100	Tiglath-pileser I of Assyria			1100
1000		Very few tablets extant from this period		1000
900	Neo-Assyrian Empire →		Copies of the Gilgamesh epic from Assyria	900
800	Sargon II	Spread of Aramaic in Assyria and Babylonia		800
700	Sennacherib / Esarhaddon	Royal libraries at Nineveh		700
650	Ashurbanipal / Fall of Nineveh			650
600	Neo-Babylonian Empire / Nebuchadnezzar II	Spoken Akkadian dying out		600
500	Persian Empire / Darius, Xerxes			500
400	Alexander the Great	Babylonian literature copied out and preserved in libraries of temples and scholars →	Copies of the Gilgamesh epic from Uruk and Babylon →	400
300	Greek (Hellenistic) period			300
200		Last cuneiform tablets	Last copies of the Gilgamesh epic	200
100 BC	Parthian period			100 BC
BC–AD	Decline of Babylon →			BC–AD
100 AD	Roman wars			100 AD

*N.B. Dates before 1100 BC are approximate.

Dramatis personae

An acute accent marks the vowel of a stressed syllable. Where such a vowel falls in an open syllable it will often be long (e.g., Humbaaba). In some names the position of the stress is conjectural.

Gilgámesh, king of the city-state of Úruk
Nínsun, a goddess, his mother
Enkídu, his friend and companion
Shámhat, a prostitute of Uruk
Shámash, the Sun God
Humbába, the guardian of the Forest of Cedar
Íshtar, the principal goddess of Uruk
Shidúri, a minor goddess of wisdom
Ur-shanábi, the ferryman of Uta-napishti
Úta-napíshti, survivor of the Flood

A comprehensive list of the proper nouns that occur in the texts translated in this book is given on pp. 222ff.

I

The Standard Version of
the Babylonian Gilgamesh Epic:
'He who saw the Deep'

Tablet I. The Coming of Enkidu

Prologue and paean. King Gilgamesh tyrannizes the people of Uruk, who complain
to the gods. To divert his superhuman energies the gods create his counterpart,
the wild man Enkidu, who is brought up by the animals of the wild. Enkidu is
spotted by a trapper, who lures him away from the herd with a prostitute. The
prostitute shows him her arts and proposes to take him to Uruk, where Gilgamesh
has been seeing him in dreams.

He who saw the Deep, the country's foundation,
   [who] knew . . . , was wise in all matters!
[Gilgamesh, who] saw the Deep, the country's foundation,
   [who] knew . . . , was wise in all matters!

[He] . . . everywhere . . .   I 5
   and [*learnt*] of everything the sum of wisdom.
He saw what was secret, discovered what was hidden,
   he brought back a tale of before the Deluge.

He came a far road, was weary, found peace,
   and set all his labours on a tablet of stone.   I 10
He built the rampart of Uruk-the-Sheepfold,
   of holy Eanna, the sacred storehouse.

See its wall like a strand of *wool*,
   view its parapet that none could copy!
Take the stairway of a bygone era,   I 15
   draw near to Eanna, seat of Ishtar the goddess,
that no later king could ever copy!

Climb Uruk's wall and walk back and forth!
   Survey its foundations, examine the brickwork!
Were its bricks not fired in an oven?   I 20
   Did the Seven Sages not lay its foundations?

[A square mile is] city, [a square mile] date-grove, a square mile is
      clay-pit, half a square mile the temple of Ishtar:
   [three square miles] and a half is Uruk's expanse.

[*See*] the tablet-box of cedar,
   [*release*] its clasp of bronze!   I 25
[*Lift*] the lid of its secret,
   [*pick*] *up* the tablet of lapis lazuli and read out
the travails of Gilgamesh, all that he went through.

Surpassing all other kings, heroic in stature,
   brave scion of Uruk, wild bull on the rampage!   I 30
Going at the fore he was the vanguard,
   going at the rear, one his comrades could trust!

A mighty bank, protecting his warriors,
   a violent flood-wave, smashing a stone wall!
Wild bull of Lugalbanda, Gilgamesh, the perfect in strength,   I 35
   suckling of the august Wild Cow, the goddess Ninsun!

Gilgamesh the tall, magnificent and terrible,
   who opened passes in the mountains,
who dug wells on the slopes of the uplands,
   and crossed the ocean, the wide sea to the sunrise;   I 40

who scoured the world ever searching for life,
   and reached through sheer force Uta-napishti the Distant;
who restored the cult-centres destroyed by the Deluge,
   and set in place for the people the rites of the cosmos.

Who is there can rival his kingly standing,   I 45
   and say like Gilgamesh, 'It is I am the king'?
Gilgamesh was his name from the day he was born,
   two-thirds of him god and one third human.

It was the Lady of the Gods drew the form of his figure,
    while his build was perfected by divine Nudimmud.   I 50

*   *   *

A triple cubit was his foot, half a rod his leg.   I 56
Six cubits was his stride,
    . . . cubits the *front part* of his . . .

His cheeks were bearded like those of . . . ,
    the hair of his head grew thickly [as barley.]   I 60
When he grew tall his beauty was consummate,
    by earthly standards he was most handsome.

In Uruk-the-Sheepfold he *walks [back and forth,]*
    like a wild bull lording it, head held aloft.
He has no equal when his weapons are brandished,   I 65
    his companions are kept on their feet by his *contests.*

The young men of Uruk he harries without warrant,
    Gilgamesh lets no son go free to his father.
By day and by night his tyranny grows harsher,
    Gilgamesh, [*the guide of the teeming people*!]   I 70

It is he who is shepherd of Uruk-the-Sheepfold,
    [but Gilgamesh] lets no [daughter go free to her] mother.
[*The women voiced*] their [*troubles to the goddesses,*]
    [*they brought their*] complaint before [*them:*]

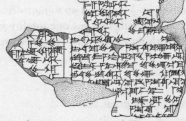

2 *'Like a wild bull lording it, head held aloft'.*

'[Though powerful, pre-eminent,] expert [and *mighty*,]   I 75
  [Gilgamesh] lets [no] girl go free to [her *bridegroom*.]'
The warrior's daughter, the young man's bride,
  to their complaint the goddesses paid heed.

The gods of heaven, the lords of *initiative*,
  [*to the god Anu they spoke*] . . . :   I 80
'A savage wild bull you have bred in Uruk-the-Sheepfold,
  he has no equal when his weapons are brandished.

'His companions are kept on their feet by his *contests*,
  [the young men of Uruk] he harries without warrant.
Gilgamesh lets no son go free to his father,   I 85
  by day and by [night his tyranny grows] harsher.

'Yet he is the shepherd of Uruk-the-Sheepfold,
  Gilgamesh, [*the guide of the*] teeming [*people.*]
Though he is their shepherd and *their* [*protector*,]
  powerful, pre-eminent, expert [and *mighty*,]   I 90
Gilgamesh lets no girl go free to her *bride*[*groom*.]'

The warrior's daughter, the young man's bride:
  to their complaint the god [Anu] paid heed.   I 93

The stanza which gives Anu's reaction has been dropped in the late edition of
the epic, but by good fortune it is preserved as a short extract from an older
version of the text, which was written by a student scribe on an exercise tablet
found in the city of Nippur:

'[Let] them summon [Aruru,] the great one,   MB Ni
  [she it was created them,] mankind so numerous:
[let her create the *equal* of Gilgamesh,] one mighty in strength,
  [and let] him vie [with him,] so Uruk may be rested!'

The text of Tablet I resumes:

They summoned Aruru, the great one:
  'You, Aruru, created [mankind:]
now fashion what Anu has thought of!   I 95

'Let him be a *match* for the *storm* of his heart,
    let them vie with each other, so Uruk may be rested!'
The goddess Aruru heard these words,
    what Anu had thought of she fashioned within her.   I 100

The goddess Aruru, she washed her hands,
    took a pinch of clay, threw it down in the wild.
In the wild she created Enkidu, the hero,
    offspring of silence, knit strong by Ninurta.

All his body is matted with hair,   I 105
    he bears long tresses like those of a woman:
the hair of his head grows thickly as barley,
    he knows not a people, nor even a country.

Coated in hair like the god of the animals,
    with the gazelles he grazes on grasses,   I 110
joining the throng with the game at the water-hole,
    his heart *delighting* with the beasts in the water.

A hunter, a trapper-man,
    did come upon him by the water-hole.
One day, a second and then a third,   I 115
    he came upon him by the water-hole.
When the hunter saw him, his expression froze,
    but he with his herds – he went back to his lair.

[The hunter was] troubled, subdued and silent,
    his mood [*was despondent,*] his features gloomy.
In his heart there was sorrow,   I 120
    his face resembled [one come from] afar.

The hunter opened [his mouth] to speak, saying [to his father:]
    'My father, there was a man came [*by the water-hole.*]
Mightiest in the land, strength [he possesses,]
    [his strength] is as mighty [as a rock] from the sky.   I 125

'Over the hills he [*roams all day,*]
  [always] with the herd [*he grazes on grasses,*]
[always] his tracks [*are found*] by the water-hole,
  [I am afraid and] I dare not approach him.

'[He fills in the] pits that I [myself] dig,   I 130
  [he pulls up] the snares that I lay.
[He sets free from my grasp] all the beasts of the field,
  [he stops] me doing the work of the wild.'

[His father opened his mouth to] speak, saying to the hunter:
  '[My son, *in the city of*] Uruk [*go, seek out*] Gilgamesh!   I 135
. . . . in his presence,
  his strength is as mighty [as a rock from the sky.]

'[Take the road,] set your face [toward Uruk,]
  [*do not rely on*] the strength of a man!
[Go, my son, and] fetch [Shamhat the harlot,]   I 140
  [*her allure is a match*] for even the mighty!

'[When the herd comes] down [to] the water-hole,
  [she should strip off] her [raiment to reveal] her charms.
[He will] see her, and will approach her,
  his herd will spurn him, [though he grew up] amongst it.'   I 145

[*Paying heed*] to the advice of his father,
  the hunter went off, [*set out on the journey.*]
He took the road, set [his face] toward Uruk,
  before Gilgamesh *the king* [*he spoke these words:*]

'There was a man [came *by the water-hole,*]   I 150
  mightiest in the land, strength [he possesses,]
[his strength] is as mighty as a rock from the sky.

'Over the hills he roams all [*day,*]
  always with the herd [*he grazes on grasses,*]
always his tracks [*are found*] by the water-[hole,]   I 155
  I am afraid and I dare not approach [him.]

'He fills in the pits that I [myself] dig,
    he pulls up the snares [that I lay.]
He sets free from my grasp all the beasts of the field,
    he stops me doing the work of the wild.'   I 160

Said Gilgamesh to him, to the hunter:
    'Go, hunter, take with you Shamhat the harlot!

'When the herd comes down to the water-hole,
    she should strip off her raiment to reveal her charms.
He will see her, and will approach her,   I 165
    his herd will spurn him, though he grew up amongst it.'

Off went the hunter, taking Shamhat the harlot,
    they set out on the road, they started the journey.
On the third day they came to their destination,
    hunter and harlot sat down there *to wait*.   I 170

One day and a second they waited by the water-hole,
    then the herd came down to drink the water.
The game arrived, their hearts *delighting in* water,
    and Enkidu also, born in the uplands.

With the gazelles he grazed on grasses,   I 175
    joining the throng with the game at the water-hole,
his heart *delighting* with the beasts in the water:
    then Shamhat saw him, the child of nature,
the savage man from the midst of the wild.

'This is he, Shamhat! Uncradle your bosom,   I 180
    bare your sex, let him take in your charms!
Do not recoil, but take in his scent:
    he will see you, and will approach you.

'Spread your clothing so he may lie on you,
    do for the man the work of a woman!   I 185
Let his passion caress and embrace you,
    his herd will spurn him, though he grew up amongst it.'

Shamhat unfastened the cloth of her loins,
    she bared her sex and he took in her charms.
She did not recoil, she took in his scent: I 190
    she spread her clothing and he lay upon her.

She did for the man the work of a woman,
    his passion caressed and embraced her.
For six days and seven nights
    Enkidu was erect, as he coupled with Shamhat.

When with her delights he was fully sated,   I 195
    he turned his gaze to his herd.
The gazelles saw Enkidu, they started to run,
    the beasts of the field shied away from his presence.

Enkidu had defiled his body so pure,
    his legs stood still, though his herd was in motion.   I 200
Enkidu was weakened, could not run as before,
    but now he had *reason*, and wide understanding.

He came back and sat at the feet of the harlot,
    watching the harlot, observing her features.
Then to the harlot's words he listened intently,   I 205
    [as Shamhat] talked to him, to Enkidu:

'You are handsome, Enkidu, you are just like a god!
    Why with the beasts do you wander the wild?
Come, I will take you to Uruk-the-Sheepfold,
    to the sacred temple, home of Anu and Ishtar,   I 210

'where Gilgamesh is perfect in strength,
    like a wild bull lording it over the menfolk.'
So she spoke to him and her word found favour,
    he knew by instinct, he should seek a friend.

Said Enkidu to her, to the harlot: I 215
    'Come, Shamhat, take me along
to the sacred temple, holy home of Anu and Ishtar,
    where Gilgamesh is perfect in strength,
like a wild bull lording it over the menfolk.

'I will challenge him, for [*my strength*] is mighty,   I 220
    I will vaunt myself in Uruk, saying "I am the mightiest!"
[*There*] I shall change the way things are ordered:
    [one] born in the wild is mighty, strength he possesses.'

Shamhat:

'Let [*the people*] see your face,
    . . . . . . that exists I know indeed.   I 225
Go, Enkidu, to Uruk-the-Sheepfold,
    where young men are girt with waistbands!

'Every day [*in Uruk*] there is a festival,
    the drums there rap out the beat.
And there are harlots, most comely of figure,   I 230
    graced with charm and full of delights.

'Even the aged they rouse from their beds!
    O Enkidu, [as yet so] ignorant of life,
I will show you Gilgamesh, a man happy and carefree,
    look at him, regard his features!   I 235

'He is fair in manhood, dignified in bearing,
    graced with charm is his whole person.
He has a strength more mighty than yours,
    unsleeping he is by day and by night.

'O Enkidu, cast aside your sinful thoughts!   I 240
    Gilgamesh it is whom divine Shamash loves.
The gods Anu, Enlil and Ea have broadened his wisdom.

'Before you even came from the uplands,
  Gilgamesh in Uruk was seeing you in dreams:
Gilgamesh rose to relate a dream, saying to his mother: I 245
  "O mother, this is the dream I had in the night –

' "The stars of the heavens appeared above me,
  like a rock from the sky one fell down before me.
I lifted it up, but it weighed too much for me,
  I tried to roll it, but I could not dislodge it.   I 250

' "The land of Uruk was standing around it,
  [the land was gathered] about it.
A crowd [*was milling about*] before it,
  [the menfolk were] thronging around it.

' "[Like a babe-in]-arms they were kissing its feet,   I 255
  like a wife [I loved it,] caressed and embraced it.
[I lifted it up,] set it down at your feet,
  [and you, O mother, you] made it my equal."

'[The mother of Gilgamesh] was clever and wise,
  well versed in everything, she said to her son –
[Wild-Cow] Ninsun was clever and wise,   I 260
  well versed in everything, she said to Gilgamesh:

' "The stars of heaven [appeared] above you,
  [like a] rock from the sky one fell down before you.
You lifted it up, but it weighed too much for you,
  you tried to roll it, but you could not dislodge it.

' "You lifted it up, set it down at my feet,   I 265
  and I, Ninsun, I made it your equal.
Like a wife you loved it, caressed and embraced it:
  a mighty comrade will come to you, and be his friend's saviour.

' "Mightiest in the land, strength he possesses,
  his strength is as mighty as a rock from the sky.   I 270
Like a wife you'll love him, caress and embrace him,
  he will be mighty, and often will save you."

'Having had a second dream,
　　he rose and entered before the goddess, his mother.
Said Gilgamesh to her, to his mother,   I 275
　　"Once more, O mother, have I had a dream –

'"[In a street] of Uruk-the-Town-Square,
　　an axe was lying with a crowd gathered round.
The land [of Uruk] was standing around it,
　　[the country was] gathered about it.   I 280

'"A crowd *was milling about* before it,
　　[the menfolk were] thronging around it.
I lifted it up and set it down at your feet,
　　like a wife [I loved] it, caressed and embraced it,
[and you, O mother,] you made it my equal."   I 285

'The mother of Gilgamesh was clever and wise,
　　well versed in everything, she said to her son –
Wild-Cow Ninsun was clever and wise,
　　well versed in everything, she said to Gilgamesh:

'"My son, the axe you saw is a friend,
　　like a wife you'll love him, caress and embrace him,
and I, Ninsun, I shall make him your equal.   I 290
　　A mighty comrade will come to you, and be his friend's saviour,
mightiest in the land, strength he possesses,
　　his strength is as mighty as a rock from the sky."

'Said Gilgamesh to her, to his mother,
　　"May it befall me, O mother, by Counsellor Enlil's
　　　　command!   I 295
Let me acquire a friend to counsel me,
　　a friend to counsel me I will acquire!"

'[So did Gilgamesh] see his dreams.'
　　[After] Shamhat had told Enkidu the dreams of Gilgamesh,
the two of them together [began making] love.   I 300

Tablet II. The Taming of Enkidu

The prostitute takes Enkidu to a shepherds' camp, where he is instructed in the ways of men and becomes the shepherds' watchman. A passing stranger tells him how in Uruk Gilgamesh exercises *droit de seigneur* at wedding ceremonies. Enkidu, shocked by this practice, enters Uruk and interrupts the proceedings. Gilgamesh and Enkidu fight until Enkidu accepts Gilgamesh's supremacy, whereupon the pair become firm friends. In search of fame and glory Gilgamesh proposes an expedition to the Forest of Cedar, ignoring Enkidu's warning of the dangers. They kit themselves out with weapons. Gilgamesh announces his plans to the assembly of Uruk. The elders try to dissuade him.

[Enkidu] was sitting before her, . . .   II 1

A lacuna follows the opening line of Tablet II, and when the text resumes the lines are still not fully recovered. The big Old Babylonian Pennsylvania tablet (P) supplies a better-preserved account, though one that partly overlaps with Tablet I:

While the two of them together were making love,   P 46
    he forgot the wild where he was born.
For seven days and seven nights
    Enkidu was erect and coupled with *Shamhat.   P 50

The harlot opened her mouth,
    saying to Enkidu:
'As I look at you, Enkidu, you are like a god,
    why with the beasts do you wander the wild?   P 55

'Come, I will lead you to Uruk-the-Town-Square,
    to the sacred temple, the home of Anu!
Enkidu, arise, let me take you
    to the temple Eanna, the home of Anu,   P 60

'where [men] are engaged in labours of skill,
    you, too, *like a man*, will *find a place for* yourself.'   P 63

    * * *

Her words he heard, her speech found favour: P 66
  the counsel of a woman struck home in his heart.
She stripped and clothed him in part of her garment,   P 70
  the other part she put on herself.

The text of Tablet II resumes:

By the hand she took him, like a god [she led him,]   II 36
  to the shepherds' camp, the site of the sheep-pen.
The band of shepherds was gathered around him,
  talking about him among themselves:

'This fellow – how like in build he is to Gilgamesh,   II 40
  tall in stature, *proud* as a battlement.
For sure it's Enkidu, born in the uplands,
  his strength is as mighty as a rock from the sky.'

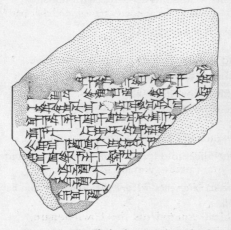

3 *'For sure it's Enkidu, born in the uplands'.*

Bread they set before him,
  ale they set before him.   II 45
Enkidu ate not the bread, but looked *askance*.

Here Tablet II becomes fragmentary again, and the episode is best taken from
the Old Babylonian Pennsylvania tablet:

How to eat bread Enkidu knew not,   P 90
  how to drink ale he had never been shown.

The harlot opened her mouth,
  saying to Enkidu: P 95
'Eat the bread, Enkidu, essential to life,
  drink the ale, the lot of the land!'

Enkidu ate the bread until he was sated,   P 100
  he drank the ale, a full seven goblets.
His mood became free, he started to sing,
  his heart grew merry, his face lit up.   P 105

The barber groomed his body so hairy,
  anointed with oil he turned into a man.
He put on a garment, became like a warrior,   P 110
  he took up his weapon to do battle with lions.

The text of Tablet II resumes again:

[When at night the shepherds lay sleeping,]
  [he struck] down wolves, he [chased off lions.]   II 60
Sleeping lay the senior shepherds,
  their shepherd boy Enkidu, a [man wide] awake.

[A certain] fellow had [*been invited*] to a wedding,
  [to] Uruk-the-Sheepfold [*he was going*] for the [*banquet.*]   II 64

Here another lacuna intervenes in Tablet II, which the Old Babylonian tablet
again helps to fill:

Enkidu was having his pleasure with *Shamhat.   P 135
He lifted his eyes, caught sight of the man,
  and thus he spoke to the harlot:

'*Shamhat, bring the man over: P 140
  why he came here, let me *learn* his reason.'
The harlot hailed the man,
  went up to him, spoke to him:

'Where do you hurry to, fellow?   P 145
  What is your journey so toilsome?'
The fellow opened his mouth,
  saying to Enkidu:

'I was invited to a wedding banquet,
  it is the lot of the people to contract a marriage.   P 150
I shall load the ceremonial table
  with tempting foods for the wedding feast.

'For the king of Uruk-the-Town-Square,
  the *veil* will be parted for the one who picks first;   P 155
for Gilgamesh, the king of Uruk-the-Town-Square,
  the *veil* will be parted for the one who picks first.

'He will couple with the wife-to-be,
  he first of all, the bridegroom after.   P 160
By divine consent it is so ordained:
  when his navel-cord was cut, for him she was destined.'

At the fellow's words his face paled in anger.   P 166

    *   *   *

  Off goes Enkidu, with *Shamhat following.   P 175

He entered the city of Uruk-the-Town-Square,
  and a crowd gathered around.
He came to a halt in the street of Uruk-the-Town-Square,   P 180
  all gathered about, the people discussed him:

'In build he is the image of Gilgamesh,
  but shorter in stature, and bigger of bone.   P 185
For [sure it's the one who] was born in the uplands,
  animals' milk is what he was suckled on.'

In Uruk they held regular festivals of sacrifice,   P 190
  young men made merry, set up a *champion*:
for the fellow whose features were fair,
  for Gilgamesh, like a god, was set up a rival.   P 195

For the goddess of weddings the bed was laid out,
    Gilgamesh met with the maiden by night.
Forward came (Enkidu), he stood in the street,   P 200
    blocking the path of Gilgamesh.

The text of Tablet II becomes legible once more:

The land of Uruk was standing [around him,]   II 103
    the land was gathered [about him.]
A crowd was *milling about* before [him,]   II 105
    the menfolk were thronging [around him.]

Like a babe-in-arms they were [kissing his feet,]
    already the fellow . . . . . .
For the goddess of weddings was ready the bed,
    for Gilgamesh, like a god, was set up a substitute.   II 110

Enkidu with his foot blocked the door of the wedding house,
    not allowing Gilgamesh to enter.
They seized each other at the door of the wedding house,
    in the street they joined combat, in the Square of the Land.

The door-jambs shook, the wall did shudder,   II 115
    [in the street Gilgamesh and Enkidu joined combat, in the Square
        of the Land.]
[The door-jambs shook, the wall did shudder.]

Another lacuna intervenes, again partly to be filled by the Old Babylonian
Pennsylvania tablet:

Gilgamesh knelt, one foot on the ground,
    his anger subsided, he broke off from the fight.   P 230
After he broke off from the fight,
    said Enkidu to him, to Gilgamesh:

'As one unique your mother bore you,   P 235
    the wild cow of the fold, the goddess Ninsun!
High over warriors you are exalted,
    to be king of the people Enlil made it your destiny!'   P 240

At this point the Old Babylonian Pennsylvania tablet ends. Its sequel, the Yale tablet (Y), is less well preserved. In the first intelligible episode Enkidu is speaking to Gilgamesh:

'Why do you desire to do this thing?
    ... anything ... do you want so much?   Y 15
Let me . . . . ,
    a feat that never was done in the land.'

They kissed each other and formed a friendship.

After another lacuna Tablet II resumes with an episode in which Gilgamesh introduces Enkidu to his mother:

    'The mightiest [in the land, strength he possesses.]   II 162
[His strength is as mighty as a] rock from the sky,
    he is tall in [stature, *proud* as a battlement.]'

The mother of Gilgamesh [opened her mouth to speak,]   II 165
    saying to [her son –]
Wild-Cow Ninsun [opened her mouth to speak,]
    [saying to Gilgamesh:]

'My son, in his gate . . . . . . ,
    bitterly you . . . . . . '   II 169

        *   *   *

'You hold . . . . ,   II 172
    ... in his gate . . . . . .

'Bitterly he . . . . . . ,
    Enkidu possesses no [*kith or kin*.]   II 175
Shaggy hair hanging loose . . . . . .
    he was born in the wild and [*has*] no [*brother*.]'

Standing there, Enkidu heard [what she said,]
    and thinking it over, he sat [down *weeping*.]
His eyes brimmed with [tears,]   II 180
    his arms fell limp, [his] strength [*ebbed away*.]

They took hold of each other and . . . . . . ,
    they [*linked*] their hands like . . . . . .
Gilgamesh . . . . ,
    to Enkidu he spoke a word, [saying:]   II 185

'Why, my friend, [did your eyes] brim [with tears,]
    your arms fall limp, [your strength *ebb away*?]'
Said Enkidu to him, [to Gilgamesh:]
    'My friend, my heart is aggrieved . . .

'Through sobbing [my *legs* do] tremble,   II 190
    terror has entered my heart.'

The Old Babylonian Yale tablet fills the gap in the standard version:

Gilgamesh opened his mouth,
    saying to Enkidu: Y 90

        *   *   *

' . . . . . . ferocious *Humbaba,   Y 97
    . . . [let us] slay him, [so *his power*] is no more!

'In the Forest of Cedar, [where *Humbaba] dwells,   Y 100
    let us frighten him in his lair!'
Enkidu opened his mouth,
    saying to Gilgamesh: Y 105

'I knew him, my friend, in the uplands,
    when I roamed here and there with the herd.
For sixty leagues the forest is a wilderness,
    who is there would venture inside it?

'*Humbaba, his voice is the Deluge,   Y 110
    his speech is fire, and his breath is death!
Why do you desire to do this thing?
    An unwinnable battle is *Humbaba's ambush!'   Y 115

Gilgamesh opened his mouth,
  saying to Enkidu:
'I will climb, my friend, [*the forest's*] slopes.'   Y 119

The text of Tablet II resumes:

Enkidu [opened his] mouth [to speak, saying to Gilgamesh:]   II 216
  '[My friend], how can we [go to the home of Humbaba?]
So to keep safe the cedars,
  Enlil made it his lot to terrify men.

'That is a journey [which must not be made,]
  [that is a man who must not be looked on.]
He who guards the [Forest of Cedar, his *reach* is wide,]   II 220
  Humbaba, his voice is the Deluge.

'His speech is fire, his breath is death,
  he hears the forest murmur at sixty leagues' distance.
Who is there would venture into his forest?
  Adad ranks first, and Humbaba second.   II 225

'Who is there would oppose him among the Igigi?
  So to keep safe the cedars,
Enlil made it his lot to terrify men;
  if you penetrate his forest you are seized by the tremors.'

Gilgamesh opened his mouth to speak,   II 230
  saying [to Enkidu:]
'Why, my friend, do you speak like a weakling?
  With your spineless words you [make me] despondent.

'As for man, [his days] are numbered,
  whatever he may do, it is but wind,   II 235
. . . exists not for me . . . . . .

'You were born and grew up [in the wild:]
  even lions were afraid of you, [you experienced] all.
Grown men fled away [from your presence,]
  your heart is tried and [tested in] combat.   II 240

'Come, my friend, [let us hie] to the forge!'

A short lacuna follows. It can be filled from the Old Babylonian Yale tablet:

'[Let] them cast [us hatchets] in our presence!'   Y 162

They took each other by the hand and hied to the forge,
   where the smiths were sitting in consultation.
Great hatchets they cast,   Y 165
   and axes weighing three talents apiece.

Great daggers they cast:
   two talents apiece were the blades,
one half of a talent the crests of their handles,
   half a talent apiece the daggers' gold mountings.   Y 170
Gilgamesh and Enkidu bore ten talents each.

He bolted the sevenfold gates of Uruk,
   he convened [the assembly,] the crowd gathered round.
. . . in the street of Uruk-the-Town-Square,
   Gilgamesh [seated himself on] his throne.   Y 175

[In the street of Uruk]-the-Town-Square,
   [the crowd was] sitting before him.
[Thus Gilgamesh] spoke
   [to the elders of Uruk]-the-Town-Square:

'[Hear me, O elders of Uruk-the-Town]-Square!   Y 180
   [I would tread the path to ferocious *Humbaba,]
I would see the god of whom men talk,
   whose name the lands do constantly repeat.

'I will conquer him in the Forest of Cedar:
   let the land learn Uruk's offshoot is mighty!   Y 185
Let me start out, I will cut down the cedar,
   I will establish for ever a name èternal!'

The text of Tablet II resumes:

[Then Gilgamesh spoke]   II 258
  [to the young men of Uruk-the-Sheepfold:]

'Hear me, O young men [of Uruk-the-Sheepfold,]   II 260
  O young men of Uruk, who understand [*combat*!]
Bold as I am I shall tread the distant path [to the home of
        Humbaba,]
  I shall face a battle I know not.

'[I shall ride] a road [I know not:]
  give me your blessing as I go on my journey,   II 265
[so I may see again] your faces [in safety,]
  and return [glad at heart] through Uruk's gate!

'On my return [I will celebrate] New Year [twice over,]
  I will celebrate the festival twice in the year.
Let the festival take place, the merriment begin,   II 270
  let the drums resound before [Wild-Cow] Ninsun!'

Enkidu [offered] counsel to the elders,
  and the young men of Uruk, who understood *combat*:

'Tell him not to go to the Forest of Cedar!
  That is a journey which must not be made,   II 275
that is a man [who must not be] looked on.
  He who guards the Forest of Cedar, his [*reach*] is wide.

'This *Humbaba*, [his voice is the Deluge,]
  [his speech is fire,] his breath is death!
[He hears] the forest murmur [at sixty leagues' distance:]   II 280
  [who is there would venture] into his forest?

'[Adad ranks first, and Humbaba] second:
  [who is there would oppose him] among the Igigi?
[So to keep safe the cedars,]
  Enlil made it his lot to terrify men;   II 285
if you penetrate his forest you are seized by the tremors.'

The senior advisers rose,
   good counsel they offered Gilgamesh:
'You are young, Gilgamesh, borne along by emotion,
   all that you talk of you don't understand.   II 290

'This Humbaba, his voice is the Deluge,
   his speech is fire, his breath is death!
He hears the forest murmur at sixty leagues' distance:
   who is there would venture into his forest?   II 295

'Adad ranks first, and Humbaba second:
   who is there would oppose him among the Igigi?
So to keep safe the cedars,
   Enlil made it his lot to terrify men.'

Gilgamesh heard the words of the senior advisers,   II 300
   he looked with a [laugh at] Enkidu . . . :
['Now, my friend, how frightened I am!]
   [In fear of him shall I change my mind?']

The rest of Tablet II, perhaps twenty lines containing Gilgamesh's reply to his
counsellors, is lost.

Tablet III. Preparations for the Expedition
to the Forest of Cedar

The elders give Gilgamesh and Enkidu advice for their journey. The two heroes
visit the goddess Ninsun, who enlists the help of the Sun God, Shamash, and
the aid of his wife, Aya. Ninsun adopts the orphan Enkidu. Gilgamesh gives
instructions for the governing of Uruk in his absence. The heroes depart.

[The elders of Uruk-the-Sheepfold]   II end
   [spoke to Gilgamesh:]

'To Uruk's [quay come back in safety,]   III 1
   do not rely, O Gilgamesh, on your strength alone,
look long and hard, land a blow you can count on!

' "Who goes in front saves his companion,
     who knows the road protects his friend."   III 5
Let Enkidu go before you,
     he knows the journey to the Forest of Cedar.

'He is tested in battle and tried in combat,
     he shall guard his friend and keep safe his companion,
Enkidu shall bring him safe home to his *wives*!   III 10

(To Enkidu)

'In our assembly we place the King in your care:
     you bring him back and replace him in ours!'
Gilgamesh opened his mouth to speak,
     saying to Enkidu:

'Come, my friend, let us go to the Palace Sublime,   III 15
     into the presence of the great Queen Ninsun.
Ninsun is clever and wise, well versed in everything,
     she will set our feet in steps of good counsel.'

Taking each other hand in hand,
     Gilgamesh and Enkidu went to the Palace Sublime.   III 20
Into the presence of the great Queen Ninsun,
     Gilgamesh rose and entered before [her.]

Said Gilgamesh to her, to [Ninsun:]
     '[I shall tread,] O Ninsun, bold as I am,
the distant path to the home of Humbaba,   III 25
     I shall face a battle I know not,

'I shall ride a road I know not:
     I beseech you, give me your blessing for my journey!
Let me see your face again in safety,
     and return glad at heart through Uruk's gate.   III 30

'On my return I will celebrate New Year twice over,
   I will celebrate the festival twice in the year.
Let the festival take place, the merriment begin,
   let the drums resound in your presence!'

[Wild-Cow] Ninsun listened long and with sadness   III 35
   to the words of Gilgamesh, her son, and Enkidu.
Into the bath-house she went seven times,
   [she bathed] herself in water of tamarisk and soapwort.

[*She donned*] a fine dress to adorn her body,
   [*she chose a jewel*] to adorn her breast.   III 40
Having put on [*her cap,*] she donned her tiara,
   . . . . . . the harlots . . . the ground.

She climbed the staircase and went up on the roof,
   on the roof she set up a censer to Shamash.
Scattering incense she lifted her arms in appeal to the Sun
                           God: III 45
   'Why did you afflict my son Gilgamesh with so restless a spirit?

'For now you have touched him and he will tread
   the distant path to the home of Humbaba.
He will face a battle he knows not,
   he will ride a road he knows not.   III 50

'During the days of his journey there and back,
   until he reaches the Forest of Cedar,
until he slays ferocious Humbaba,
   and annihilates from the land the Evil Thing you abhor,

'each day when [*you travel*] the circuit [*of the earth,*]   III 55
   may Aya the Bride unfearing remind you:
"Entrust him to the care of the watches of the night!"'
   At eventide . . .   III 58

       *   *   *

'You opened, O [Shamash, *the gates* for] the herd to go out,
    for . . . you came forth for the land. ·
The uplands [*took shape*,] the heavens grew [bright,]   III 65
    the beasts of the wild . . . your ruddy glow.

*   *   *

'At the coming forth [of your light] is gathered the crowd,
    the divine Anunnaki await [your brilliance.]
May [Aya the Bride] unfearing [remind you:]
    "[Entrust] him to [the care of the watches of the night!]"   III 75

*   *   *

'Also . . . .   III 80
    while Gilgamesh travels to the Forest of Cedar,
let the days be long, let the nights be short,
    let his loins be girt, let his *stride* [be *sure*!]

'Let him pitch at nightfall a camp for the night,
    [let] nighttime . . . . . .   III 85
May Aya the Bride unfearing remind you:
    "The day Gilgamesh and Enkidu encounter Humbaba,

'"O Shamash, rouse against Humbaba the mighty gale-winds:
    South Wind, North Wind, East Wind and West Wind,
Blast, Counterblast, Typhoon, Hurricane and Tempest,   III 90
    Devil-Wind, Frost-Wind, Gale and Tornado.

'"Let rise thirteen winds and Humbaba's face darken,
    let the weapons of Gilgamesh then reach Humbaba!"
After your very own *fires* are kindled,
    at that time, O Shamash, turn your face to the *supplicant*!   III 95

'Your fleet-footed mules shall [*bear*] you [*onwards*.]
    A restful seat, a bed [for the night] shall be [*what awaits*] you.
The gods, your brothers, shall bring food [*to delight*] you,
    Aya the Bride shall wipe your face dry with the fringe of her
        garment.'

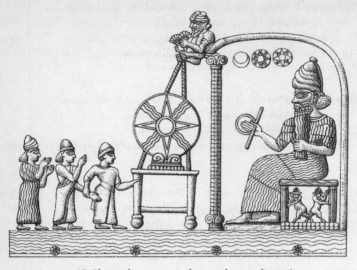

4 'O Shamash, turn your face to the supplicant!'

Again Wild-Cow Ninsun made her request before Shamash: III 100
  'O Shamash, will not Gilgamesh . . . the gods?
Will he not share the heavens with you?
  Will he not share with the moon a sceptre and crown?

'Will he not grow wise with Ea of the Ocean Below?
  Will he not rule with Irnina the black-headed people?   III 105
Will he not dwell with Ningishzida in the Land-of-No-Return?

'Let me make him, O Shamash, . . . ,
  lest he . . . , lest he . . . in the Forest of Cedar.'

    *   *   *

After Wild-Cow Ninsun had charged Shamash thus,   III 116

[Wild-Cow] Ninsun was clever [and wise, well versed in
    everything,]
  [*the mother of*] Gilgamesh . . . . . .
She smothered the censer and *came* [*down from the roof,*]
  she summoned Enkidu and declared her will: III 120

'O mighty Enkidu, you are not sprung from my womb,
    but henceforth your brood will belong with the votaries of
        Gilgamesh,
the priestesses, the hierodules and the women of the temple.'
    She put the symbols on Enkidu's neck.

'The priestesses took in the foundling,   III 125
    and the Divine Daughters brought up the foster-child.
Enkidu, whom [I *love*,] I take for my son,
    Enkidu in [*brotherhood*,] Gilgamesh shall favour him!'

'Also . . . .
    while [you] travel [*together*] to the Forest of Cedar,   III 130
let [the days be] long, let the nights be short,
    [let your loins be girt, let] your *stride* [be *sure*!]

'[At nightfall pitch a camp for the] night,
    let . . . protect . . . . . . '

After another lacuna there follows an episode in which Gilgamesh and Enkidu
apparently perform rituals in aid of a safe journey, but it remains very badly
damaged:

    Gilgamesh . . . .   III 147
His . . . . ,
    [to] the Gate of Cedar . . . . . .
Enkidu in the chapel . . . . . . ,   III 150
    and Gilgamesh in the chapel of . . . . . .
Juniper, incense, ... ,
    members of the . . . *were present* . . .

        *   *   *

    'By the command of Shamash you will attain [*your desire*.]   III 166
In the Gate of Marduk . . . . . . ,
    on the breast of the water . . . . . .
The back . . . . ,
    in the Gate of Cedar not . . . . . .   III 170
Gilgamesh . . . . . . ,

and Enkidu . . . . . .
At twenty leagues [*you should* break bread!]'

After a long lacuna, Gilgamesh gives instructions for the running of the city in
his absence:

'[During the days of our journey there and] back,   III 202
    [until we reach the Forest of] Cedar,

'[until we] slay [ferocious Humbaba,]
    [and annihilate] from [the land the Evil Thing Shamash
        abhors,]   III 205
. . . .
    may you acquire no . . . . . .

'[*The officers*] must not assemble young men in the street.
    Judge the lawsuit of the weak, seek out . . . ,
while we attain our desire like babes-in-arms,   III 210
    and plant our [weapons] in Humbaba's gate!'

The officers stood there wishing him well,
    the young men of Uruk ran behind in a mob,
and the officers kissed his feet:
    'To Uruk's quay come back in safety!   III 215

'Do not rely, O Gilgamesh, on your strength alone,
    look long and hard, land a blow you can count on!
"Who goes in front will save his comrade,
    who knows the road shall [guard] his friend."

'Let Enkidu go before you,   III 220
    he knows the journey to the Forest of Cedar.
He is tested in battle and [tried] in combat,
    through the mountain passes [*he often has journeyed.*]

'He shall [guard] his friend [and keep safe his companion,]
    [Enkidu shall bring him safe] home to his *wives*!   III 225

(To Enkidu)

In our assembly [we place the King in your care:]
　　you bring him back and replace [him in ours!]'

Enkidu [opened] his mouth [to speak,]
　　saying [to Gilgamesh:]
'My friend, turn back ......,   III 230
　　do not [*pursue*] this journey ......'

The rest of Tablet III, perhaps ten lines, is missing. The departure of the
heroes is described in the Old Babylonian Yale tablet, though the text becomes
increasingly fragmentary:

Enkidu opened his mouth,   Y 272
　　saying to Gilgamesh:
'Where you've *set your mind* begin the journey,
　　let your heart have no fear, keep your eyes on me!

'[In the] forest I knew his lair,   Y 275
　　[and the ways, too,] that *Humbaba wanders.
Speak [*to the crowd*] and send them home!
　　............

'...... [they should not] go with me,
　　......... to you.'   Y 280
... The crowd with happy heart,
　　... they [heard] what he had said.

The young men *made a fervent prayer* ...:
　　'Go, Gilgamesh, let ......
May your god go [before you!]   Y 285
　　May [Shamash] let you attain [your goal!]'

Gilgamesh and Enkidu *went forth* ...

Tablet IV. The Journey to the Forest of Cedar

Every three days in the course of their journey Gilgamesh and Enkidu pitch camp on a hillside and conduct a ritual to provoke a dream. Each time Gilgamesh wakes from a nightmare, but Enkidu reassures him that his dream is favourable after all. After at least five such dreams the heroes draw near to the Forest of Cedar. Shamash advises a speedy attack in order to catch unawares the ogre Humbaba, who guards the cedar cloaked in his seven auras. As the heroes anxiously try to allay each other's fears they arrive at the forest.

[At twenty] leagues they broke bread,
   [at] thirty leagues they pitched camp:
[fifty] leagues they travelled in the course of a day,
   by the third day [a march] of a month and a half;
nearer they drew to Mount Lebanon.

[Facing the sun they] dug [a well,]   IV 5
   [they put *fresh water* in . . .]
[Gilgamesh climbed to the top of the mountain,]
   [to the hill he poured out an offering of flour:]
['O mountain, bring me a dream, so I see a good sign!']

[Enkidu made for Gilgamesh a House of the Dream God,]   IV 10
   [he fixed a door in its doorway to keep out the weather.]
[In the circle *he had drawn* he made him lie down,]
   [and *falling flat* like a net lay himself in the doorway.]

[Gilgamesh rested his chin on his knees,]
   [sleep fell upon him, that spills over people.]   IV 15
[In the middle of the night he reached his sleep's end,]
   [he rose and spoke to his friend:]

['My friend, did you not call me? Why have I wakened?]
   [Did you not touch me? Why am I startled?]
[Did a god not pass by? Why is my flesh frozen numb?]   IV 20
   [My friend, I have had the first dream!]

'[The] dream that I had [was an utter confusion:]
   [in] a mountain valley . . . . . .
[The mountain] fell down on top of . . . . . . ,
   [then] we like . . . .'   IV 25

[The one] born in the [wild knew how to give counsel,]
   Enkidu spoke to his friend, [gave his dream meaning:]
'My friend, [your] dream is a good omen,
   the dream is precious [*and bodes us well.*]

'My friend, the mountain you saw [*could not be Humbaba*:]   IV 30
   [we] shall capture Humbaba, [him] we [shall *slay,*]
we shall [cast down] his corpse on the field of battle.
   And next morning [we shall see a good] sign [from the Sun
     God.]'

At twenty leagues they broke [bread,]
   at thirty leagues they pitched [camp:]   IV 35
fifty leagues they travelled in the course of [a day,]
   by the third day a march of [a month and] a half;
nearer they drew to Mount [Lebanon.]

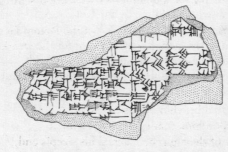

5 *'At twenty leagues they broke bread'.*

Facing the sun they dug a well,
   [they put *fresh*] *water* [in . . .]
Gilgamesh climbed to the top [of the mountain,]   IV 40
   [to the hill] he poured out an offering of flour:
'O mountain, bring me a dream, [so I see a good sign!]'

Enkidu made for [Gilgamesh a House of the Dream God,]
  [he fixed a door in its doorway to keep out the weather.]
[In the circle *he had drawn* he made him lie down,]   IV 45
  [and *falling flat* like a net lay himself in the doorway.]

[Gilgamesh rested his chin on his knees,]
  [sleep fell upon him, that spills over people.]
[In the middle of the night he reached his sleep's end,]
  [he rose and spoke to his friend:]   IV 50

['My friend, did you not call me? Why have I wakened?]
  [Did you not touch me? Why am I startled?]
[Did a god not pass by? Why is my flesh frozen numb?]
  [My friend, I have had the second dream!']   IV 54

                    *   *   *

Gilgamesh's relation of his second dream has not survived in Tablet IV, but the
gap can be filled by a paraphrase of an earlier version of the epic which comes
from the Hittite capital, Hattusa, and dates to the Middle Babylonian period:

  'My second dream sur[passes] the first.   Bo₂ 12'
In my dream, my friend, a mountain . . . ,
  it threw me down, it held me by my feet . . .
The brightness grew more intense. A man [*appeared*,]   Bo₂ 15'
  the comeliest in the land, his beauty . . .
[From] beneath the mountain he pulled me out and . . .
  He gave me water to drink and my heart grew [calm.]
[On] the ground he set [my] feet.'

Enkidu [spoke] to him,   Bo₂ 20'
  [saying] to Gilgamesh:
'My friend, we shall . . . , he is different altogether.
  *Humbaba . . . is not the mountain,
he is different altogether . . .
  Come, *cast aside* [your] fear . . . '   Bo₂ 24'

The text of Tablet IV resumes:

[At twenty leagues they broke bread,]
  [at thirty leagues they pitched camp:]   IV 80
[fifty leagues they travelled in the course of a day,]
  [by the third day a march of a month and a half;]
[nearer they drew to Mount Lebanon.]

[Facing the sun they dug a well,]
  [they put *fresh water* in] . . .
[Gilgamesh climbed to the top of] the mountain,   IV 85
  [to the] hill [he poured out an offering of flour:]
'[O mountain], bring me a dream, so I see [a good sign!]'

[Enkidu] made for [Gilgamesh a] House of the Dream God,
  [he fixed] a door in its doorway to keep out the weather.
[In the circle *he had*] *drawn* he made him lie down,   IV 90
  [and *falling flat*] like a net lay himself in the doorway.

Gilgamesh rested his chin on his knees,
  sleep fell upon him, that spills over people.
[In the] middle of the night he reached his sleep's end,
  he rose and spoke to his friend: IV 95

'My friend, did you not call me? Why have I wakened?
  Did you not touch me? Why am I startled?
Did a god not pass by? Why is my flesh frozen numb?
  My friend, I have had the third dream!

'The dream that I had was an utter confusion: IV 100
  heaven cried aloud, while earth did rumble.
The day grew still, darkness came forth,
  there was a flash of lightning, fire broke out.

'[*The flames*] flared up, death rained down.
  . . . and the flashes of fire went out,   IV 105
[where] it had fallen turned into cinders.
  [You were] born in the wild, can we take counsel?'

[Having heard the words of his friend,]
   Enkidu gave the dream meaning, saying to Gilgamesh:
'[My friend,] your dream is a good omen, fine is [*its*
      message.]'   IV 109

The rest of Enkidu's explanation of the third dream is lost, but this lacuna in
Tablet IV can be filled in part from the Old Babylonian school tablet from
Nippur:

'We draw, my friend, ever nearer the forest,   OB Ni 1
   the dreams are close, the battle soon.
You will see the radiant auras of the god,
   of *Humbaba, whom in your thoughts you fear so much.

'Locking horns like a bull you will batter him,   OB Ni 5
   and force his head down with your strength.
The old man you saw is your powerful god,
   the one who begot you, divine Lugalbanda.'

The text of Tablet IV becomes available again:

[At twenty] leagues they [broke bread,]   IV 120
   [at thirty] leagues they pitched [camp:]
[fifty] leagues they travelled [in the course of a day,]
   by the third [day a march] of a month and a half;
nearer they drew to Mount Lebanon.

[Facing] the sun they dug [a well,]   IV 125
   they put [*fresh water*] in . . .
Gilgamesh [climbed] to the top [of the mountain,]
   to the [hill he poured] out an offering [of flour.]
['O mountain, bring me a] dream, [so I see a good sign!]'

[Enkidu made for Gilgamesh a House of the Dream God,]   IV 130
   [he fixed a door in its doorway to keep out the weather.]
[In the circle *he had drawn* he made him lie down,]
   [and *falling flat* like a net lay himself in the doorway.]

[Gilgamesh rested his chin on his knees,]
   [sleep fell upon him, that spills over people.]   IV 135
[In the middle of the night he reached his sleep's end,]
   [he rose and spoke to his friend:]

['My friend, did you not call me? Why have I wakened?]
   [Did you not touch me? Why am I startled?]
[Did a god not pass by? Why is my flesh frozen numb?]   IV 140
   [My friend, I have had the fourth dream!']

The details of the fourth dream and its explanation are not well preserved in
Tablet IV, but the Old Babylonian tablet from Nippur supplies a more complete
version of the text:

'My friend, I have had the fourth,
   it surpasses my other three dreams!   OB Ni 10
I saw a Thunderbird in the sky,
   up it rose like a cloud, soaring above us.

'It was a . . . , its visage distorted,
   its mouth was fire, its breath was death.
[There was also a] man, he was strange of form,   OB Ni 15
   he . . . and stood there in my dream.

'[He *bound*] its wings and took hold of my arm,
   . . . . . . he cast it down [before] me,
. . . . upon it.'

After a short lacuna, Enkidu explains the dream:

'[You saw a Thunderbird in the sky,]   OB Ni 20'
   [up] it [rose like a] cloud, soaring above us.

'It was a . . . , its visage distorted,
   its mouth was fire, its breath was death.
You will fear its awesome splendour,
   I shall . . . its foot and let you arise!   OB Ni 25'

'The man you saw was mighty Shamash . . . '

The text of Tablet IV resumes, though badly broken:

'[My friend, favourable is] your dream . . . . . . ,   IV 155
    . . . . . . this . . . . . .
. . . Humbaba like . . . . . . ,
    . . . will be kindled . . . upon [him.]

'We shall bring about his . . . , we shall bind his wings,
    . . . . we shall . . .   IV 160
His . . . . . . , we shall stand upon him.
    [And next] morning we shall [see] a good sign from the Sun
        God.'

[At twenty leagues] they broke bread,
    [at thirty leagues] they pitched camp:
[fifty leagues they] travelled in the course [of a day.]   IV 165

[Facing the sun] they dug a [well,]
    they put [*fresh water*] in . . .
Gilgamesh [climbed] to the top [of the mountain,]
    to [the hill he] poured out an offering of [flour.]
'[O mountain, bring me] a dream, [so I see a good] sign!'   IV 170

Enkidu [made] for [Gilgamesh a House of the Dream God,]
    he fixed [a door in its doorway to keep out the weather.]
In the circle [*he had drawn* he made him lie down,]
    [and *falling*] flat [like a net] lay [himself in the doorway.]

[Gilgamesh] rested his [chin on his knees,]   IV 175
    [sleep fell] upon [him, that spills over people.]
[In the middle of the night he reached his sleep's end,]
    [he rose and spoke to his friend:]

['My friend, did you not call me? Why have I wakened?]
    [Did you not touch me? Why am I startled?]   IV 180
[Did a god not pass by? Why is my flesh frozen numb?]
    [My friend, I have had the fifth dream!']

Lacuna. Another account of one of the dreams and Enkidu's explanation of it survives in an Old Babylonian tablet from Tell Harmal, ancient Shaduppûm:

'My friend, I had a dream: Ha₁ 3
   how *ominous* it was, how *desolate*, how unclear!

'I had taken me hold of a bull from the wild:
   as it clove the ground with its bellows,   Ha₁ 5
the clouds of dust it raised thrust deep in the sky,
   and I, in front of it, *leaned myself forward*.

'Taking hold of . . . . . . enclosed my arms.
. . . he extricated [me] . . . *by force* . . .
My cheek . . . , my . . . ,
   [he gave] me water [to drink] from his waterskin.'

'The [god,] my friend, we are going against,   Ha₁ 10
   he's not the wild bull, he's different altogether.
The *wild bull* you saw was shining Shamash,
   he will grasp our hands in time of peril.

'The one who gave you water to drink from his skin
   was your god who respects you, divine Lugalbanda.   Ha₁ 15
We shall join forces and do something unique,
   a feat that never has been in the land!'

When the text of Tablet IV resumes, the heroes have almost reached the Forest of Cedar, and Enkidu is giving Gilgamesh courage:

'[*Why, my friend*, do your tears] flow?   IV 195
   [O offshoot sprung from] Uruk's midst, . . .
. . . now stand and . . . ,
   Gilgamesh [the king,] offshoot sprung from Uruk's midst, . . . '

[Shamash] heard what he had spoken,
   [straight] away [from the sky there cried out] a voice: IV 200
'Hurry, stand against him! Humbaba must not [enter his forest,]
   [he must not] go down to the grove, he must not . . . !

'He [must not] wrap himself in his seven cloaks . . . !
    [One] he is wrapped in, six he has shed.'
They . . . .   IV 205
    like a fierce wild bull, horns locked . . .

He bellowed once, a bellow full of terror,
    the guardian of the forests was bellowing,
. . . .
    Humbaba was [thundering] like the God of the Storm.   IV 210

A long lacuna intervenes, then:

[Enkidu] opened his [mouth] to speak,   IV 239
    [saying to Gilgamesh:]
' . . . have come down . . . . . . ,   IV 240
    . . . . . . and [my arms] grow stiff!'

[Gilgamesh] opened his mouth to speak,
    saying [to Enkidu:]
'[Why,] my friend, do we [speak] like weaklings?
    [Was it not we] crossed all of the mountains?

'[Did not] . . . . before us?   IV 245
    Before we withdraw . . . . . .
My [friend,] experienced in combat,
    who . . . battle . . . . . .

'You . . . and you fear not . . . ,
    . . . like a *dervish*, and change . . .   IV 250
Let [your shout] resound [like] a kettle drum,
    let the stiffness leave your arms, the tremors [your knees!]

'Take my hand, friend, and we shall go [on] together,
    [let] your thoughts dwell on combat!
Forget death and [seek] life!   IV 255
    . . . . . . the careful man.

' "[Let him who] goes first be on guard for himself and bring his
    comrade to safety!"
  It is they made a name [for days] long in the future!'
[At the] *distant* . . . the two of them arrived,
  [they ceased] their talking and came to a halt.   IV 260

Tablet V. The Combat with Humbaba

After admiring the mountain dense-grown with cedar, the heroes draw their
weapons and creep into the forest. Humbaba confronts them, and accuses Enkidu
of treachery. Enkidu urges swift action. Gilgamesh and Humbaba fight, and
Shamash sends the thirteen winds to blind Humbaba and win victory for his
protégé. Humbaba pleads for his life. Enkidu again urges haste, telling Gilgamesh
to kill Humbaba before the gods find out. Humbaba curses the heroes, who
promptly kill him and begin felling cedar in the sacred groves. From one espe-
cially magnificent cedar Enkidu vows to make a great door to adorn the temple
of the god Enlil.

They stood there marvelling at the forest,
  gazing at the lofty cedars,
gazing at forest's entrance –
  where Humbaba came and went there was a track.

The path was straight and the way well trodden.   V 5
  They saw the Mountain of Cedar, seat of gods and goddesses'
    throne.
[On the] face of the mountain the cedar proffered its abundance,
  its shade was sweet and full of delight.

[Thick] tangled was the thorn, the forest a shrouding canopy,
  . . . cedar, *ballukku*-trees . . . . . .   V 10

          *   *   *

After a lacuna intervenes, the text continues, though it is not completely recovered:

At once the dirks . . . . . . ,   V 53
  and from the scabbards . . . . . .
The axes were smeared . . . . . . ,   V 55

hatchet [and] dirk in . . . . . .
One . . . . ,
   they stole into . . . .
Humbaba . . . .   V 59

    *   *   *

Gilgamesh [opened his mouth to speak,]   V 65
   [saying to Enkidu:]

'What, [my friend,] . . . . . .

    *   *   *

   '[For] Enlil . . . . '

Enkidu [opened] his mouth [to speak,]   V 70
   [saying to Gilgamesh:]
'My [friend], Humbaba . . . . ,
   one-to-one . . . .

'[Two] garments, however, ... ,
   even a glacis-slope two [*climbing can conquer.*]
Two . . . .   V 75
   a three-ply rope [*is not easily broken.*]

'[Even] a mighty lion two cubs [*can overcome.*]'

A fragment of this conversation is also preserved on a second Old Babylonian
tablet from Tell Harmal (Ha₂):

'We have come to a place where a man shouldn't go . . . ,
   let us set our weapons in the gate of *Humbaba!'
. . . [Enkidu] declared to his friend:
   'A tempest's onslaught is [ferocious *Humbaba!]
[Like] the god of the storm he will trample us down.'

When the text of Tablet V resumes, the heroes are face to face with the forest's
guardian:

Humbaba opened his mouth to speak,   V 85
   saying to Gilgamesh:
'Let fools take counsel, Gilgamesh, with the rude and brutish!
   Why have you come here into my presence?

'Come, Enkidu, you spawn of a fish, who knew no father,
   hatchling of terrapin and turtle, who sucked no mother's milk!
In your youth I watched you, but near you I went not,
   would your . . . *have filled* my belly?   V 90

'[Now] in treachery you bring before me Gilgamesh,
   and stand there, Enkidu, like a warlike stranger!
I will slit the throat and gullet of Gilgamesh,
   I will feed his flesh to the locust bird, ravening eagle and vulture!'

Gilgamesh opened his mouth to speak, saying to Enkidu: V 95
   'My friend, Humbaba's features have changed!
Though boldly we came up to his lair to defeat him,
   yet my heart will not quickly . . . '

Enkidu opened his mouth to speak,
   saying to Gilgamesh:
'Why, my friend, [do you] speak like a weakling?   V 100
   With your spineless words you [make] me despondent.

'Now, my friend, but one is [*our task*,]
   the copper is already pouring into the mould!
To stoke the furnace for an hour? To . . . the coals for an hour?
   To send the Deluge is to crack the whip!   V 105

'[Don't] draw back, don't make a retreat!
   . . . . . . make your blow mighty!'   V 107

    *   *   *

   He smote the ground and . . . faced him head on.   V 132

At the heels of their feet the earth burst asunder,
   they shattered, as they whirled, Mounts Sirion and Lebanon.
Black became the clouds of white,   V 135
   raining down on them death like a mist.

Shamash roused against Humbaba the mighty gale-winds:
   South Wind, North Wind, East Wind and West Wind,
Blast, Counterblast, Typhoon, Hurricane and Tempest,
   Devil-Wind, Frost-Wind, Gale and Tornado: V 140

there rose thirteen winds and the face of Humbaba darkened –
   he could not charge forwards, he could not kick backwards –
the weapons of Gilgamesh then reached Humbaba.
   In a plea for his life said Humbaba to Gilgamesh:

'You are so young, Gilgamesh, your mother just bore you,   V 145
   but indeed you are the offspring of [Wild-Cow Ninsun!]
By Shamash's command the mountains *you flattened*,
   O offshoot sprung from Uruk's midst, Gilgamesh the king!

'. . . , Gilgamesh, a dead man cannot . . . ,
   . . . alive for his lord . . . . . .   V 150
Spare my life, O Gilgamesh, ... ,
   let me dwell here for you in [the Forest of Cedar!]

'Trees as many as you command . . . . . . ,
   I will guard you myrtle, ...
timber to be the pride of [your] palace!'   V 155

Enkidu opened his mouth to speak,
   [saying to Gilgamesh:]
'Do not listen, my [friend,] to Humbaba's words,
   [*ignore*] his supplications . . . . . . '   V 158

    *   *   *

[Humbaba opened his mouth to speak,]   V 174
   [saying to Enkidu:]

'You are experienced in the ways of my forest, the ways . . . ,   V 175
    also you know all the arts of speech.
I should have picked you up and hanged you from a sapling at the
        way into the forest,
    I should have fed your flesh to the locust bird, ravening eagle and
        vulture.

'Now, Enkidu, [my] release lies with you:
    tell Gilgamesh to spare me my life!'   V 180
Enkidu opened his mouth to speak,
    saying to Gilgamesh:

'My friend, Humbaba who guards the Forest of [Cedar:]
    finish him, slay him, do away with his power!
Humbaba who guards the Forest [of Cedar:]   V 185
    finish him, slay him, do away with his power,
before Enlil the foremost hears what we do!

The [great] gods will take against us in anger,
    Enlil in Nippur, Shamash in [Larsa] . . . ,
Establish for ever [*a fame*] that endures,
    how Gilgamesh [*slew ferocious*] Humbaba!'

Humbaba heard [*what Enkidu was saying,*]   V 190
    he [lifted] his head and . . .

            *   *   *

[Humbaba opened his mouth to speak,]
    [saying to Enkidu:]

' . . . You sit before [him] like a shepherd,   V 236
    like his hireling [*doing his bidding.*]
Now, Enkidu, [my release] lies with you . . . ,
    tell Gilgamesh to [spare] me my life!'

Enkidu opened his mouth to speak,   V 240
    saying [to Gilgamesh:]
'My friend, Humbaba who guards the Forest [of Cedar –]
    [finish him,] slay him, [do away with his power,]
before [Enlil] the foremost hears what we do!

The [great] gods will take against us in anger,
    Enlil in Nippur, Shamash in [Larsa] . . .
Establish for ever [*a fame*] that endures,
    how Gilgamesh *slew* [*ferocious*] Humbaba!'   V 245

Humbaba heard . . . and . . . [*bitterly cursed them*:]

          *   *   *

'May the pair of them not grow old,   V 256
    besides Gilgamesh his friend, none shall bury Enkidu!'

Enkidu opened his mouth to speak,
    saying to Gilgamesh:
'My friend, I speak to you but you do not hear me!
    While the curses . . . . ,   V 260
[*let those curses return*] to his mouth.'

[Gilgamesh heard the words] of his friend,
    he drew forth [the dirk at] his side.
Gilgamesh [smote him] in the neck,
    Enkidu . . . while he pulled out the lungs.   V 265

[. . .] . . . springing up,
    [from] the head he took the tusks as booty.
[*Rain*] in plenty fell on the mountain,
    . . . in plenty fell on the mountain.   V 269

A different version of the slaying of Humbaba and his minions, but better
preserved, is given in an Old Babylonian tablet from Ishchali:

6 '*Gilgamesh smote him in the neck*'.

[Said] Gilgamesh to [him,] to Enkidu: Ish 10'
    'Now, my friend, we must impose our victory.
The auras slip away in the thicket,
    the auras slip away, their radiance *grows dim*.'

Said Enkidu to him, to Gilgamesh:
    'My friend, catch a bird and where go its chicks?   Ish 15'
Let us look for the auras later,
    as the chicks run here and there in the thicket!

'Smite him again, slay his servant *alongside him*!'
    Gilgamesh heard the word of his companion.
He took up his axe in his hand,   Ish 20'
    he drew forth the dirk from his belt.

Gilgamesh smote him in the neck,
  his friend Enkidu *gave encouragement*.
He . . . . he fell,
  the ravines did run with his blood.   Ish 25′

*Humbaba the guardian he smote to the ground,
  for two leagues afar . . .
With him he slew . . . . . . ,
  the woods he . . . . . .

He slew the ogre, the forest's guardian,   Ish 30′
  at whose yell *were sundered* the peaks of Sirion and Lebanon,
. . . the mountains did *quake*,
  . . . all the hillsides did tremble.

He slew the ogre, the cedar's guardian,
  the broken . . . . . .   Ish 35′
As soon as he had slain all seven (of the auras),
  the war-net of *two talents' weight*, and the dirk of eight,

a load of ten talents he took up,
  he went down to trample the forest.
He discovered the secret abode of the gods,
  Gilgamesh felling the trees, Enkidu choosing the *timber*.   Ish 39′

After a gap the text of Tablet V resumes:

Enkidu opened his mouth to speak,   V 292
  saying to Gilgamesh:
'My friend, we have felled a lofty cedar,
  whose top thrust up to the sky.

'I will make a door, six rods in height, two rods in breadth, one
          cubit in thickness,   V 295
  whose pole and pivots, top and bottom, will be all of a piece.'

At this point Tablet V is badly damaged. A better-preserved version of the episode
is known from an Old Babylonian tablet of unknown provenance, now in
Baghdad:

. . . he went trampling through the Forest of Cedar,   IM 17
   he discovered the secret abode of the gods.
The Wild-Born knew how to give counsel,
   he said to his friend:

'By your strength alone you slew the guardian,   IM 20
   what can bring you dishonour? Lay low the Forest of [Cedar!]
Seek out for me a lofty cedar,
   whose crown is high as the heavens!

'I will make a door of a reed-length's breadth,
   let it not have a pivot, let it travel in the door-jamb.
Its side will be a cubit, a reed-length its breadth,   IM 25
   let no stranger draw near it, let a god have love for [it.]

'To the house of Enlil the Euphrates shall bear it,
   let the folk of Nippur rejoice over it!
Let the god Enlil delight in it!'   IM 29

The text of Tablet V resumes for the final three lines:

They bound together a raft, they laid [*the cedar on it.*]   V 300
Enkidu was helmsman . . . . ,
   and Gilgamesh [*carried*] the head of Humbaba.

Tablet VI. Ishtar and the Bull of Heaven

Back in Uruk Gilgamesh's beauty provokes the desire of the goddess Ishtar and
she proposes to him. Gilgamesh scorns her, reminding her of the fates suffered
by her many former conquests. Ishtar is enraged and rushes up to heaven. She
persuades Anu, her father, to give her the fiery Bull of Heaven (the constellation
Taurus) so that she can punish Gilgamesh with death. The Bull of Heaven causes
havoc in Uruk, but Gilgamesh and Enkidu discover its weak spot and kill it.
They insult Ishtar further and return to the palace in triumph to celebrate their
victory.

He washed his matted hair, he cleaned his equipment,
   he shook his hair down over his back.
Casting aside his dirty gear he clad himself in clean,
   wrapped cloaks round him, tied with a sash.
Then did Gilgamesh put on his crown.   VI 5

On the beauty of Gilgamesh Lady Ishtar looked with longing:
   'Come, Gilgamesh, be you my bridegroom!
Grant me your fruits, O grant me!
   Be you my husband and I your wife!

'Let me harness you a chariot of lapis lazuli and gold,   VI 10
   its wheels shall be gold and its horns shall be amber.
Driving lions in a team and mules of great size,
   enter our house amid the sweet scent of cedar!

'As you enter our house
   doorway and footstool shall kiss your feet!   VI 15
Kings, courtiers and nobles shall kneel before you,
   produce of mountain and lowland they shall bring you as tribute!

'Your goats shall bear triplets, your ewes shall bear twins,
   your donkey when laden shall outpace any mule!
Your horse shall gallop at the chariot in glory,   VI 20
   no ox shall match yours at the yoke!'

[Gilgamesh] opened his mouth to speak,
   [saying] to the Lady Ishtar:
'[And if indeed I] take you in marriage,

' . . . . . . body and clothing,   VI 25
   [*whence would come*] my food and my sustenance?
[*Would you feed me*] bread that is fit for a god,
   [*and pour me ale*] that is fit for a king?'   VI 28

     *   *   *

'[*Who is there*] would take you in marriage?   VI 32
  [You, *a frost* that congeals no] ice,
a louvre-door [that] stays [not] breeze nor draught,
  a palace that massacres . . . warriors,   VI 35

'an elephant which . . . its *hoods*,
  bitumen that [*stains the hands*] of its bearer,
a waterskin that [*cuts the hands*] of its bearer,
  limestone that [*weakens*] a wall of ashlar,

'a battering ram that destroys [*the walls of*] the enemy,   VI 40
  a shoe that bites the foot of its owner!
What bridegroom of yours did endure for ever?
  What brave warrior of yours went up [*to the heavens?*]

'Come, let me tell [you the tale] of your lovers:
  of . . . . his arm.   VI 45
Dumuzi, the lover of your youth,
  year upon year, to lamenting you doomed him.

'You loved the speckled *allallu*-bird,
  but struck him down and broke his wing:
now he stands in the woods crying "My wing!"   VI 50
  You loved the lion, perfect in strength,
but for him you dug seven pits and seven.

'You loved the horse, so famed in battle,
  but you made his destiny whip, spur and lash.
You made his destiny a seven-league gallop,   VI 55
  you made his destiny to drink muddy water,
and doomed Silili his mother to perpetual weeping.

'You loved the shepherd, the grazier, the herdsman,
  who gave you piles of loaves baked in embers,
and slaughtered kids for you day after day.   VI 60

'You struck him and turned him into a wolf,
  now his very own shepherd boys chase him away,
and his dogs take bites at his haunches.

'You loved Ishullanu, your father's gardener,
      who used to bring you dates in a basket,   VI 65
daily making your table gleam.
      You eyed him up and went to meet him:

' "O my Ishullanu, let us taste your vigour:
      Put out your 'hand' and stroke my quim!"
But Ishullanu said to you: VI 70

' "Me! What do you want of me?
      Did my mother not bake? Have I not eaten,
that now I should eat the bread of slander and insults?
      Should I let only rushes cover me in winter?"

'When you heard what [he'd] said,   VI 75
      you struck him and turned him into a *dwarf*.
You sat him down in the midst of his labours,
      he cannot go up . . . , he cannot go down . . .
Must you love me also and [deal with me] likewise?'

The goddess Ishtar [heard] these words,   VI 80
      she [went up] to heaven in a furious rage.
[Weeping] she went to Anu, her father,
      before Antu, her mother, her tears did flow:

'O father, again and again does Gilgamesh scorn me,
      telling a tale of foulest slander,   VI 85
slander about me and insults too.'

Anu opened his mouth to speak,
      saying to the Lady Ishtar:
'*Ah*, but was it not you who provoked King Gilgamesh,
      so he told a tale of foulest slander,   VI 90
slander about you and insults too?'

Ishtar opened her mouth to speak,
      saying to her father, Anu:
'Father, give me, please, the Bull of Heaven,
      so in his dwelling I may slay Gilgamesh!   VI 95

'If you do not give me the Bull of Heaven,
    I shall *smash [the gates of the Netherworld, right down]* to its
        dwelling,
to the world below I shall *grant [manumission,]*
    I shall bring up the dead to consume the living,
I shall make the dead outnumber the living.'   VI 100

Anu opened his mouth to speak,
    saying to the Lady Ishtar:
'If you want from me the Bull of Heaven,
    let the widow of Uruk gather seven years' chaff,
[and the farmer *of Uruk*] grow seven years' hay.'   VI 105

[Ishtar opened her mouth] to speak,
    [saying to] her father, Anu:
'. . . . . already I stored,
    . . . . already I grew.

'The widow [of Uruk has] gathered [seven] years' chaff,   VI 110
    the farmer [*of Uruk* has grown seven years'] hay.
With the wrath of the Bull I shall [*have vengeance.*]'
    Anu heard this speech of Ishtar,
the Bull of Heaven's nose-rope he placed in her hands.

[Down came] Ishtar, leading it onward: VI 115
    when it reached the land of Uruk,
it dried up the woods, the reed-beds and marshes,
    down it went to the river, lowered the level by seven full cubits.

As the Bull of Heaven snorted a pit opened up,
    one hundred men of Uruk fell down it.   VI 120
The second time it snorted a pit opened up,
    two hundred men of Uruk fell down it.

The third time it snorted a pit opened up,
    and Enkidu fell in as far as his waist.
Enkidu sprang up and seized the Bull by the horns.   VI 125
    In his face the Bull spat slaver,
with the tuft of its tail . . . . . .

Enkidu opened his mouth [to speak,]
   saying to Gilgamesh, [his friend:]
'My friend, we vaunted ourselves [in our] city: VI 130
   how shall we answer the thronging people?

'My friend, I have tested the might of the Bull . . . ,
   so learning [its] strength, [and knowing its] purpose.
Let me [test] again the might of the Bull,
   I [shall get myself] behind [the Bull of Heaven,]   VI 135
I will seize [it by the tuft of the tail.]

'I will set [my foot on the back of] its [leg,]
   in . . . . [it.]
Then [you] like a [butcher, brave and] skilful,
   between the yoke of the horns and the slaughter-spot thrust in
      your knife!'   VI 140

Enkidu rushed round to the rear of the Bull,
   he seized it by the [tuft] of the tail.
[He set] his foot on [the back of] its [leg,]
   [in] . . . . it.

Then Gilgamesh like a butcher, brave and skilful,   VI 145
   between the yoke of the horns and the slaughter-spot [he thrust
      in] his knife.

After they had slain the Bull of Heaven,
   they bore its heart aloft and set it before Shamash.
Stepping back they fell prostrate in the presence of the Sun God,
   then both of them together sat down.   VI 150

Ishtar went up on the wall of Uruk-the-Sheepfold,
   hopping and stamping, she wailed in woe:
'Alas! Gilgamesh, who mocked me, has killed the Bull of Heaven.'

Enkidu heard these words of Ishtar,
   and tearing a haunch off the Bull he hurled it towards her. VI 155
'Had I caught you too, I'd have treated you likewise,
   I'd have draped your arms in its guts!'

7 'Between the yoke of the horns and the slaughter-spot he thrust
in his knife'.

Ishtar assembled the courtesans, prostitutes and harlots,
    over the Bull of Heaven's haunch she began rites of
        mourning.
Gilgamesh summoned all the smiths and the craftsmen,   VI 160
    the size of the horns the craftsmen admired.

Thirty minas of lapis lazuli in a solid block,
    two minas each their *rims*,
six kor of oil, the capacity of both.
    He gave them to his god Lugalbanda, to hold oil for
        anointment,   VI 165
he took them in to hang in his chamber.

They washed their hands in the river Euphrates,
    took each other by the hand and in they came.
As they drove along the streets of Uruk,
    the people were gathered to gaze [on them.]   VI 170

Gilgamesh spoke a word to the serving girls of [*his palace*:]
    'Who is the finest among men?
Who the most glorious of fellows?'
    'Gilgamesh is the finest among men!
[Gilgamesh the most] glorious of fellows!'   VI 175

   *   *   *

Gilgamesh made merry in his palace.   VI 179

At night the men lay asleep on their beds,   VI 180
    and Enkidu as he slept was having a dream.
Enkidu rose to relate the dream,
    saying to his friend:

Tablet VII. The Death of Enkidu

In a dream Enkidu sees the gods in assembly decree his doom. In anguished
delirium he pictures before him the great door of cedar he made for Enlil's
temple, and he curses it because it has failed to secure for him the god's favour.
He then turns his thoughts to the trapper and the prostitute, the instruments of
his introduction to civilization, whom he also blames for his plight. Shamash
persuades him to relent, and he returns to bless the prostitute. He has a second
dream, in which he is dragged down to the Netherworld by the Angel of Death
and granted a vision of hell. After describing the dream to Gilgamesh he falls
sick. Languishing on his deathbed he complains to Gilgamesh of the ignominy
of his fate, compared with death in battle. He dies.

'My friend, why were the great gods in counsel?'   VII 1

What followed the opening line of Tablet VII is still not recovered. The missing
episode is known from a fragmentary prose paraphrase, written in Hittite, which
was based on an older version of the epic:

... and dawn broke.   III(?) col. i

Enkidu began to speak to Gilgamesh: 'My brother, this night what
a dream [I dreamed!] The gods Anu, Enlil, Ea and celestial Shamash
[held assembly], and Anu spoke unto Enlil: "These, because they slew
the Bull of Heaven, and slew *Humbaba that [guarded] the mountains
dense-[wooded] with cedar," so said Anu, "between these two [let
one of them die!]"

'And Enlil said: "Let Enkidu die, but let not Gilgamesh die!"'

'Celestial Shamash began to reply to the hero Enlil: "Was it not at
your word that they slew him, the Bull of Heaven – and also *Hum-
baba? Now shall innocent Enkidu die?"

'Enlil was wroth at celestial Shamash: "How like a comrade you
marched with them daily!"'

Enkidu lay down before Gilgamesh, his tears [flowed] down like
streams: 'O my brother, dear to me is my brother! They will [never]
raise me up again for my brother. [Among] the dead I shall sit, the
threshold of the dead [I shall cross,] never again [shall I set] eyes on
my dear brother.'

The text of Tablet VII resumes with Enkidu's delirium:

Enkidu lifted [his eyes *as though to the door*,]   VII 37
    he talked with the door as if [*with a man*:]

'O door of the woodland, that has no [sense,]
    I have understanding that [you] have not.   VII 40
For twenty leagues I sought for you the [*finest*] timber,
    until [*in the forest*] I found a tall cedar.

'Your tree had no rival [*in the Forest of Cedar*:]
    six rods is your height, two rods your breadth, one [cubit] your
        thickness,
your pole and your pivots, top and bottom, are all of a piece. VII 45
    I fashioned you, I lifted you, I hung you in Nippur.

'Had I but known, O door, that so you would [*repay* me,]
    had I but known, O door, that so you would reward me,
I would have lifted my axe, I would have cut you down,
    I would have floated you down as a raft to Ebabbara.   VII 50

'[To] Ebabbara, the temple of Shamash, I would have brought
        [you,]
    I would have set [up] the cedar [*in the gate*] of Ebabbara.
[In] its doorway I would have stood thunderbird [and *bull*
        colossus,]
    . . . . . . your entrance I would have [*placed*.]

'I would have . . . the city . . . Shamash,   VII 55
    and in Uruk . . . . :
because Shamash heard what I said,
    and in time of [*peril*] . . . *he* [*gave*] *me* a weapon.

'Now, O door, it was I who fashioned you, who lifted you up:
    can I now [*break you up*, can I] now tear you down?   VII 60
May a king who comes after me bear for you hatred,
    or . . . . . . hang you [*where you cannot be seen*,]
may he remove my name and write upon you his own!'

He tore out . . . , he cast it . . . ,
    as he listened to his words, all of a sudden his [tears were
        flowing –]   VII 65
as Gilgamesh listened to the words of Enkidu, his friend,
    [all of a sudden his] tears were [flowing.]

Gilgamesh opened his mouth to speak,
    saying to Enkidu:
['My friend,] . . . in . . . . . . pre-eminent,
    [*do you*, who] had *understanding* and reason, [*now speak*]
        profanity?   VII 70

'Why, my friend, does your heart talk *profanity* . . . ?
    [the dream] was special, great the anxiety.
[*Your feverish lips*] were buzzing like flies,
    [the misgivings were] great, the dream was rare.

'To the one who survives [*the gods*] leave grieving: VII 75
   the dream leaves sorrow to the one who survives.
The great gods [I'll] beseech in supplication,
   let me seek out [*Shamash*,] I'll appeal to your god.

'*In* [*your presence*] *I will pray* [*to* Anu,] father of the gods,
   [may] *great* counsellor Enlil [hear] my prayer in your
                               presence,
                                                             VII 80
may [*my entreaty find favour with Ea*!]
   I will fashion your statue in gold without limit,
. . . . '

['My friend,] give no silver, *give* no gold, *give* no . . . !
The word [*Enlil*] spoke is not like the . . . gods',   VII 85
   [what he] commands, he doesn't erase,
[what] he sets down . . . , he doesn't erase.

'My friend, fixed [*is my destiny*,]
   people go to their doom before their time.'
At the very first glimmer of brightening dawn,   VII 90
   Enkidu lifted his head, lamenting to Shamash.

Under the rays of the sun his tears were flowing:
   'I appeal to you, Shamash, for my life so precious:
[as for] the hunter, the trapper-man,
   who let me be not as great as my friend: VII 95

'may the hunter be not as great as his friend!
   Destroy his profit, diminish his income!
May his share be cut in your presence!
   [*The house*] where he enters, may [*its god*] leave by the
                               window!'

[After] he had cursed the hunter to his heart's content,   VII 100
   he decided [also] to curse Shamhat [the harlot:]
'Come, Shamhat, I will fix your destiny,
   a doom to endure for all eternity:

'[I will] curse you with a mighty curse,
    my curse shall afflict you now and forthwith!   VII 105
A household to delight in [you shall not] acquire,
    [never to] reside *in the* [*midst*] of a family!

'In the young women's [*chamber* you shall not] sit!
    Your finest [garment] the ground shall defile!
Your festive gown [the drunkard] shall stain [in the dirt!]   VII 110
    Things of beauty [you shall never acquire!]

'. . . . . of the potter.
    No . . . shall you have . . . . . . !
No table [for a banquet,] the people's abundance, shall be laid in
        your house!
    [The bed you] delight in shall be a miserable *bench*!   VII 115

'[The junction] of highways shall be where you sit!
    [A field of ruins shall be] where you sleep!
The shadow of the rampart shall be where you stand!
    [Thorn and] briar shall skin your feet!

'[Drunk and] sober shall strike your cheek!
    . . . *shall* be plaintiff, and claim against you!   VII 120
[*The roof of your house*] no builder shall plaster!
    [*In your bedroom*] the owl shall roost!

'[*At your table* never shall] banquet take place!   VII 123

            *   *   *

'Because [you made] me [weak, who was undefiled!]   VII 130
    Yes, in the wild [you weakened] me, who was undefiled!'
Shamash heard what he had spoken,
    straight away from the sky there cried out a voice:

'O Enkidu, why curse Shamhat the harlot,
    who fed you bread that was fit for a god,   VII 135
and poured you ale that was fit for a king,
    who clothed you in a splendid garment,
and gave you as companion the handsome Gilgamesh?

'And now Gilgamesh, your friend and your brother,
   [will] lay you out on a magnificent bed.   VII 140
[On] a bed of honour he will lay you out,
   [he will] place you on his left, on a seat of repose;
[the rulers] of the underworld will all kiss your feet.

'The people of Uruk [he will have] mourn and lament you,
   the [thriving] people he will fill full of woe for you.   VII 145
After you are gone his hair will be matted in mourning,
   [clad] in the skin of a lion, he will wander the [wild.]'

Enkidu [heard] the words of Shamash the hero,
   . . . his heart so angry grew calm,
. . . [his heart] so furious grew calm: VII 150
   'Come, [Shamhat, I will fix your destiny!]

'[My] mouth [that] cursed you shall bless [you] as well!
   [Governors] shall love you and noblemen too!
[At one league off] men shall slap their thighs,
   [at two leagues off] they shall shake out their hair!   VII 155

'No soldier shall [be slow] to drop his belt for you,
   obsidian he shall [give you], lapis lazuli and gold!
Ear[rings] and *jewellery* shall be what he gives you!

'Ishtar, [the ablest] of gods, shall gain you entrance
   to the man whose home [*is established*] and wealth heaped
      high!   VII 160
[For you] his wife shall be deserted, though mother of seven!'

[As for Enkidu], his mind was troubled,
   he lay on his own and [began to ponder.]
What was on his mind he told to his friend:
'My friend, in the course of the night I had such a dream!   VII 165

8 *'Ishtar, the ablest of gods'.*

'The heavens thundered, the earth gave echo,
    and there was I, standing between them.
A man there was, grim his expression,
    just like a Thunderbird his features were frightening.

'His hands were a lion's paws, his claws an eagle's talons,   VII 170
    he seized me by the hair, he overpowered me.
I struck him, but back he sprang like a skipping rope,
    he struck me, and like a raft capsized me.

'Underfoot [he] crushed me, like a mighty wild bull,
    [*drenching*] my body with poisonous slaver.   VII 175
"Save me, my friend! . . . . . . "
    You were afraid of him, but you . . . . . .   VII 177

*   *   *

'[*He struck me and*] turned me into a dove.   VII 182

'[He bound] my arms like the wings of a bird,
    to lead me captive to the house of darkness, seat of Irkalla:
to the house which none who enters ever leaves,   VII 185
    on the path that allows no journey back,

'to the house whose residents are deprived of light,
    where soil is their sustenance and clay their food,
where they are clad like birds in coats of feathers,
    and see no light, but dwell in darkness.   VII 190

'On door [and bolt the dust lay thick,]
    on the House [of Dust was poured a deathly quiet.]
In the House of Dust that I entered,

'I looked around me, saw the "crowns" in a throng,
    there were the crowned [heads] who'd ruled the land since days
        of yore,   VII 195
who'd served the roast [at the] tables of Anu and Enlil,
    who'd proffered baked bread, and poured them cool water from
        skins.

'In the House of Dust that I entered,
    there were the *en*-priests and *lagar*-priests,
there were lustration-priests and *lumahhu*-priests,   VII 200
    there were the great gods' *gudapsû*-priests,

'there was Etana, there was Shakkan,
    [there was] the queen of the Netherworld, the goddess
        Ereshkigal.
Before her sat [Belet]-ṣeri, the scribe of the Netherworld,
    holding [a tablet], reading aloud in her presence.   VII 205

'[She raised] her head and she saw me:
    "[Who was] it fetched this man here?
[Who was it] brought here [*this fellow*?]"'   VII 208

The remainder of Enkidu's vision of hell is lost. At the end of his speech he
commends himself to Gilgamesh:

'I who [endured] all hardships [with you,]   VII 251
    remember [me, my friend,] don't [forget] all I went through!'

Gilgamesh:

'My friend saw a vision which will never [*be equalled*!]'

The day he had the dream [his strength] was exhausted,
    Enkidu was cast down, he lay one day sick [and then a
        second.]   VII 255
Enkidu [lay] on his bed, [his sickness *worsened*,]
    a third day and a fourth day, [the sickness of Enkidu *worsened*.]

A fifth day, a sixth and a seventh, an eighth, a ninth [and a tenth,]
    the sickness of Enkidu *worsened* . . .
An eleventh day and a twelfth, ...   VII 260
    Enkidu [lay] on the bed, ...
He called for Gilgamesh [*and spoke to his friend*:]

'[*My god*] has taken against me, my friend, . . . ,
    [*I do not die*] like one who [falls] in the midst of battle.
I was afraid of combat, and . . . . . .   VII 265
    My friend, one who [falls] in combat [*makes his name*,]
but I, [*I do not fall*] in [*combat, and shall make not my name*.]'

The description of Enkidu's final death throes, which no doubt filled the remaining
thirty or so lines of Tablet VII, is still to be recovered.

Tablet VIII. The Funeral of Enkidu

Gilgamesh offers up a great lament for Enkidu. He summons his craftsmen and
makes a funerary statue of his friend, and from his treasury he selects the grave
goods that Enkidu will take to the Netherworld to win the goodwill of the deities
who dwell there. As part of the wake a great banquet is held, and then treasures
are offered to the gods of the Netherworld and ritually displayed in public.

At the very first glimmer of brightening dawn,
  Gilgamesh [began mourning] his friend:
'O Enkidu, [whom] your mother, a gazelle,
  and your father, a wild donkey, [*did raise,*]

'whom the wild [asses] did rear with their milk,   VIII 5
  whom the beasts [of the wild *did teach*] all the pastures –
O Enkidu, may the paths [of] the Forest of Cedar
  mourn you [without pause,] by day and by night!

'May the elders of teeming Uruk-the-Sheepfold mourn you!
  May the crowd who gave us their blessings [mourn you!]   VIII 10
May the high [*peaks*] of hills and mountains mourn you,
  . . . . pure.
May the pastures lament like your mother!

'May [*boxwood,*] cypress and cedar mourn you,
  through whose midst we crept in our fury!   VIII 15
May the bear mourn you, the hyena, the panther, the *cheetah*, the
       stag and the *jackal*,
  the lion, the wild bull, the deer, the ibex, all the beasts of the
       wild!

'May the sacred river Ulay mourn you,
  along whose banks we walked in our vigour!
May the pure Euphrates mourn you,
  whose water we poured in libation from skins!   VIII 20

'May the young men of Uruk-the-Sheepfold mourn you,
  [who] witnessed our battle when we slew the Bull of Heaven!
May the ploughman mourn you in [*his furrow*],
  [when he] extols your name with his sweet yodel!

'May the . . . of teeming Uruk-the-Sheepfold mourn you,   VIII 25
  [who] sends [forth] your name [with] the first . . . !
May the shepherd mourn you [*in his sheepfold,*]
  [who] made sweet [for your mouth] the milk and *butter*!

'May [the shepherd boy] mourn you . . . ,
   [who] provided the ghee for your *lips*!   VIII 30
May the *brewer* . . . . . . mourn you,
   [who] provided the ale for your mouth!

'May the harlot . . . . . . mourn you,
   [who] . . . anointed you with sweet-smelling oil!
May . . . [in the house] of the wedding ceremony mourn
      [you,]   VIII 35
   who . . . a wife . . . . . . !

'May . . . . mourn you!
   May . . . . . . mourn you [like] brothers!
May their tresses be loosed [down their backs] like sisters!
   . . . for Enkidu, your mother and father . . .   VIII 40
   [On this] very [day] I [*myself*] shall mourn you!

'Hear me, O young men, hear [me!]
   Hear me, O elders [of teeming Uruk,] hear me!
I shall weep for Enkidu, my friend,
   like a hired mourner-woman I shall bitterly wail.   VIII 45

9 *'I shall weep for Enkidu, my friend!'*

'The axe at my side, in which my arm trusted,
   the dirk at my belt, the shield at my face,
my festive garment, my girdle of delight:
   a wicked wind rose up and robbed me.

'O my friend, wild ass on the run, donkey of the uplands, panther
      of the wild,   VIII 50
   my friend Enkidu, wild ass on the run, donkey of the uplands,
      panther of the wild!
Having joined forces we climbed the [mountains,]
   seized and [slew] the Bull of Heaven,
destroyed Humbaba, who [dwelt in the] Forest [of Cedar.]

'Now what is this sleep that has seized [you?]   VIII 55
   You've become unconscious, you do not [hear me!]'
But he, he lifted not [his head.]
   He felt his heart, but it beat no longer.

He covered, like a bride, the face of his friend,
   like an eagle he circled around him.   VIII 60
Like a lioness deprived of her cubs,
   he paced to and fro, this way and that.

His curly [hair] he tore out in clumps,
   he ripped off his finery, [*like*] something taboo he cast it away.
At the very first glimmer of brightening dawn,   VIII 65
   Gilgamesh sent forth a call to the land:

'O forgemaster! [*Lapidary*!] Coppersmith! Goldsmith! Jeweller!
   Fashion my friend, ... !'
. . . he made a statue of his friend:
   'The limbs of my friend shall be of . . .   VIII 70

'Your *eyebrows* shall be of lapis lazuli, your chest of gold,
   your body shall be of . . . . . .   VIII 72

    *   *   *

'[I shall lay you out on a magnificent bed,]   VIII 84
  [I shall lay you out] on a bed [of honour.]   VIII 85
I shall place you [on my left, on a seat of repose;]
  the rulers of the underworld [will all kiss your feet.]

'The people [of Uruk] I shall have mourn [and lament you,]
  the thriving people [I shall fill full of woe for you.]
After you are gone [my hair will be matted in mourning,]   VIII 90
  clad in the skin of [a lion I shall wander] the wild.'

At the very first glimmer of brightening dawn,
  [*Gilgamesh arose and entered his treasury.*]
He undid its sealings, inspected the gems:
  obsidian, carnelian, [*lapis lazuli*,] . . . alabaster.   VIII 95

. . . . *skilfully worked*,
. . . . he provided for his friend.
. . . . he provided for his friend,
. . . . . . of *x*+10 minas of gold he provided for his friend.
. . . . . . of *x* minas of gold he provided for his friend.   VIII 100
. . . . . . of *x* minas of gold he provided for his friend.
. . . . . . of *x* minas of gold he provided for his friend.
. . . .
. . . . . . between them, mounted in thirty minas of gold,
. . . . . . was their . . . , he provided for his friend.   VIII 105
. . . . . . was their . . . , he provided for his friend.
. . . . was their thickness,
. . . . . . was their . . . , he provided for his friend.
. . . . large
. . . . he provided for his friend.   VIII 110
. . . . of his waist
. . . . he provided for his friend.
. . . . he provided for his friend.
. . . . he provided for his friend.
. . . . he provided for his friend.   VIII 115
. . . .
. . . . he provided for his friend.
. . . . of his feet, he provided for his friend.
. . . . . . of *x* talents of ivory . . . ,

...... of which the handle [was *x* minas] of gold, he provided for
    his friend.   VIII 120
      mighty ... of its arm, he provided for his friend.
... of which the quiver was ..., and the handle a talent of gold, he
    provided for his friend.
         . of his arm was ivory,
...... of which the handle was forty minas of gold, he provided
    for his friend.
         , three cubits was its length,   VIII 125
.... was its thickness, he provided for his friend.
.... of fine gold,
.... of carnelian, *rod* of iron,
.... *holder*, a wild bull,
.... for his friend,   VIII 130
he butchered fattened [oxen] and sheep, piled them high for his
    friend.
...... *Shamash* ...,
...... they carried all the meat to the rulers of the underworld.

... the great queen Ishtar.
[a *throw*]*stick* of ..., the gleaming wood,   VIII 135
    [for] the great queen Ishtar he displayed to the Sun God:
['May] the great queen Ishtar ... accept this,
    may she [welcome] my friend [and walk at his side!]'

....
    for the god Namra-[ṣit, ..., he displayed to the Sun
        God:]   VIII 140
'May [Namra-ṣit, ..., accept this,]
    may he [welcome my friend and walk at his side!]'

A flask of lapis lazuli ......
....
    for Ereshkigal, [the queen of the Netherworld, he displayed to
        the Sun God:]   VIII 145
'May Ereshkigal, the [queen of the teeming Netherworld,] accept
    this,
    may she welcome [my friend and walk at his side!]'

A flute of carnelian . . . . . .
    for Dumuzi, the shepherd beloved of [Ishtar, he displayed to the
        Sun God:]
'May Dumuzi, the shepherd beloved of [Ishtar,] accept this,   VIII 150
    may he welcome my friend and [walk at his side!]'

A chair of lapis lazuli . . . . . .
    a staff of lapis lazuli . . . . . .
    for Namtar, [the vizier of the Netherworld, he displayed to the
        Sun God:]
'May [Namtar, the vizier of the teeming Netherworld,]
    accept this,   VIII 155
    [may he welcome my friend and walk at his side!]'

. . . .
    for [Hushbisha, the stewardess of the Netherworld, he displayed
        to the Sun God:]
'May [Hushbisha, the stewardess of the teeming Netherworld,
    accept this,]   VIII 160
    [may she welcome my friend and walk at his side!]'

He had made . . . .
    a *clasp* of silver, a *bracelet of* . . . . . .
    for Qassu-ṭabat, the sweeper of [Ereshkigal, he displayed to the
        Sun God:]
'[May] Qassu-ṭabat, the sweeper [of Ereshkigal,] accept this, VIII 165
    may he welcome my friend and [walk at his side!]
    May my friend not . . . , nor become sick at heart!'

. . . of alabaster, the inside inlaid with lapis lazuli and carnelian,
    [*depicting an image*] of the Cedar Forest,
    . . . . . . inlayed with carnelian   VIII 170
    for Ninshuluhha . . . the cleaner of the house, he displayed to the
        Sun God:
'May Ninshuluhha . . . the cleaner of the house, accept this,
    may she welcome my friend and walk at his side!
[May she] . . . before my friend,
    may my [friend] not . . . , nor become sick at heart!'

A double-edged dagger with a haft of lapis lazuli,   VIII 175
  adorned with an image of the pure Euphrates,
  for Bibbu, the butcher of the Netherworld, he displayed to the
    Sun God:
'[May Bibbu, the butcher] of the teeming Netherworld, [accept this,]
  [may he] welcome [my friend] and walk at his side!'

. . . . . . with a back of alabaster   VIII 180
  [for *Dumuzi*-abzu, the] *scapegoat* of the Netherworld, he
    displayed to the Sun God:
'[May *Dumuzi*]-abzu, the *scapegoat* of the teeming Netherworld,
    [accept this,]
  may he welcome my [friend] and walk at his side!'

. . . . . . the top of which was lapis lazuli,
  . . . . . . inlaid with carnelian,   VIII 185
  [for . . . . . . he displayed to the Sun God:]
['May . . . . . . accept this,]
  [may he welcome my friend and walk at his side!']   VIII 188

When the text resumes after a lacuna the speaker is someone other than Gilgamesh:

'. . . . . . which we . . .   VIII 208
. . . their . . . , their names . . .
  . . . judge of the Anunnaki . . . '   VIII 210
Gilgamesh heard these words,
  he conceived [the idea] of *damming* the river.

At the very first glimmer of brightening dawn,
  Gilgamesh opened [*his gate*.]
He brought out a great table of *elammaku*-wood,   VIII 215
  he filled with honey a dish of carnelian.

He filled with ghee a dish of lapis lazuli,
  he decorated . . . and displayed it to the Sun God.
. . . . . . [*he displayed to the Sun*] God.

The rest of the description of Enkidu's funeral, which would have occupied the
remaining thirty or so lines of Tablet VIII, is yet to come to light.

Tablet IX. The Wanderings of Gilgamesh

In mourning for Enkidu, whose death has brought home to him his own mortality, Gilgamesh leaves Uruk to wander the earth in search of the immortal Uta-napishti, whose secret he covets. Pressing on to the end of the world he comes to the mountains where the Sun sets and rises and asks the help of the scorpion-man who guards the way under the mountains. Unable to convince Gilgamesh of the danger he courts the scorpion-man allows him to pass, and Gilgamesh races against time to complete the Path of the Sun before the Sun can catch up with him. He reaches the far end of the tunnel just in time and finds himself in a garden of jewels.

For his friend Enkidu Gilgamesh
   did bitterly weep as he wandered the wild:
'I shall die, and shall I not then be as Enkidu?
   Sorrow has entered my heart!

'I am afraid of death, so I wander the wild,   IX 5
   to find Uta-napishti, son of Ubar-Tutu.
On the road, travelling swiftly,
   I came one night to a mountain pass.

'I saw some lions and grew afraid,
   I lifted my head to the moon in prayer,   IX 10
to [Sîn, the] *lamp* of the gods, went my supplications:
   "[O Sîn and . . . ,] keep me safe!"'

[That night he] lay down, then woke from a dream:
   . . . in the presence of the moon he grew glad of life,
he took up his axe in his hand,   IX 15
   he drew forth [the dirk from] his belt.

Like an arrow among them he fell,
   he smote the [lions, he] killed them and scattered them.

The lacuna that intervenes here can be filled in part with text from an Old Babylonian tablet reportedly from Sippar:

[He] clad himself in their skins, he ate their flesh.   Si i 2'
Gilgamesh [*dug*] wells that never existed before,
    [*he*] *drank* the water, as he chased the winds.

Shamash grew worried, and *bending down*,   Si i 5'
    he spoke to Gilgamesh:
'O Gilgamesh, where are you wandering?
    The life that you seek you never will find.'

Said Gilgamesh to him, to the hero Shamash:
    'After *roaming*, wandering all through the wild,   Si i 10'
when I enter the Netherworld will rest be scarce?
    I shall lie there sleeping all down the years!

'Let my eyes see the sun and be sated with light!
    The darkness is *hidden*, how much light is there left?
When may the dead see the rays of the sun?'   Si i 15'

The text of Tablet IX resumes:

To Mashu's twin mountains he came,   IX 38
    which daily guard the rising [sun,]
whose tops [support] the fabric of heaven,   IX 40
    whose base reaches down to the Netherworld.

There were scorpion-men guarding its gate,
    whose terror was dread, whose glance was death,
whose radiance was fearful, overwhelming the mountains –
    at sunrise and sunset they guarded the sun.   IX 45

Gilgamesh saw them, in fear and dread he covered his face,
    then he collected his wits, and drew nearer their presence.
The scorpion-man called to his mate:
    'He who has come to us, flesh of the gods is his body.'

The scorpion-man's mate answered him: IX 50
    'Two-thirds of him is god, and one third human.'
The scorpion-man called out,
    saying a word [to King Gilgamesh,] flesh of the gods:

10 'At sunrise and sunset they guarded the sun'.

'[*How did you come here,*] such a far road?
  [*How did you get here,*] to be in my presence?   IX 55
[*How did you cross the seas,*] whose passage is perilous?
      . . . . . . let me learn of your [*journey!*]

' . . . . . . *where* your [*face*] is turned,
      . . . . . . let me learn [*of your journey!*]'   IX 59

When the text resumes after a lacuna, Gilgamesh is explaining his quest:

  '[*I am seeking*] the [*road*] of my forefather, Uta-napishti,   IX 75
who attended the gods' assembly, and [found life eternal:]
  of death and life [*he shall tell me the secret.*]'

The scorpion-man opened his mouth [to speak,]
  saying to [Gilgamesh:]
'Never [before], O Gilgamesh, was there [one like you,]   IX 80
  never did anyone [*travel the path*] of the mountain.

'For twelve double-hours its interior [*extends*,]
  the darkness is dense, and [light is] there none.
For the rising of the sun . . . . ,
  for the setting of the sun . . . .   IX 85

'For the setting of the . . . . ,
  they sent forth . . . .
And you, how will you . . . . . . ?
  Will you go in . . . . ?'   IX 90

After a long lacuna, the text resumes with the end of Gilgamesh's reply:

'Through sorrow . . . .   IX 125
  by frost and by sunshine [my face is burnt.]
Through exhaustion . . . .
  now you . . . .'

The scorpion-man [opened his mouth to speak,]
  [saying a word] to King Gilgamesh, [flesh of the gods:]   IX 130
'Go, Gilgamesh! . . . .
  May the mountains of Mashu [*allow you to pass*!]

'[May] the mountains and hills [*watch over your going*!]
  Let [them *help you*] in safety [*to continue your journey*!]
[May] the gate of the mountains [*open before you*!]'   IX 135

Gilgamesh [*heard these words*,]
  what [the scorpion-man] told him [he took to heart,]
he [took] the path of the Sun God . . . . . .

At one double-hour . . . . ,
  the darkness was dense, [and light was there none:]   IX 140
it did not [allow him to see behind him.]

At two double-hours . . . . ,
    the darkness was dense, [and light was there none:]
it did not [allow him to see behind him.]

At three double-hours . . . . ,   IX 145
    [the darkness was dense, and light was there none:]
[it did not allow him to see behind him.]

At four double-hours . . . . ,
    [the darkness] was dense, [and light was there none:]
it did not [allow him to see behind him.]   IX 150

At five double-hours . . . . ,
    the darkness was dense, [and light was there none:]
it did not allow [him to see behind him.]

On [*reaching*] six double-hours,
    the darkness was dense, [and light was there none:]   IX 155
it did not allow [him to see behind him.]

On reaching seven double-hours . . . ,
    the darkness was dense, and [light was there] none:
it did not allow him to see behind [him.]

At eight double-hours he was hurrying . . . ,   IX 160
    the darkness was dense, and light was [there none:]
it did not [allow him to] see behind him.

At nine double-hours . . . . . . the north wind,
    . . . . his face.
[The darkness was dense, and] light was [there none:]   IX 165
    [it did not allow him to] see behind him.

[On] reaching [ten double-hours,]
    . . . . was very near.
[*On reaching* eleven double-hours *a journey remained*] of one
      double-hour,
    [at twelve double-hours Gilgamesh came] out in advance of the
      Sun.   IX 170

...... there was brilliance:
  he went straight, as soon as he saw them, to . . . the trees of the
     gods.
A carnelian tree was in fruit,
  hung with bunches of grapes, lovely to look on.

A lapis lazuli tree bore foliage,   IX 175
  in full fruit and gorgeous to gaze on.

  *   *   *

  . . . *cypress* . . . .
. . . cedar . . . . ,   IX 185
  its leaf-stems were of *pappardilû*-stone and . . .
Sea *coral* . . . . . . *sasu*-stone,
  instead of thorns and briars [*there grew*] stone *vials*.
He touched a carob, [*it was*] *abashmu*-stone,
  agate and haematite . . . . . .   IX 190

  *   *   *

As Gilgamesh walked about . . . ,   IX 195
  she lifted [her head in order] to watch him.

Tablet X. At the Edge of the World

Beyond the garden, by the sea-shore, lives a wise old goddess. She spies a
forbidding figure in the distance and, taking him to be a hunter, bars the door
of her tavern. Gilgamesh hears her and threatens to break in. She asks who he
is. He tells her how his friend has died and how much he now fears death, and
he asks her aid in crossing the sea to find Uta-napishti. She warns him of the
futility of his quest and the dangers of the Waters of Death, but at length tells
him where to find Uta-napishti's ferryman, Ur-shanabi, with his crew of Stone
Ones. Gilgamesh rushes down on the ferryman and his strange companions.
When the fighting is over he explains his quest to Ur-shanabi and asks his aid in
finding Uta-napishti. Ur-shanabi reveals that Gilgamesh has hindered his own
progress by smashing the Stone Ones, but he instructs Gilgamesh to make
punting-poles of immense length as an alternative means of propulsion. They
embark on the boat with the poles. When the poles are all gone Gilgamesh uses
the ferryman's garment to make a sail, and they cross the Waters of Death.

Having landed Gilgamesh tells his story to Uta-napishti. Uta-napishti reminds
him of the duties of kings and discourses on the inevitability of death and the
fleeting nature of life.

Shiduri was a tavern-keeper who lived by the sea-shore,
    there she dwelt, [*in an inn by the sea-shore.*]
Potstands she had, and [*vats all of gold,*]
    she was swathed in hoods and [*veiled with*] veils.

Gilgamesh came wandering . . . . . . ,   X 5
    he was clad in a pelt, and fearful [*to look on.*]
The flesh of the gods he had in [*his body,*]
    but in [his heart] there was sorrow.

His face resembled one come from afar.
    As the tavern-keeper watched him in the distance,   X 10
talking to herself she spoke a word,
    taking counsel in her own mind:

'For sure this man is a hunter of wild bulls,
    but where does he come from, making straight for my gate?'
Thus the tavern-keeper saw him, and barred her gate,   X 15
    barred her gate and went up on the roof.

But Gilgamesh gave ear to . . . ,
    he lifted his chin, and *turned* [*towards her.*]
[Said] Gilgamesh to her, [to the tavern]-keeper:
  'Tavern-keeper, why [did you bar] your [gate] as soon as you
      saw [me?]   X 20

'You barred your gate, [and went up on the] roof.
    I shall smash down the door, I shall [shatter the bolts!]'   X 22

    ✻   ✻   ✻

[Said the tavern-keeper] to him, [to] Gilgamesh: X 25
  ' . . . . . . I barred my gate,
. . . . . . [I went up on] the roof.
    . . . . . . let me learn of [*your journey!*]'

[Said Gilgamesh to] her, [to the tavern]-keeper:
   '[My friend Enkidu and I . . . . :]   X 30

'[having joined forces we climbed the] mountains,
   [seized and slew the Bull of Heaven,]
[destroyed Humbaba, who dwelt in the Forest of] Cedar,
   [killed] lions [in the mountain *passes*.]'

Said [the tavern-keeper to him,] to Gilgamesh: X 35
   '[If *you and Enkidu were*] the ones who slew the Guardian,
[destroyed] Humbaba, who dwelt in the Forest of Cedar,
   killed lions [in the] mountain [*passes*,]
[seized] and slew [the] Bull come down from heaven –

'[why are your] cheeks [so hollow,] your face so sunken,   X 40
   [your mood so wretched,] your visage [so] wasted?
[Why] in your heart [does sorrow reside,]
   and your face resemble one [come from afar?]
[Why are] your features burnt [by frost and by sunshine,]
   [and why do] you wander the wild [in lion's garb?]'   X 45

[Said Gilgamesh to her,] to the tavern-keeper:
   '[Why should my cheeks not be hollow, my face not sunken,]
[my mood not wretched, my visage not wasted?]

'[Should not sorrow reside in my heart,]
   [and my face not resemble one come from afar?]   X 50
[Should not my features be burnt by frost and by sunshine,]
   [and should I not wander the wild in lion's garb?]

'[My friend, a wild ass on the run,]
   [donkey of the uplands, panther of the wild,]
[my friend Enkidu, a wild ass on the run,]
   [donkey of the uplands, panther of the wild,]

'[my friend, whom I loved so dear,]   X 55
   [who with me went through every danger,]
[my friend Enkidu, whom I loved so dear,]
   [who with me went through every danger:]

'[*the doom of mortals* overtook him.]
  [Six days I wept for him and seven nights.]
[I did not surrender his body for burial,]
  [until a maggot dropped from his nostril.]   X 60

'[Then I was afraid *that I too would die*,]
  [I grew fearful of death, and so wander the wild.]
What became of my friend [*was too much* to bear,]
  [so on a far road I wander the] wild;
what became of [my friend] Enkidu [*was too much* to bear,]   X 65
  [so on a far path] I wander [the wild.]

'How can I keep silent?] How can I stay quiet?
  [My friend, whom I loved, has turned] to clay,
my friend Enkidu, whom I loved, has [turned to clay.]
  [Shall I not be like] him, and also lie down,   X 70
[never] to rise again, through all eternity?'

Said Gilgamesh to her, to the tavern-keeper:
  'Now, O tavern-keeper, where is the road to Uta-napishti?
What is its landmark? Tell me!
  Give me its landmark!   X 75
If it may be done, I will cross the ocean,
  if it may not be done, I will wander the wild!'

Said the tavern-keeper to him, to Gilgamesh:
  'O Gilgamesh, there never has been a way across,
nor since olden days can anyone cross the ocean.   X 80
  Only Shamash the hero crosses the ocean:
apart from the Sun God, who crosses the ocean?

'The crossing is perilous, its way full of hazard,
  and midway lie the Waters of Death, blocking the passage
      forward.
So besides, Gilgamesh, once you have crossed the ocean,   X 85
  when you reach the Waters of Death, what then will you do?

'Gilgamesh, there is Ur-shanabi, the boatman of Uta-napishti,
   and the Stone Ones are with him, as he *picks a pine clean* in the
      midst of the forest.
Go then, let him see your face!
   If [it may be] done, go across with him,   X 90
if it may not be done, turn around and go back!'

Gilgamesh heard these words,
   he took up his axe in his hand,
he drew forth the dirk [from] his [belt,]
   forward he crept and on [them] rushed down.   X 95

Like an arrow he fell among them,
   in the midst of the forest his shout resounded.
Ur-shanabi saw the *bright . . . . . .* ,
   he took up an axe, and he . . . him.

But he, Gilgamesh, struck his head . . . ,   X 100
   he seized his arm and . . . *pinned him down.*
They took fright, the Stone [Ones, *who crewed*] the boat,
   who were not [*harmed by* the Waters] of Death.

. . . . the wide ocean,
   at the waters . . . he stayed [not his hand]:   X 105
he smashed [them in his fury, *he threw them*] in the river.

What happens next is best preserved in the Old Babylonian tablet reportedly
from Sippar:

He came back to stand over him,   Si iv 2
   as *Ur-shanabi looked him in the eye.

Said *Ur-shanabi to him, to Gilgamesh:
   'Tell me, what is your name?   Si iv 5
I am *Ur-shanabi, of *Uta-napishti the Distant.'
   Said Gilgamesh to him, to *Ur-shanabi:

'Gilgamesh is my name,
   who came from Uruk-Eanna,
who wound a way around the mountains,   Si iv 10
   the hidden road where rises the sun.'

The text of Tablet X resumes:

Said Ur-shanabi to him, to Gilgamesh: X 112
   'Why are your cheeks so hollow, [your face so] sunken,
   your mood so wretched, [your visage so wasted?]

'[Why in your heart] does sorrow reside,   X 115
   and [your face resemble one] come from afar?
Why are [your features] burnt by frost and by sunshine,
   [and why] do you [wander the wild in lion's garb?]'

Said [Gilgamesh to him,] to [the boatman Ur-shanabi:]
   '[Why should] my cheeks [not be hollow, my face] not
      [sunken,]   X 120
my [mood not wretched, my visage] not wasted?

'[Should not] sorrow [reside] in [my heart,]
   [and my] face [not resemble one come from afar?]
[Should] not [my features be] burnt [by frost and by sunshine,]
   and should I not [wander the wild in lion's garb?]   X 125

'[My friend, a wild ass on the run,]
   [donkey of the uplands, panther of the wild,]
[my friend Enkidu, a wild ass on the run,]
   [donkey of the uplands, panther of the wild −]

'[having joined forces we climbed the mountains,]
   [seized and slew the Bull of Heaven,]
[destroyed Humbaba, who dwelt in the Forest of Cedar,]   X 130
   [killed lions] in [the mountain *passes* −]

'my friend [whom I loved so dear,]
   [who with me went through every danger,]
[my friend] Enkidu, [whom I loved so dear,]
   [who with me went through every danger:]
[*the doom of mortals*] overtook [him.]

'Six days [I wept for him and seven nights:]   X 135
   [I did not surrender his body for burial]
until [a maggot dropped from his nostril.]
   Then I was afraid [*that I too would die,*]
[I grew fearful of death, so wander the wild.]

'What became of my [friend *was too much* to bear,]   X 140
   so on a far road I [wander the wild;]
[what became of my friend Enkidu *was too much* to bear,]
   so on a far path [I wander the wild.]

'How can I keep [silent? How can I stay quiet?]
   My friend, whom I loved, has [turned to clay,]   X 145
[my friend Enkidu, whom I loved, has turned to clay.]
   Shall I not be like him, and also lie [down,]
[never to rise again, through all eternity?]'

Said Gilgamesh to him, to Ur-[shanabi, the boatman:]
   'Now, Ur-shanabi, where [is the road to Uta-napishti?]   X 150
What is its landmark? Tell me!
   Give [me its landmark!]
If it may be done, I will cross the ocean,
   if it may not be done, [I will wander the wild!]'

Said Ur-shanabi to him, to Gilgamesh: X 155
   'Your own hands, O Gilgamesh, have prevented [*your crossing:*]
you smashed the Stone Ones, *threw* [*them in the river,*]
   the Stone Ones are smashed, and the *pine* is not [*stripped.*]

'Take up, O Gilgamesh, your axe in [your] hand,
   go down to the forest and [cut three hundred] punting-poles,
      each five rods in length.   X 160
Trim them and furnish them each with a boss,
   then bring [*them here into my presence.*]'

Gilgamesh heard these words,
   he took up his axe in his hand,
he drew forth [the dirk from his belt,]   X 165
   he went down to the forest and [cut three hundred]
      punting-poles, each five rods in length.
He trimmed them and furnished them each with a boss,
   then he brought [*them to Ur-shanabi, the boatman.*]

Gilgamesh and Ur-shanabi crewed [the boat,]
   they launched the craft, and [crewed it] themselves.   X 170
In three days they made a journey of a month and a half,
   and Ur-shanabi came to the Waters of [Death.]

[Said] Ur-shanabi to him, [to Gilgamesh:]
   '*Set to*, O Gilgamesh! Take the first [punting-pole!]
Let your hand not touch the Waters of Death, lest you
     wither [it!]   X 175

'Take a second punting-pole, Gilgamesh, a third and a fourth!
   Take a fifth punting-pole, Gilgamesh, a sixth and a seventh!
Take an eighth punting-pole, Gilgamesh, a ninth and a tenth!
   Take an eleventh punting-pole, Gilgamesh, and a twelfth!'

At one hundred and twenty double-furlongs Gilgamesh had used all
     the punting-poles,   X 180
   so he, [Ur-shanabi,] undid his clothing,
Gilgamesh stripped off [his] garment,
   with arms held aloft he made a yard-arm.

Uta-napishti was watching Gilgamesh in the distance,
    talking to himself he [spoke] a word,   X 185
[taking counsel] in his own mind:
    'Why are the boat's [Stone Ones] all broken,
and aboard it one who is not its master?

'He who comes is no man of mine,
    but on the right . . . . . .   X 190
I am looking, but he is no [man of] mine . . . '

        *   *   *

'He is not mine . . . . . . ,
    . . . .
The boatman . . . . ,
    the man who . . . . ,
who . . . . '   X 200

        *   *   *

Gilgamesh [*drew near*] to the quayside.   X 204

        *   *   *

    Said Gilgamesh to him, [to Uta-napishti:]
'. . . Uta-napishti . . . . . . ,
    . . . who after the Deluge . . . . . .

'. . . . . . what . . . . . . ?   X 210
    . . . . '

[Said Uta-napishti to] him, to [Gilgamesh:]
    '[Why are your cheeks so hollow, your face so] sunken,
[your mood so wretched, your visage] so wasted?

'[Why in your heart] does sorrow reside,   X 215
    [and your face resemble] one come from afar?
[Why are your features burnt by frost] and by sunshine,
    and why do you wander the wild in lion's garb?'

[Said] Gilgamesh to him, [to Uta-napishti:]
  'Why should my cheeks not be hollow, [my face not
      sunken,]   X 220
my mood not wretched, my visage not wasted?

'Should not sorrow reside in my heart,
  and my [face] not resemble one come from afar?
[Should not] my features be [burnt] by frost and by sunshine,
  [and should I not] wander the wild in lion's garb?   X 225

'[My friend, a wild ass on the run,]
  [donkey of the uplands,] panther of the wild,
[my friend Enkidu, a wild ass on the run,]
  [donkey of the uplands, panther of the wild –]

'[having joined forces we climbed] the mountains,
  [seized and] slew [the Bull] of Heaven,
[destroyed Humbaba, who] dwelt [in the] Forest of Cedar,   X 230
  killed lions [in the mountain *passes* –]

'[my friend, whom I loved so dear,]
  [who with me went through] every danger,
[my friend Enkidu, whom I loved so dear,]
  [who with me] went through every danger:
[*the doom of mortals* overtook him.]

'[Six days] I wept for him [and seven nights:]   X 235
  [I did not surrender his body for] burial
[until a maggot dropped from] his [nostril.]
  [Then I was afraid *that I too would die*,]
[I grew] fearful of death, [and so wander the] wild.

'What became of [my friend *was too much*] to [bear,]   X 240
  so on a far road [I wander the] wild;
what became of my friend Enkidu [*was too much* to bear,]
  so on a far path [I wander the wild.]

'How can I keep silent? How can I stay quiet?
   My friend, whom I loved, has turned to clay,   X 245
my friend Enkidu, [whom I loved, has turned to clay.]
   [Shall] I not be like him and also lie down,
never to rise again, through all [eternity?]'

Said Gilgamesh to him, to Uta-napishti:
   'I thought, "I will find Uta-napishti the Distant, of whom men
       tell,"   X 250
and I wandered journeying through every land.
   Many times I passed through terrible mountains,
many times I crossed and recrossed all the oceans.

'Of slumber sweet my face had too little,
   I scourged myself by going sleepless.   X 255
I have filled my sinews with sorrow,
   and what have I achieved by my toil?

'I had yet to reach the tavern-keeper, my clothing was worn out.
   [I killed] bear, hyena, lion, panther, *cheetah*,
deer, ibex, the beasts and game of the wild: X 260
   I ate their flesh, their pelts I *flayed*.

'Now let the gate of sorrow be barred,
   let [*its door be sealed*] with tar and pitch,
for my sake they shall [*interrupt*] the dancing no more,
   [for] me, happy and carefree . . . . . . '   X 265

Said Uta-napishti to him, to [Gilgamesh:]
   'Why, Gilgamesh, do you ever [chase] sorrow?
You, who are [built] from gods' flesh and human,
   whom the [gods did fashion] like your father and mother!

'[Did *you*] ever, Gilgamesh, [*compare your lot*] with the fool? X 270
   They placed a throne in the assembly, and [*told you*,] "*Sit!*"
The fool gets left-over yeast instead of [*fresh*] ghee,
   bran and grist instead of [*best flour*.]

'He is clad in a *rag*, instead of [*fine garments*,]
    instead of a belt, *he is girt* [*with old rope*.]   X 275
Because he has no *advisers* [*to guide him*,]
    his affairs lack counsel . . . . . .

'Have thought for him, Gilgamesh, ... ,
    [*who is*] their master, as many as . . . . . . ?
. . . .   X 280
    . . . the moon and the gods [*of the night*.]

'[At] night the moon travels . . . . . . ,
    the gods stay awake, and . . . . . .
Wakeful, unsleeping, ... ,
    from olden times is set . . . . . .   X 285

'Now consider . . . . . . ,
    your support . . . .
If, Gilgamesh, the temples of the gods [*have no*] *provisioner*,
    the temples of the goddesses . . . . . .

'They . . . . . . , the gods . . . ,   X 290
    for . . . . . . he made . . .
. . . . . . for a gift he . . . ,
    . . . . . . they will cast down . . . '   X 293

          *   *   *

'[*Enkidu indeed*] they took to his doom.   X 296
    [But you,] you toiled away, and what did you achieve?
You exhaust yourself with ceaseless toil,
    you fill your sinews with sorrow,

'bringing forward the end of your days.   X 300
    Man is snapped off like a reed in a canebrake!
The comely young man, the pretty young woman –
    all [*too soon in*] their [*prime*] Death abducts them!

'No one at all sees Death,
    no one at all sees the face [of Death,]   X 305
no one at all [hears] the voice of Death,
    Death so savage, who hacks men down.

'Ever do we build our households,
  ever do we make our nests,
ever do brothers divide their inheritance,   X 310
  ever do feuds arise in *the land*.

'Ever the river has risen and brought us the flood,
  the mayfly floating on the water.
On the face of the sun its countenance gazes,
  then all of a sudden nothing is there!   X 315

11 *'Then all of a sudden nothing is there!'*

'The abducted and the dead, how alike is their lot!
  But never was drawn the likeness of Death,
never in the land did the dead greet a man.

'The Anunnaki, the great gods, held an assembly,
  Mammitum, maker of destiny, fixed fates with them: X 320
both Death and Life they have established,
  but the day of Death they do not disclose.'

Tablet XI. Immortality Denied

Gilgamesh asks Uta-napishti how he gained eternal life, and hears how Uta-napishti survived the Deluge and was given immortality by the gods as a result. Uta-napishti suggests Gilgamesh go without sleep for a week. Gilgamesh fails the test and realizes in despair that if he cannot beat Sleep he has no hope of conquering Death. Uta-napishti commands his ferryman to have Gilgamesh bathe and dress himself in more kingly garments, and to escort him back to Uruk. Uta-napishti's wife counsels him to give the departing hero the customary present for his journey. Uta-napishti tells Gilgamesh how, deep under the sea, a plant-like coral grows that has the property of rejuvenation. Gilgamesh dives to the sea-bed and retrieves it. He and Ur-shanabi leave for Uruk. Stopping at a welcoming pool, Gilgamesh bathes in its water, and a snake seizes on his inattention to steal the precious 'plant'. Knowing that he will never rediscover the exact spot where he dived, Gilgamesh realizes at last that all his labours have been in vain. His hopes are destroyed: it would have been better not to have met Uta-napishti at all. He and Ur-shanabi arrive in Uruk, where, with words that echo the prologue, Gilgamesh shows the ferryman the walls that will be his enduring monument.

Said Gilgamesh to him, to Uta-napishti the Distant:
    'I look at you, Uta-napishti:
your form is no different, you are just like me,
    you are not any different, you are just like me.

'I was fully intent on making you fight,   XI 5
    but now in your presence my hand is stayed.
How was it you stood with the gods in assembly?
    How did you find the life eternal?'

Said Uta-napishti to him, to Gilgamesh:
    'Let me disclose, O Gilgamesh, a matter most secret,
to you I will tell a mystery of gods.   XI 10

'The town of Shuruppak, a city well known to you,
    which stands on the banks of the river Euphrates:
this city was old – the gods once were in it –
    when the great gods decided to send down the Deluge.

'Their father Anu swore on oath,   XI 15
    and their counsellor, the hero Enlil,
their chamberlain, the god Ninurta,
    and their sheriff, the god Ennugi.

'Princely Ea swore with them also,
    repeating their words to a fence made of reed: XI 20
"O fence of reed! O wall of brick!
    Hear this, O fence! Pay heed, O wall!

'"O man of Shuruppak, son of Ubar-Tutu,
    demolish the house, and build a boat!
Abandon wealth, and seek survival!   XI 25
    Spurn property, save life!
Take on board the boat all living things' seed!

'"The boat you will build,
    her dimensions all shall be equal:
her length and breadth shall be the same,   XI 30
    cover her with a roof, like the Ocean Below."

'I understood, and spoke to Ea, my master:
    "I obey, O master, what thus you told me.
I understood, and I shall do it,
    but how do I answer my city, the crowd and the elders?"   XI 35

'Ea opened his mouth to speak,
    saying to me, his servant:
"Also you will say to them this:
    'For sure the god Enlil feels for me hatred.

'"'In your city I can live no longer,   XI 40
    I can tread no more [on] Enlil's ground.
[I must] go to the Ocean Below, to live with Ea, my master,
    and he will send you a rain of plenty:

' " '[an abundance] of birds, a *profusion* of fishes,
    [*he will provide*] a harvest of riches.   XI 45
In the morning he will send you a shower of bread-cakes,
    and in the evening a torrent of wheat.' "

'At the very first glimmer of brightening dawn,
    at the gate of Atra-hasis assembled the land:
the carpenter carrying [his] hatchet,   XI 50
    the reed-worker carrying [his] stone,
[*the shipwright bearing his*] heavyweight axe.

'The young men were . . . . . . ,
    the old men bearing ropes of palm-fibre;
the rich man was carrying the pitch,   XI 55
    the poor man brought the . . . tackle.

'By the fifth day I had set her hull in position,
    one acre was her area, ten rods the height of her sides.
At ten rods also, the sides of her roof were each the same length.
    I set in place her body, I drew up her design.

'Six decks I gave her,   XI 60
    dividing her thus into seven.
Into nine compartments I divided her interior,
    I struck the bilge plugs into her middle.
I saw to the punting-poles and put in the tackle.   XI 65

'Three myriad measures of pitch I poured in a furnace,
    three myriad of tar I . . . within,
three myriad of oil fetched the workforce of porters:
    aside from the myriad of oil consumed in *libations*,
there were two myriad of oil stowed away by the boatman.   XI 70

'For my workmen I butchered oxen,
    and lambs I slaughtered daily.
Beer and ale, oil and wine
    like water from a river [I gave my] workforce,
so they enjoyed a feast like the days of New Year.   XI 75

'At sun-[*rise*] I set my hand [to] the oiling,
   [before] the sun set the boat was complete.
.... were very arduous:
   from back to front we moved poles for the slipway,
[*until*] two-thirds of [the boat *had entered the water*.]   XI 80

'[Everything I owned] I loaded aboard:
   all the silver I owned I loaded aboard,
all the gold I owned I loaded aboard,
   all the living creatures I had I loaded aboard.
I sent on board all my kith and kin,   XI 85
   the beasts of the field, the creatures of the wild, and members of
      every skill and craft.

'The time which the Sun God appointed –
   "In the morning he will send you a shower of bread-cakes,
and in the evening a torrent of wheat.
   Go into the boat and seal your hatch!" –

'that time had now come: XI 90
   "In the morning he will send you a shower of bread-cakes,
and in the evening a torrent of wheat."
   I examined the look of the weather.

'The weather to look at was full of foreboding,
   I went into the boat and sealed my hatch.
To the one who sealed the boat, Puzur-Enlil the shipwright,   XI 95
   I gave my palace with all its goods.

'At the very first glimmer of brightening dawn,
   there rose on the horizon a dark cloud of black,
and bellowing within it was Adad the Storm God.
   The gods Shullat and Hanish were going before him,   XI 100
bearing his throne over mountain and land.

'The god Errakal was uprooting the mooring-poles,
   Ninurta, passing by, made the weirs overflow.
The Anunnaki gods carried torches of fire,
   scorching the country with brilliant flashes.   XI 105

'The stillness of the Storm God passed over the sky,
   and all that was bright then turned into darkness.
[He] charged the land like a *bull* [*on the rampage,*]
   he smashed [it] in pieces [*like a vessel of clay.*]

'For a day the gale [winds *flattened the country,*]
   quickly they blew, and [*then came*] the [*Deluge.*]   XI 110
Like a battle [the cataclysm] passed over the people.
   One man could not discern another,
nor could people be recognized amid the destruction.

'Even the gods took fright at the Deluge,
   they left and went up to the heaven of Anu,   XI 115
lying like dogs curled up in the open.
   The goddess cried out like a woman in childbirth,
Belet-ili wailed, whose voice is so sweet:

'"The olden times have turned to clay,
   because I spoke evil in the gods' assembly.   XI 120
How could I speak evil in the gods' assembly,
   and declare a war to destroy my people?

'"It is I who give birth, these people are mine!
   And now, like fish, they fill the ocean!"

12 *'And now, like fish, they fill the ocean!'*

The Anunnaki gods were weeping with her,   XI 125
   wet-faced with sorrow, they were weeping [with her,]
their lips were parched and stricken with fever.

'For six days and [seven] nights,
    there blew the wind, the downpour,
the gale, the Deluge, it flattened the land.

'But the seventh day when it came,   XI 130
    the gale relented, the Deluge *ended*.
The ocean grew calm, that had thrashed like a woman in labour,
    the tempest grew still, the Deluge ended.

'I looked at the weather, it was quiet and still,
    but all the people had turned to clay.   XI 135
The flood plain was flat like the roof of a house.
    I opened a vent, on my cheeks fell the sunlight.

'Down sat I, I knelt and I wept,
    down my cheeks the tears were coursing.
I scanned the horizons, the edge of the ocean,   XI 140
    in fourteen places there rose an island.

'On the mountain of Nimush the boat ran aground,
    Mount Nimush held the boat fast, allowed it no motion.
One day and a second, Mount Nimush held the boat fast, allowed
        it no motion,
a third day and a fourth, Mount Nimush held the boat fast,
        allowed it no motion,   XI 145
a fifth day and a sixth, Mount Nimush held the boat fast, allowed
        it no motion.

'The seventh day when it came,
    I brought out a dove, I let it loose:
off went the dove but then it returned,
    there was no place to land, so back it came to me.   XI 150

'I brought out a swallow, I let it loose:
    off went the swallow but then it returned,
there was no place to land, so back it came to me.

'I brought out a raven, I let it loose:
    off went the raven, it saw the waters receding,   XI 155
finding food, *bowing and bobbing*, it did not come back to me.

'I brought out an offering, to the four winds made sacrifice,
    incense I placed on the peak of the mountain.
Seven flasks and seven I set in position,
    reed, cedar and myrtle I piled beneath them.   XI 160

'The gods did smell the savour,
    the gods did smell the savour sweet,
the gods gathered like flies around the man making sacrifice.

'Then at once Belet-ili arrived,
    she lifted the flies of lapis lazuli that Anu had made for their
          courtship: XI 165
"O gods, let these great beads in this necklace of mine
    make me remember these days, and never forget them!

' "All the gods shall come to the incense,
    but to the incense let Enlil not come,
because he lacked counsel and brought on the Deluge,   XI 170
    and delivered my people into destruction."

'Then at once Enlil arrived,
    he saw the boat, he was seized with anger,
filled with rage at the divine Igigi:
    "[From] where escaped this living being?   XI 175
No man was meant to survive the destruction!"

'Ninurta opened his mouth to speak,
    saying to the hero Enlil:
"Who, if not Ea, could cause such a thing?
    Ea alone knows how all things are done."   XI 180

'Ea opened his mouth to speak,
 saying to the hero Enlil:
"You, the sage of the gods, the hero,
 how could you lack counsel and bring on the Deluge?

'"On him who transgresses, inflict his crime!   XI 185
 On him who does wrong, inflict his wrongdoing!
'Slack off, lest it snap! Pull tight, lest it [slacken!]'

'"Instead of your causing the Deluge,
 a lion could have risen, and diminished the people!
Instead of your causing the Deluge,   XI 190
 a wolf could have risen, and diminished the people!

'"Instead of your causing the Deluge,
 a famine could have happened, and slaughtered the land!
Instead of your causing the Deluge,
 the Plague God could have risen, and slaughtered the land! XI 195

'"It was not I disclosed the great gods' secret:
 Atra-hasis I let see a vision, and thus he learned our secret.
And now, decide what to do with him!"

'Enlil came up inside the boat,
 he took hold of my hand and brought me on board.   XI 200
He brought aboard my wife and made her kneel at my side,
 he touched our foreheads, standing between us to bless us:

'"In the past Uta-napishti was a mortal man,
 but now he and his wife shall become like us gods!
Uta-napishti shall dwell far away, where the rivers flow
   forth!"   XI 205
 So far away they took me, and settled me where the rivers flow
   forth.

'But you now, who'll convene for you the gods' assembly,
 so you can find the life you search for?
For six days and seven nights, come, do without slumber!'

As soon as Gilgamesh squatted down on his haunches,   XI 210
   sleep like a fog already breathed over him.
Said Uta-napishti to her, to his wife:
   'See the fellow who so desired life!
Sleep like a fog already breathes over him.'

Said his wife to him, to Uta-napishti the Distant: XI 215
   'Touch the man and make him awake!
The way he came he shall go back in well-being,
   by the gate he came forth he shall return to his land!'

Said Uta-napishti to her, to his wife:
   'Man is deceitful, he will deceive you.   XI 220
Go, bake for him his daily bread-loaf, and line them up by his
      head,
   and mark on the wall the days that he sleeps!'

So she baked for him his daily bread-loaf, she lined them up by his
      head,
   noting on the wall the days that he slept.
His first bread-loaf was all dried up,   XI 225
   the second was leathery, soggy the third,

the fourth flour-cake had turned to white,
   the fifth had cast a mould of grey,
fresh-baked was the sixth,
   the seventh still on the coals:
then he touched him and the man awoke.   XI 230

Said Gilgamesh to him, to Uta-napishti the Distant:
   'No sooner had sleep spilled itself over me,
than forthwith you touched me and made me awake!'
   [Said] Uta-napishti [to him,] to Gilgamesh:

'Come, Gilgamesh, count me your bread-loaves,   XI 235
   then you will learn [the days that you slept.]
Your [first] bread-loaf [was all dried up,]
   the second was leathery, soggy the third,

'the fourth flour-cake had turned to white,
  the fifth had cast a mould of grey,
fresh-baked was the sixth,   XI 240
  [the seventh still on] the coals:
and only then did I touch you.'

Said Gilgamesh to him, to Uta-napishti the Distant:
  'O Uta-napishti, what should I do and where should I go?
A thief has taken hold of my [*flesh*!]
  For there in my bed-chamber Death does abide,   XI 245
and wherever [I] turn, there too will be Death.'

[Said] Uta-napishti to [him,] to the boatman Ur-shanabi:
  '[May] the quay [reject] you, Ur-shanabi, and the ferry scorn
     you!
You who used to walk this shore, be banished from it now!
  As for the man that you led here,   XI 250

'his body is tousled with matted hair,
  the pelts have ruined his body's beauty.
Take him, Ur-shanabi, lead him to the washtub,
  have him wash his matted locks as clean as can be!

'Let him cast off his pelts, and the sea bear them off,   XI 255
  let his body be soaked till fair!
Let a new kerchief be made for his head,
  let him wear royal robes, the dress fitting his dignity!

'Until he goes home to his city,
  until he reaches the end of his road,   XI 260
let the robes show no mark, but stay fresh and new!'
  Ur-shanabi took him, and led him to the washtub.

He washed his matted locks as clean as could be,
  he cast off his pelts, and the sea bore them off.
His body was soaked till fair,   XI 265
  he made a new [kerchief for] his head,

he wore royal robes, the dress fitting his dignity.
   'Until he goes [home to his city,]
until he reaches the end of his road,
   let [the robes show no mark, but stay fresh and] new!'   XI 270

Gilgamesh and Ur-shanabi crewed the boat,
   they launched the [craft,] and crewed it themselves.
Said his wife to him, to Uta-napishti the Distant:
   'Gilgamesh came here by toil and by travail,

'what have you given for his homeward journey?'   XI 275
   And Gilgamesh, he picked up a punting-pole,
he brought the boat back near to the shore.
   [Said] Uta-napishti to him, to Gilgamesh:

'You came here, O Gilgamesh, by toil and by travail,
   what do I give for your homeward journey?   XI 280
Let me disclose, O Gilgamesh, a matter most secret,
   to you [I will] tell a mystery of [gods.]

'There is a plant that [looks] like a box-thorn,
   it has prickles like a *dogrose*, and will [prick *one who plucks it*.]
But if you can possess this plant,   XI 285
   [*you'll be again as you were in your youth*.]'

Just as soon as Gilgamesh heard what he said,
   he opened a [channel] . . . . . .
Heavy stones he tied [to his feet,]
   and they pulled him down . . . to the Ocean Below.   XI 290

He took the plant, and pulled [it up, *and lifted it*,]
   the heavy stones he cut loose [from his feet,]
and the sea cast him up on its shore.
   Said Gilgamesh to him, to Ur-shanabi the boatman:

'This plant, Ur-shanabi, is the "Plant of Heartbeat",   XI 295
   with it a man can regain his vigour.
To Uruk-the-Sheepfold I will take it,
   to an ancient I will feed some and put the plant to the test!

'Its name shall be "Old Man Grown Young",
    I will eat it myself, and be again as I was in my youth!'   XI 300
At twenty leagues they broke bread,
    at thirty leagues they stopped for the night.

Gilgamesh found a pool whose water was cool,
    down he went into it, to bathe in the water.
Of the plant's fragrance a snake caught scent,   XI 305
    came up [in silence], and bore the plant off.

As it turned away it sloughed its skin.
    Then Gilgamesh sat down and wept,
down his cheeks the tears were coursing.
    . . . [*he spoke*] to Ur-shanabi the boatman: XI 310

'[For whom,] Ur-shanabi, toiled my arms so hard,
    for whom ran dry the blood of my heart?
Not for myself did I find a bounty,
    [for] the "Lion of the Earth" I have done a favour!

'Now far and wide the tide is rising.   XI 315
    Having opened the channel I abandoned the tools:
what thing would I find that served as my landmark?
    Had I only turned back, and left the boat on the shore!'

At twenty leagues they broke bread,
    at thirty leagues they stopped for the night.   XI 320
When they arrived in Uruk-the-Sheepfold,
    said Gilgamesh to him, to Ur-shanabi the boatman:

'O Ur-shanabi, climb Uruk's wall and walk back and forth!
    Survey its foundations, examine the brickwork!
Were its bricks not fired in an oven?   XI 325
    Did the Seven Sages not lay its foundations?

'A square mile is city, a square mile date-grove, a square mile is
        clay-pit, half a square mile the temple of Ishtar:
    three square miles and a half is Uruk's expanse.'

Tablet XII. Appendix

The last Tablet in the 'Series of Gilgamesh', Tablet XII, is not part of the epic at all, but an Akkadian translation of the latter part of the Sumerian poem of Bilgames and the Netherworld. It was appended to the epic presumably because of the relevance of the material: it describes conditions in the Netherworld, where after his death Gilgamesh presided over the shades of the dead. A translation is given in Chapter 5, following that of the original Sumerian poem.

2

Babylonian Texts of the
Early Second Millennium BC

The Pennsylvania tablet: 'Surpassing all other kings' Tablet II

The Pennsylvania tablet, often known as Gilgamesh P, comes from southern Babylonia and probably dates to the late eighteenth century BC. It was bought by the University Museum, Philadelphia, in 1914 and is now CBS 7771. It is Tablet II of an Old Babylonian edition of the epic known in antiquity as 'Surpassing all other kings'. The text it contains runs parallel, though with some differences in language and in the order of the episodes, with Tablets I–II of the standard version of the epic, and much of it has already been used in Chapter 1 to restore Tablet II. Gilgamesh relates his dreams to his mother, the goddess Ninsun, who interprets them for him. Enkidu and the prostitute, who is here known as Shamkatum, make love, and she suggests that he leave the wild and come to Uruk. They arrive at the shepherds' camp, where Enkidu is introduced to bread and beer. He is washed, groomed and dressed, and becomes the shepherds' nightwatchman. Learning from a passer-by how Gilgamesh at weddings has the privilege of *droit de seigneur*, Enkidu leaves for Uruk. There he arrives at the very moment when, as it seems, the young men choose one of their number to challenge the king. Presumably we are to understand that Enkidu then fills this role, for he interrupts the wedding procession and wrestles with Gilgamesh. The tablet ends with his acceptance that Gilgamesh's kingship is legitimate.

Gilgamesh rose to relate the dream,
    saying to his mother:
'O mother, during the course of my night
    I walked hale and hearty among the young men.

'Then the stars of the sky *hid* from me,
   a *piece* of the sky fell down to me.
I picked it up, but it was too heavy for me,
   I pushed at it but I could not dislodge it.

'The land of Uruk was gathered about it,   P 10
   the young men were kissing its feet.
I braced my forehead and they helped me push,
   I picked it up and carried it off to you.'

The mother of Gilgamesh, well versed in everything,   P 15
   said to Gilgamesh:
'For sure, Gilgamesh, someone like yourself
   was born in the wild and the upland has reared him.

'You will see him and you will rejoice,   P 20
   the young men will kiss his feet.
You will embrace him and bring him to me.'
   He lay down, and he had another dream.

He rose and spoke to his mother: P 25
   'O mother, I have had another dream.
. . . in the street of Uruk-the-Town-Square,
   an axe was lying with a crowd gathered around.   P 30

'The axe itself, it was strange of shape;
   I saw it and I grew glad.
Like a wife I loved it, caressed and embraced it,
   I took it up and set it at my side.'*   P 35

The mother of Gilgamesh, well versed in everything,
   [said] to [Gilgamesh:]   P 38

Because of a lacuna, only the end of Ninsun's reply is preserved:

---

*Also, 'I made it into my brother.'

' . . . so that I shall make him your equal.'   P 43
As Gilgamesh related the dream,
   Enkidu was sitting before the harlot.   P 45

While the two of them together were making love,
   he forgot the wild where he was born.
For seven days and seven nights
   Enkidu was erect and coupled with Shamkatum.   P 50

13 *'Enkidu was erect and coupled with Shamkatum'.*

The harlot opened her mouth,
   saying to Enkidu:
'As I look at you, Enkidu, you are like a god,
   why with the beasts do you wander the wild?   P 55

'Come, I will lead you to Uruk-the-Town-Square,
   to the sacred temple, the home of Anu!
Enkidu, arise, let me take you
   to the temple Eanna, the home of Anu,   P 60

'where [men] are engaged in labours of skill,
   you, too, *like a man*, will *find a place for* yourself.
You have been enough in the shepherds' *domain*.'   P 65

Her words he heard, her speech found favour,
   the counsel of a woman struck home in his heart.
She stripped and clad him in part of her garment,   P 70
   the other part she put on herself.

By the hand she took him, like a god she led him,
   to the shepherds' camp, the site of the sheep-pen.
The shepherds gathered about him,   P 75
   like . . . .

'[In build he is the image of Gilgamesh,]   P 80
   [but shorter in stature, and bigger of bone.]
[For sure it's the one who was born in the uplands,]
   the milk of the beasts is what he was suckled on.'   P 85

Bread they put before him,
   he peered at it, gazing and staring.
How to eat bread Enkidu knew not,   P 90
   how to drink ale he had never been shown.

The harlot opened her mouth,
   saying to Enkidu: P 95
'Eat the bread, Enkidu, essential to life,
   drink the ale, the lot of the land!'

Enkidu ate the bread until he was sated,   P 100
   he drank the ale, a full seven goblets.
His mood became free, he started to sing,
   his heart grew merry, his face lit up.   P 105

The barber groomed his body so hairy,
    anointed with oil he turned into a man.
He put on a garment, became like a warrior,   P 110
    he took up his weapon to do battle with lions.

When at night, asleep, the shepherds lay down,
    he struck down wolves, he chased off lions.   P 115
Sleeping lay the senior herdsmen,
    their watchman Enkidu, a [man wide] awake.

A certain fellow *had been invited to a wedding*,   P 120
    in . . . .

A lacuna intervenes, then the narrative continues:

Enkidu was having his pleasure with Shamkatum.   P 135
He lifted his eyes, he caught sight of the man,
    and he said to the harlot:

'Shamkatum, bring the man over: P 140
    why he came here, let me *learn* his reason.'
The harlot hailed the man,
    went up to him, spoke to him:

'Where do you hurry to, fellow?   P 145
    What is your journey so toilsome?'
The fellow opened his mouth,
    saying to Enkidu:

'I was invited to a wedding banquet,
    it is the lot of the people to contract a marriage.   P 150
I shall load the ceremonial table
    with tempting foods for the wedding feast.

'For the king of Uruk-the-Town-Square,
    the *veil* will be parted for the one who picks first; P 155
for Gilgamesh, the king of Uruk-the-Town-Square,
    the *veil* will be parted for the one who picks first.

'He will couple with the wife-to-be,
   he first of all, the bridegroom after.   P 160
By divine consent it is so ordained;
   when his navel-cord was cut, for him she was destined.'

At the fellow's words his face paled in anger.   P 165

The rest of Enkidu's reaction is lost in a lacuna, after which the text resumes:

There goes Enkidu, with Shamkatum following.   P 175

He entered the city of Uruk-the-Town-Square,
   and a crowd gathered around.
He came to a halt in the street of Uruk-the-Town-Square,   P 180
   all gathered about, the people discussed him:

'In build he is the image of Gilgamesh,
   but shorter in stature, and bigger of bone.   P 185
For [sure it's the one who] was born in the uplands,
   animals' milk is what he was suckled on.'

In Uruk they held regular festivals of sacrifice,   P 190
   young men made merry, set up a *champion*:
for the fellow whose features were fair,
   for Gilgamesh, like a god, was set up a rival.   P 195

For the goddess of weddings the bed was laid out,
   Gilgamesh met with the maiden by night.
Forward came (Enkidu), he stood in the street,   P 200
   blocking the path of Gilgamesh.

. . . . . . they *discussed* him.   P 204

    *   *   *

Gilgamesh . . . . . . *the doorway.*
In front of him . . . . . . ,   P 210
   he was growing angry . . . . . .

Enkidu moved towards him,
   as they confronted each other in the Square of the Land.
Enkidu blocked the door with his foot,   P 215
   he did not allow Gilgamesh to enter.

They took hold of each other, backs bent like a bull,
   they smashed the door-jamb, the wall did shake;   P 220
Gilgamesh and Enkidu took hold of each other, backs bent like a
   bull,
   they smashed the door-jamb, the wall did shake.   P 225

Gilgamesh knelt, one foot on the ground,
   his anger subsided, he broke off from the fight.   P 230
After he broke off from the fight,
   said Enkidu to him, to Gilgamesh:

'As one unique your mother bore you,   P 235
   the wild cow of the fold, the goddess Ninsun!
High over warriors you are exalted,
   to be king of the people Enlil made it your destiny!'   P 240

The Yale tablet: 'Surpassing all other kings' Tablet III

The Yale tablet, often known as Gilgamesh Y, is Tablet III of the
same Old Babylonian edition of the epic as the Pennsylvania tablet.
It shares its handwriting and other physical characteristics with the
Pennsylvania tablet and must have come from the same site. The
tablet was purchased by the Yale Babylonian Collection, New Haven,
Connecticut, where it is registered as YBC 2178. The text runs parallel
with Tablets II–III of the standard version of the epic, though with
many differences. Parts of it have been used to restore the text in
Chapter 1. Gilgamesh and Enkidu become close friends, as Ninsun
predicted. For reasons that are not clear because of the broken state
of the tablet, Enkidu is overcome with misery. Gilgamesh cheers him
with a proposal to mount an expedition to the Forest of Cedar. There
they will kill the monstrous Huwawa, as Humbaba is known in this
and other Old Babylonian tablets. Enkidu advises Gilgamesh that

Huwawa was appointed to guard the cedar by the gods. Chiding him
with being afraid to die, Gilgamesh extols the glory of death in battle
and the immortal name that it would bring. They have their weapons
cast at the forge and Gilgamesh convenes the assembly of Uruk. He
announces his proposed expedition, and the elders advise caution.
Gilgamesh laughs off their counsel. After a break in the text someone,
perhaps his mother Ninsun, is wishing him well for the journey.
Gilgamesh prays to the Sun God for protection on the road, and also
to his deified father, Lugalbanda. The heroes shoulder their equipment,
and the elders offer Gilgamesh blessings and advice for the journey.
As the pair depart Enkidu tells Gilgamesh to send the young men
back inside the city. They leave alone.

Beginning broken

'Why do you desire to do this thing?
    ... anything ... do you want so much?   Y 15
Let me ....,
    a feat that never was done in the land.'

They kissed each other and formed a friendship.

After a long lacuna, the text resumes:

[His] eyes [were brimming with] tears,   Y 71
    his mood grew sad, *heavily* he sighed;
Enkidu's [eyes] were brimming with tears,
    his mood [grew sad, *heavily*] he sighed.   Y 75

[Gilgamesh] *bent* his face to him,
    [saying] to Enkidu:
'[Why,] my [friend,] do your eyes [brim with] tears,   Y 80
    your [mood grow sad, with such *heavy*] sighs?'

Enkidu opened [his mouth,]
    saying to Gilgamesh:
'Sobs, my friend, have knotted the sinews in my neck,   Y 85
    my arms go limp, my strength ebbs away.'

Gilgamesh opened his mouth,
   saying to Enkidu: Y 90

    *   *   *

' . . . . . . ferocious Huwawa,   Y 97
   . . . [let us] slay him, [so *his power*] is no more!

'[In the Forest] of Cedar, [where Huwawa] dwells,   Y 100
   [let us] frighten him in his lair!'
Enkidu opened his mouth,
   saying to Gilgamesh: Y 105

'I knew him, my friend, in the uplands,
   when I roamed here and there with the herd.
For sixty leagues the forest is a wilderness,
   who is there would venture inside it?

'Huwawa, his voice is the Deluge,   Y 110
   his speech is fire, and his breath is death!
Why do you desire to do this thing?
   An unwinnable battle is Huwawa's ambush!'   Y 115

Gilgamesh opened his mouth,
   saying to Enkidu:
'I will climb, my friend, [*the forest's*] slopes.'   Y 119

    *   *   *

Enkidu opened his mouth,   Y 127
   saying to Gilgamesh:

'How can we go, my friend, to the Forest of [Cedar?]   Y 130
   The god who guards it is Wer, mighty and unsleeping;
Huwawa [*was appointed by*] Wer,
   Adad ranks first, and Humbaba [is second.]   Y 135

'So to keep safe [the cedars,]
   [*Enlil*] assigned [him] the Seven Terrors.'
Gilgamesh opened his mouth,
   saying to Enkidu:

14 *'His speech is fire and his breath is death!'*

'Who is there, my friend, can climb to the sky?   Y 140
   Only the gods [dwell] forever in sunlight.
As for man, his days are numbered,
   whatever he may do, it is but wind.

'Here are you, afraid of death!
   What has become of your mighty valour?   Y 145
Let me walk in front of you,
   and you can call to me, "Go on without fear!"

'If I should fall, let me make my name:
   "Gilgamesh joined battle with ferocious Huwawa!"   Y 150
You were born and grew up in the wild,
   a lion attacked you, you experienced all.

'Grown men fled away from your presence,
  . . . . . . you [*in the*] evening.   Y 155
[*Why now*] do you speak like a weakling?
  [with your] spineless [words] you make me despondent.

'Let me start out, I will chop down the cedar!
  [A name that] is eternal I will establish for ever!   Y 160
[Come,] my friend, let us hie to the forge,
  let them cast [us hatchets] in our presence!'

They took each other by the hand and hied to the forge,
  where the smiths were sitting in consultation.
Great hatchets they cast,   Y 165
  and axes weighing three talents apiece.

Great daggers they cast:
  two talents apiece were the blades,
one half of a talent the crests of their handles,
  half a talent apiece the daggers' gold mountings.   Y 170
Gilgamesh and Enkidu bore ten talents each.

He bolted the sevenfold gates of Uruk,
  he convened [the assembly,] the crowd gathered round.
. . . in the street of Uruk-the-Town-Square,
  Gilgamesh [*seated himself on*] his throne.   Y 175

[In the street of Uruk]-the-Town-Square,
  [the crowd was] sitting before him.
[*Thus* Gilgamesh] spoke
  [to the elders of Uruk]-the-Town-Square:

'[Hear me, O elders of Uruk-the-Town]-Square!   Y 180
  [*I would tread the path to* ferocious Huwawa,]
I would see the god, of whom men talk,
  whose name the lands do constantly repeat.

'I will conquer him in the Forest of Cedar:
   let the land learn Uruk's offshoot is mighty!   Y 185
Let me start out, I will cut down the cedar,
   I will establish for ever a name eternal!'

The elders of Uruk-the-Town-Square
   gave answer to Gilgamesh: Y 190
'You are young, Gilgamesh, borne along by emotion,
   all that you do, you don't understand.

'We hear Huwawa is strange of aspect:
   who is there can counter his weapons?
For sixty [leagues] the forest is wilderness;   Y 195
   who is there would venture inside it?

'Humbaba, his voice is the Deluge,
   his speech is fire, and his breath is death!
Why do you desire to do this thing?
   An unwinnable battle is Huwawa's ambush!'   Y 200

Gilgamesh heard the speech of his advisers,
   he looked with a laugh at his friend:
'Now, my friend, how [*frightened I am!*]
   In fear of him shall I [*change my mind?*]'   Y 204

            *   *   *

The text resumes with the counsellors' blessing:

   'May your god [plant] your feet [on the straightest path!]   Y 213

'May he let your [*steps*] complete the journey,
   safely back to the quay of Uruk-[the-Town-Square!]'   Y 215
Gilgamesh knelt down [in the presence of] the Sun God,
   the words which he spoke . . . . . . :

'I am going, O Shamash, to the [home of Huwawa,]
   let me leave there in safety, [please keep] me alive!
Bring me back to the quay of [Uruk-the-Town-Square!]   Y 220
   Place your protection [over me!]'

Gilgamesh summoned the . . . . . .
   his instructions . . . .   Y 223

After a further lacuna, the text continues with Gilgamesh's prayer to his god,
Lugalbanda:

   [Down his] cheeks the tears were coursing:
'[I would go,] my god, on a journey I never have taken,   Y 230
   its . . . , my god, I do not know.

'[Let me come] home in safety,
   with happy heart [let me look on] your face!
[I will build] you a house to delight you,
   [I will set] you on many a throne!'   Y 235

. . . . his equipment,
   . . . . . . the great daggers.
. . . . . . bow and quiver,
   [these were placed] in their hands.

[Gilgamesh] picked up the hatchets,   Y 240
   [accepting] his quiver [with] the bow of Anshan.
In his belt [he placed] his dagger,
   [*thus equipped*] to begin the journey.

[*The young men*] came up to Gilgamesh: Y 245
   ' . . . you sent back to the city.'
The elders blessed Gilgamesh, offering advice for the road:
   '[Do not] rely, Gilgamesh, on your strength alone!
Let your eyes be sharp, guard yourself well!   Y 250

'[Let] Enkidu walk before you,
  he is versed in the path, well travelled on the road.
[He knows] the ways into the forest,
  and all the tricks of Huwawa.

' "The one who goes in front keeps safe his comrade,   Y 255
  the one whose eyes are sharp will [protect] his person!"
May Shamash permit you to win your victory,
  may your eyes be witness to the deeds you have talked of!

'May he open for you the paths that are shut,
  may he ready the road for your footsteps!   Y 260
For your feet may he ready the mountain,
  may the night bring you something to cheer you!

'May Lugalbanda assist in your victory;
  win your victory like a little child!   Y 265
In Huwawa's river, that which you strive for,
  wash your feet!

'When you camp for the night, dig a well;
  in your bottle shall be fresh water always!
You must offer chilled water to Shamash,   Y 270
  and remember your [god,] Lugalbanda.'

Enkidu opened his mouth,
  saying to Gilgamesh:
'Where you've *set your mind* begin the journey,
  let your heart have no fear, keep your eyes on me!

'[In the] forest I knew his lair,   Y 275
  [and the ways, too,] that Huwawa wanders.
Speak [*to the crowd*] and send them back home!'
  . . . . '

' . . . . . . [they should not] go with me,
        . . . . to you.'   Y 280
. . . The crowd with happy heart,
      . . . they [heard] what he had said.

The young men *made a fervent prayer* . . . :
      'Go, Gilgamesh, let . . . . . .
May your god go [before you!]   Y 285
      May [Shamash] permit you to win [your victory!']

Gilgamesh and Enkidu *went forth* . . .

A few more fragmentary lines follow. Shortly afterwards the tablet would have
concluded.

Another fragment in Philadelphia

A second piece of Old Babylonian Gilgamesh epic is kept at the
University Museum in Philadelphia (UM 29-13-570). It was most
likely found at Nippur, now Nuffar in central Babylonia, in the 1890s.
It probably dates to the early eighteenth century BC. The obverse of
the fragment treats the misery of Enkidu and the solicitude that this
awakes in Gilgamesh, providing a close parallel to the lines 79–90 of
the Yale tablet. What remains of the reverse seems to deal with a
conversation of Enkidu and Gilgamesh, probably from the episode of
the elders' warning and Gilgamesh's subsequent speech to Enkidu (cf.
Y 200ff.).

Beginning broken

obverse

'[Why, my friend, do your] eyes [brim with tears,]
      [your mood] grow sad? Let your . . . . . . !'
Said Enkidu to [him,] to [Gilgamesh:]   UM 5'
'Sobs, my [friend, *racked my being*,]
      in the heart . . . , my strength [ebbed away.]
My eyes are brimming [with tears,]

my mood grows sad . . . Let not my . . . . . . !'   UM 10'
Gilgamesh [opened his mouth,]
  [saying to Enkidu: . . .]

  *   *   *

reverse

'What *do you* . . . . . . ?
  cause to . . . . . .
In battle . . . the lair [*of Huwawa.*]'
Gilgamesh [opened his mouth,]
  saying [to Enkidu: . . .

Remainder lost

The Nippur school tablet

The Old Babylonian Nippur tablet was excavated on Tablet Hill at
Nippur in the season 1951–2, more exactly in the back room of a
private house which also served as a scribal school. It dates to the
middle of the eighteenth century BC, specifically to the years immedi-
ately before the economic crisis that devastated southern Babylonia
towards the end of that century and led to the closure of the school
and the abandonment of the house. The tablet is now stored in the
Iraq Museum, Baghdad (IM 58451). It was an apprentice's exercise,
and holds text of the episode of Gilgamesh's dreams on his approach
to the Forest of Cedar. Split into two separate passages, the piece has
already been used in Chapter 1 to restore the standard version of the
epic at Tablet IV 109, where Enkidu interprets Gilgamesh's third
dream, and 142, where the fourth dream is related and explained.

'We draw, my friend, ever nearer the forest,
  the dreams are close, the battle soon.
You will see the radiant auras of the god,
  of Huwawa, whom in your thoughts you fear so much.

'Locking horns like a bull you will batter him,   OB Ni 5
   and force his head down with your strength.
The old man you saw is your powerful god,
   the one who begot you, divine Lugalbanda.'

'My friend, I have had the fourth,
   it surpasses my other three dreams!   OB Ni 10
I saw a Thunderbird in the sky,
   up it rose like a cloud, soaring above us.

15 *'I saw a Thunderbird in the sky'*.

'It was a . . . , its visage distorted,
   its mouth was fire, its breath was death.
[There was also a] man, he was strange of form,   OB Ni 15
   he . . . and stood there in my dream.

'[He *bound*] its wings and took hold of my arm,
   . . . . . . he cast it down [before] me,
   . . . . upon it.'   OB Ni 19

     *   *   *

'[You saw a Thunderbird in the sky,]   OB Ni 20'
  [up] it [rose like a] cloud, soaring above us.

'It was a . . . , its visage distorted,
  its mouth was fire, its breath was death.
You will fear its awesome splendour,
  I shall . . . its foot and let you arise!   OB Ni 25'

'The man you saw was mighty Shamash.'

The Tell Harmal tablets

Two tablets of Old Babylonian Gilgamesh have been excavated in a
private house at Tell Harmal, the site of ancient Shaduppûm on the
eastern outskirts of Baghdad, and are now in the Iraq Museum. They
were both recovered during the third season of excavations, in August
1947, and date from the early eighteenth century BC. They appear to
be scribal exercises, like the Nippur tablet. The more legible of the
two (tablet Ha$_1$ = IM 52615) holds the text of one of Gilgamesh's
dreams on the way to the Forest of Cedar, and Enkidu's explanation
of it. Most of it has already been used in Chapter 1 to fill the lacuna
in the standard version of the epic at Tablet IV 183. The second tablet
(Ha$_2$ = IM 52760) relates a conversation between Gilgamesh and
Enkidu on their arrival at the forest, but for the most part it defies a
connected translation. Some lines from it have been used in Chapter
1 at Tablet V 77.

Tell Harmal, tablet Ha$_1$

'Go up on to the mountain crag, and look at . . .
  I have been robbed of the sleep of the gods!
My friend, I had a dream:
  how *ominous* it was, how *desolate*, how unclear!

'I had taken me hold of a bull from the wild: Ha$_1$ 5
  as it clove the ground with its bellows,
the clouds of dust it raised thrust deep in the sky,
  and I, in front of it, *leaned myself forward*.

'Taking hold of . . . . . . enclosed my arms.
    . . . he extricated [me] . . . *by force* . . .
My cheek . . . , my . . . ,
    [he gave] me water [to drink] from his waterskin.'

'The [god], my friend, we are going against,   Ha₁ 10
    he's not the wild bull, he's different altogether.
The *wild bull* you saw was shining Shamash,
    he will grasp our hands in time of peril.

'The one who gave you water to drink from his skin
    was your god who respects you, divine Lugalbanda.   Ha₁ 15
We shall join forces and do something unique,
    a feat that never has been in the land!'

The Ishchali tablet

The Ishchali tablet is often known as the Bauer tablet after its first editor, or as the Chicago tablet after its present location in the tablet collections of the Oriental Institute, University of Chicago (A 22007). It is a school exercise tablet excavated in 1935 at Ishchali, ancient Nerebtum, a town on the Diyala river just east of Baghdad, and dates to the early eighteenth century BC. The text that it contains runs roughly parallel with the end of Tablet V of the standard version of the epic, though with considerable differences. Some of it has already been used in Chapter 1 to fill out the story at Tablet V 269. Gilgamesh has just overcome the forest's guardian, Huwawa. Enkidu urges him not to spare their foe. Gilgamesh wants instead to hunt down Huwawa's 'auras', which are the radiant numinous powers that Huwawa wears as protection. Enkidu suggests that they can easily do that later. The heroes kill Huwawa, apparently also his servant and probably then the seven auras. Then they desecrate the sacred groves and fell the cedar.

Beginning broken

Said Enkidu to him, to Gilgamesh: Ish 6′
  'Smite Huwawa the [ogre, whom] your gods [abhor!]
. . . .
  [Why, my friend,] do you show him mercy?'

[Said] Gilgamesh to him, to Enkidu: Ish 10′
  'Now, my friend, we must impose our victory.
The auras slip away in the thicket,
  the auras slip away, their radiance grows dim.'

Said Enkidu to him, to Gilgamesh:
  'My friend, catch a bird and where go its chicks?   Ish 15′
Let us look for the auras later,
  as the chicks run here and there in the thicket!

'Smite him again, slay his servant alongside him!'
  Gilgamesh heard the word of his companion.
He took up his axe in his hand,   Ish 20′
  he drew forth the dirk from his belt.

Gilgamesh smote him in the neck,
  his friend Enkidu gave encouragement.
He . . . . he fell,
  the ravines did run with his blood.   Ish 25′

Huwawa the guardian he smote to the ground,
  for two leagues afar . . .
With him he slew . . . . . . ,
  the woods he . . . . . .

He slew the ogre, the forest's guardian,   Ish 30′
  at whose yell were sundered the peaks of Sirion and Lebanon,
. . . the mountains did quake,
  . . . all the hillsides did tremble.

16 *'Huwawa the guardian he smote to the ground'*.

He slew the ogre, the cedar's guardian,
   the broken . . . . . .   Ish 35′
As soon as he had slain all seven [of the auras],
   the war-net of *two talents' weight*, the dirk of eight,

a load of ten talents he took up,
   he went down to trample the forest.
He discovered the secret abode of the gods,
   Gilgamesh felling the trees, Enkidu choosing the *timber*.

Said Enkidu to him, to Gilgamesh,   Ish 40′
   '. . . , O Gilgamesh, smite the cedar!'

After a few more badly damaged lines the tablet breaks off.

A tablet in Baghdad, of unknown provenance

A fourth Old Babylonian tablet of Gilgamesh is housed in the Iraq
Museum (IM 21180x). It was acquired by donation or confiscation, and
nothing is known of its provenance except that it is from somewhere in
Iraq. The piece is badly damaged. What text is legible deals with the
episode of the felling of the cedar, overlapping slightly with the Ishchali
tablet, and has been given in Chapter 1 at Tablet V 296 (IM).

A tablet reportedly from Sippar

This tablet comprises two joining fragments, one of which is now
in the British Museum in London (BM 96974), the other in the
Vorderasiatisches Museum in Berlin (VAT 4105). The fragments were
purchased in Baghdad in 1902, and were reported to come from the
city of Sippar, on the Euphrates upstream of Babylon. The date of
the tablet is eighteenth or seventeenth century BC. The piece is not a
school exercise but a library tablet with two columns of text on each
side, and is thus most probably part of an edition of the whole epic
rather than a text in isolation. However, the recension to which
the Sippar fragment bears witness is probably not the same as that
represented by the Pennsylvania and Yale tablets. The text it holds
runs parallel to parts of Tablets IX–X of the standard version of the
epic, again with considerable differences. Some lines have been used
in Chapter 1 to supplement the standard version of the epic (col. i is
inserted at Tablet IX 18, col. iv 2–11 at Tablet X 106).

Distraught at the death of Enkidu, Gilgamesh is wandering the wild
in search of the secret of eternal life. The Sun God speaks to him from
the sky and advises him of the futility of his quest. Gilgamesh rejects
a life of easeful rest. In the knowledge that death all too soon brings
permanent repose he must extend his life if he can. After a break,
Gilgamesh is explaining to Shiduri how his friend died and how thus
he learnt the fear of death. The tavern-keeper explains that only the
gods can live for ever. The task of a man is to enjoy life while he has
it and to nurture the family that will bring him descendants. Gilgamesh
is not persuaded and insists on pursuing his quest. As the text resumes
following a second break, Gilgamesh is smashing the stone crew of

the ferryman Sursunabu (this is the name given here to the later
Ur-shanabi). Sursunabu introduces himself, and Gilgamesh relates his
journey and asks help in finding the immortal Uta-napishti, here called
Uta-naishtim. Sursunabu tells him that the Stone Ones were his means
of crossing the ocean, but asks him to prepare punting-poles for the
voyage.

Beginning lost

[He] clad himself in their skins, he ate their flesh.   Si i 2′
Gilgamesh [*dug*] wells that never existed before,
    [*he*] *drank* the water, as he chased the winds.

Shamash grew worried, and *bending down*,   Si i 5′
    he spoke to Gilgamesh:
'O Gilgamesh, where are you wandering?
    The life that you seek you never will find.'

Said Gilgamesh to him, to the hero Shamash:
    'After *roaming*, wandering all through the wild,   Si i 10′
when I enter the Netherworld will rest be scarce?
    I shall lie there sleeping all down the years!

'Let my eyes see the sun and be sated with light.
The darkness is *hidden*, how much light is there left?
    When may the dead see the rays of the sun?'   Si i 15′

After a long lacuna, the text resumes with Gilgamesh addressing the tavern-
keeper:

'[My friend, whom I loved so deeply,]
    who with me went through every danger,   Si ii 1′
Enkidu, whom I loved so deeply,
    who with me went through every danger:

'he went to the doom of mortal men.
    Weeping over him day and night,   Si ii 5′
I did not surrender his body for burial –
    "Maybe my friend will rise at my cry!" –

'for seven days and seven nights,
   until a maggot dropped from his nostril.
After he was gone I did not find life,   Si ii 10'
   wandering like a trapper in the midst of the wild.

'O tavern-keeper, I have looked on your face,
   but I would not meet death, that I fear so much.'
Said the tavern-keeper to him, to Gilgamesh:
   'O Gilgamesh, where are you wandering?   Si iii 1

'The life that you seek you never will find:
   when the gods created mankind,
death they dispensed to mankind,
   life they kept for themselves.   Si iii 5

'But you, Gilgamesh, let your belly be full,
   enjoy yourself always by day and by night!
Make merry each day,
   dance and play day and night!

'Let your clothes be clean,   Si iii 10
   let your head be washed, may you bathe in water!
Gaze on the child who holds your hand,
   let your wife enjoy your repeated embrace!

'For such is the destiny [*of mortal men,*]
   that the one who lives . . . . '   Si iii 15
[Said] Gilgamesh to her, [to the ale-wife:]

'O tavern-keeper, why do you talk [*this way?*]
   My heart is [*still very*] sick for my friend.
O tavern-keeper, why do you talk [*this way?*]
   My heart is [*still very*] sick for Enkidu.   Si iii 20

'But you dwell, O tavern-keeper, on the shore [*of the ocean,*]
   you are familiar with all [*the ways across it.*]
Show me the way, [*O show me!*]
   If it may be done [I will cross] the ocean!'

Said the tavern-keeper to him, [to Gilgamesh:]   Si iii 25
   'O Gilgamesh, never [*before*] was there one like you!
Who [*but Shamash*] can travel [*that journey?*]

17 '*Who but Shamash can travel that journey?*'

After a further lacuna, the narrative has moved on to Gilgamesh's encounter
with the Stone Ones and the ferryman:

. . . And [the Stone Ones] he smashed in his fury.   Si iv 1
[Gilgamesh] came back to stand over him,
   as Sursunabu looked him in the eye.

Said Sursunabu to him, to Gilgamesh:
   'Tell me, what is your name?   Si iv 5
I am Sursunabu, of Uta-naishtim the Distant.'
   Said Gilgamesh to him, to Sursunabu:

'Gilgamesh is my name,
   who came from Uruk-Eanna,
who wound a way around the mountains,   Si iv 10
   the hidden road where rises the sun.

'O Sursunabu, now I have met you,
   show me Uta-naishtim the Distant!'
Said Sursunabu to him, to Gilgamesh:

'   . . . .   Si iv 15
   [*to reach* Uta-naishtim the] Distant,
. . . you must crew the boat,
   . . . and I will take you to him.'

[They sat] down, talking it over between them,
   and again he said a word to him,   Si iv 20
said Sursunabu to him, to Gilgamesh:

'The Stone Ones, O Gilgamesh, enabled my crossing,
   for I must not touch the Waters of Death.
In your fury you have smashed them.
   The Stone Ones were with me to take me across.   Si iv 25

'Take up, O Gilgamesh, the axe in your hand,
   cut me three hundred punting-poles, each sixty cubits.
. . . . . . equip them with bosses . . .

Remainder lost

3

Babylonian Texts of
the Late Second Millennium BC,
from Sites in Babylonia

The Nippur exercise tablet

This piece was excavated in 1949 on Tablet Hill at Nippur and is now part of the collections of the Oriental Institute, University of Chicago (A 29934). It is a school exercise tablet written by an apprentice scribe as part of his training, probably at some time between the early fourteenth and the late thirteenth centuries BC, when the city was enjoying a period of prosperity and revival. The very short extract is from the episode of the creation of Enkidu, and some of it has been inserted in Chapter 1 at Tablet I 93–4 of the standard version.

'[Let] them summon [Aruru,] the great one,
  [she it was created them,] mankind so numerous.

'[Let her create] his [*equal*,] one mighty in strength,
  [and let] him vie [with him], so Uruk may be rested!'
They [summoned Aruru,] the sister,   MB Ni 5
  [the god *Anu*] . . . said to her:

'[You it was], Aruru, created man,
  [create now his *equal*, one mighty in strength,]
[let him vie with him, so Uruk may be rested!]'

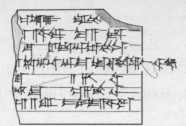

18 'Let them summon Aruru, the great one!'

The Ur tablet

This tablet was found in the course of Sir Leonard Woolley's excavations at the site of Ur of the Chaldees, in southern Babylonia just west of modern Nasiriyah, which ran from 1922 to 1934. It is now in the British Museum, where it is registered as UET 6 394. The date of the tablet is probably the twelfth century BC. The text it holds appears to be an extract from an edition of the epic very similar to the standard version. The episode is that of Enkidu on his death-bed, in which he curses the trapper and the prostitute, blesses the prostitute, and begins to relate his dream of the Netherworld. The text thus runs parallel with Tablet VII 90–171, which it helps to restore.

At the very first glimmer of brightening dawn,
    Enkidu raised his head, weeping to Shamash.
Under the rays of the sun his tears were flowing:
    'I appeal to you, Shamash, on account of the hunter, the
        trapper-man.

'*As for* the "shackler", who let me be not as great as my friend, Ur 5
    may the hunter be not as great as his friend!
May his profit be cut! Diminish his income!
    May his share be cut in your presence!'

After he had cursed the hunter to his heart's content,
    he decided to curse the harlot also.   Ur 10
'Come, Shamhat, I will fix your destiny,
    I will curse you with a mighty curse,
my curses shall afflict you now and forthwith!

'A household to delight in you shall not acquire!
    In the young women's *chamber* you shall not sit!   Ur 15
Your finest garment the ground shall defile!
    Your festive gown the drunkard shall stain in the dirt!

'A house with utensils and pots you shall never acquire,
    [the . . .] . . . of the [potter!]
. . . Shamhat, your . . . shall not acquire a pure . . . !   Ur 20
    No table [for a banquet], the people's abundance and pride, shall
        be laid *in your house*!

'The *bench* of a . . . shall be the bed you delight in!
    The crossroads of the potter shall be where you sit!
The field of ruins shall be where you bed down!
    The shadow of the city wall shall be where you stand!   Ur 25

'Briar and thorn shall skin your feet!
    Drunk and sober shall strike your cheek!
[*The rabble*] of the street shall throng to your brothel!
    [*In your tavern*] brawls shall break out!

'. . . *shall* be plaintiff, and claim against [you!]   Ur 30
    [*The roof of your house* no] builder [shall plaster!]
[*In your chamber* shall] lie [*wild*] *dogs*!
    [*At your table* no banquet shall ever] take place!   Ur 33

    * * *

'[Because] you made me weak, who was undefiled!
    [Yes,] in the wild you weakened me, who was undefiled!'   Ur 40
[Shamash heard] what he had spoken,
    [straight away] from the sky there cried out [a voice.]   Ur 42

When the text resumes after a short lacuna, Enkidu is speaking:

'Come, Shamhat, [I will fix] your [destiny,]   Ur 48
   my mouth that cursed you shall bless you as well:

'Governors shall love you and noblemen too!   Ur 50
  At one league off men shall slap their thighs,
at two leagues off they shall shake out their hair!

19 *'Governors shall love you and noblemen too!'*

'No soldier shall be slow to drop his belt for you,
  he shall give you nail and necklace!
With ear-rings of . . . he shall deck your ears!   Ur 55

'Ishtar, the ablest of gods, shall gain you entrance
  to the man whose home is established and wealth [heaped] high!
For you his wife shall be deserted, though mother of seven!'

Gilgamesh was sitting before him.
  As he pondered what was on his mind,   Ur 60
Enkidu spoke to him:

'There was something, my friend, in my dream of last night:
the heavens thundered, the earth gave echo,
   and there was I, standing between them.

'A man there was, grim his expression,   Ur 65
   just like a roaring Thunderbird were his features.
[His] hands were a lion's paws,
   [his] claws an eagle's talons.

'He seized me by the hair, he *overpowered* me.'

4

Babylonian Texts of the Late Second Millennium BC, from outside Babylonia

The fragments from Hattusa

There have been three different discoveries of pieces of the Babylonian Gilgamesh at the Hittite capital Hattusa, now Boğazköy (or Boğazkale) in central Anatolia. The first, in 1906–7, was of a tablet of thirteenth-century date which is now in the Vorderasiatisches Museum in Berlin (VAT 12890, here Bo₂). The obverse of this tablet relates the second dream of Gilgamesh on the journey to the Forest of Cedar, and part of the text of this passage has already been interpolated into the standard version of the epic at Tablet IV 55. It is given again below. The reverse holds a badly corrupted version of the episode of Ishtar and the Bull of Heaven, which is not given here.

The second discovery, in 1934, was of a tiny fragment from the dreams of Gilgamesh, now in the Museum of Anatolian Civilizations at Ankara (Bo 284/d). It is too small to warrant translation. Then in 1983 there came to light several fragments of a library tablet that contained a version of the text similar to the Old Babylonian edition represented by the Pennsylvania and Yale tablets (Bo 83/614 etc., here Bo₁). The text of two of these pieces, which date to about 1400 BC, is given here. Fragment (a) runs parallel with lines 51–102 of the Pennsylvania tablet, Fragment (d) with lines 183–95 of the Yale tablet.

Pieces found in 1983, 1: Bo₁ fragment (a)

Enkidu has been seduced by the prostitute, who now urges him to leave the wild and take his place among men. She dresses him in part of her garment. They enter the shepherds' camp, where the shepherds admire him. Enkidu learns to eat and drink like a man.

[The harlot opened her mouth,]
  [saying to] Enkidu:

'You are handsome, [Enkidu, *you are like a god,*]
  [why do you wander] with the beasts of the wild?
. . . . . . you are like a god,
  [who] among men [*is as splendid as you?*]'

[The harlot opened her mouth,]
  [saying] to Enkidu: Bo$_1$ a 5
'Come, Enkidu, [let me lead you]
  [to the shepherds' camp,] the site of the sheep-pen.'

One garment she stripped and he dressed himself,
  [the other garment she put on herself.]
She [took him by the hand] and like a god [*walked*] before him,
  [to the shepherds' camp, the site] of the sheep-pen.

[The shepherds gathered about him,]
  [the] crowd [*was talking*] among themselves:
'[In build he is the image of Gilgamesh,]
  but shorter in stature and [bigger] of bone.   Bo$_1$ a 10

'[For sure it's he who was born] in the uplands,
  the milk of the beasts [is what he was suckled on.]'
[They put bread before him,]
  [he] looked at the bread, he was perturbed.

[They put ale before him,]
  [he looked at the ale,] he was perturbed.
[The harlot opened her mouth,]
  [saying to Enkidu:]

'Eat the bread, Enkidu, [fit for a god,]
  [drink the ale,] fit for a king!'   Bo$_1$ a 15
[Enkidu ate the bread until he was sated,]
  [he] drank [the] ale, seven [goblets full.]

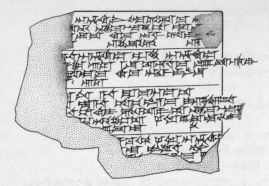

20 *'Eat the bread, Enkidu, fit for a god!'*

Pieces found in 1983, 2: Bo₁ fragment (d)

Gilgamesh announces his expedition to the elders of Uruk, who counsel
him of the danger he courts.

'[I would see the god, of whom men talk,]
  [whose name] the earth [does constantly] repeat.

'[I will conquer him in the Forest of Cedar,]
  [I] will have the [land] learn [Uruk's offshoot is mighty.]
[Let me start out, I will chop down the cedar!]
  [A name] of eternity I [will establish forever!]'

[The elders of Uruk *gave answer to Gilgamesh*:]
  'Why do you desire [to do this thing?]   Bo₁ d 5
[An unwinnable battle] is Huwawa's ambush,
  [*who is there can oppose his weapons?*]
[For *sixty*] leagues [the forest is] [wilderness.]'

Tablet found in 1906−7: Bo₂

On the way to the Forest of Cedar Gilgamesh has his second dream.
Enkidu interprets it for him and reassures him of its good portent.

Beginning missing

> They took each other by the hand and travelled on.   Bo$_2$ i 5′
> [They made] camp for the night . . .
>   Sleep, which spills forth at night, overcame [Gilgamesh.]
> In the middle of the night [his] sleep abandoned him.
>   [He rose and] related the dream to Enkidu:
> '[My] friend, [I have had a dream!]
>   If you did not rouse me why [am I awake?]
> Enkidu, my friend, I have had a dream!   Bo$_2$ i 10′
>   [If] you did [not] rouse me why [am I awake?]
> My second dream sur[passes] the first:
>   in my dream, my friend, a mountain . . .
> It threw me down, it held me by my feet . . .
>   The brightness grew more intense. A man [*appeared*,]   Bo$_2$ i 15′
> the comeliest in the land, his beauty . . .
>   [From] beneath the mountain he pulled me out and . . .
> He gave me water to drink and my heart grew [calm.]
>   [On] the ground he set [my] feet.'
> Enkidu [spoke] to him,   Bo$_2$ i 20′
>   [saying] to Gilgamesh:
> 'My friend, we shall . . . he is different altogether.
>   Huwawa . . . is not the mountain,
> he is different altogether . . .
>   Come, *cast aside* [your] fear . . . '

The fragments from Emar

Fragments of two tablets of Gilgamesh were found in 1974 at Tell
Meskene on the middle Euphrates in Syria, the ancient city of Emar,
and are now in the museum at Aleppo (Msk 74104z, etc.). They come
from a scriptorium that flourished in the thirteenth and early twelfth

centuries BC. The piece here translated as Fragment 1 (Emar₁) is from
a small tablet carrying material parallel with Tablet V of the standard
version of the epic. The other pieces are from a tablet – here Tablet
2 (Emar₂) – which relates the story of Ishtar and the Bull of Heaven,
and thus runs parallel with Tablet VI of the standard version.

Fragment 1

As the heroes approach the Forest of Cedar Gilgamesh emboldens
Enkidu. To fail would shame them in front of the people of Uruk,
and two together can conquer all.

Gilgamesh took [*his hand*]
[*and*] opened his mouth to speak, [saying:]
' . . . what, my friend,
[how] shall we answer the thronging [people?]
[*Shamash*] indeed may be lord of the heavens,   5'
. . . *shod twofold,*
. . . even a glacis-slope, two [. . .]'
Enkidu [opened] his mouth
[to speak, saying:] . . .

Tablet 2

The goddess Ishtar has proposed to Gilgamesh, and describes the life
of power and plenty that she has in store for him. Gilgamesh scorns
her, and relates the fates suffered by her former lovers. Infuriated by
his insults Ishtar asks her father for the Bull of Heaven. He gives it
to her, and she takes it down to Uruk.

'[As you enter our house]
   [doorway and footstool shall] kiss [your] hands!
[Kings shall kneel before you,] *lords will come* [*up to you,*]
   [produce of mountain and lowland they shall] bring you as
      tribute!
[Your nanny-goats] shall bear [triplets, your ewes shall bear twins,]
   [no] ox shall [match yours at the yoke!]'   a 5'

[Gilgamesh opened his mouth] to speak,
   [saying to the lady] Ishtar:
'And if indeed [I take] you [in marriage,]
. . . body [and clothing,]
   . . . . . . sustenance and *food*,
. . . [rings] to decorate [your] hands?'   a 10'

      *   *   *

'[You, *a frost* that congeals no] ice,
   [a louvre-door] that stays not breeze [nor draught,]
[an elephant that] . . . its hoods,   b 5'
   bitumen [that *stains the hands*] of its bearer,
a waterskin [that] cuts [*the hands of its bearer*,]
[a battering]-ram that destroys a wall of stone,
   [a shoe that bites the foot when] walking the street!
[What bridegroom of yours] did ever grow old?'

      *   *   *

'[Dumuzi, the lover of your] youth,
   [year upon year, to lamenting] you doomed him.
[You] loved the [speckled] *allallu*-bird,
   very soon [*you were sated with*] his [*delights*!]
[You] struck him down and broke [his wing:]   c i 5'
   now he stands in [the woods] crying "My wing!"
You loved the . . . Sutean,
   your house . . . your . . . you . . .
in a tent you *made him spend every night*,
   [in] battle you did not . . . . . .   c i 10'
You loved, [when] you dwelt [in the] fold,
   [the shepherd, the herdsman, who] always killed a sheep for you,
[who every day gave] you piles of loaves baked in embers,
   [you struck him and] turned [him into a] wolf.'

      *   *   *

[Anu opened his mouth] to [speak,]
   [saying to the] Lady Ishtar:
'*Ah*, [but did you not provoke King] Gilgamesh,
   so he [told slanders] about you and insults too?'
[Ishtar] opened her mouth to speak,   d 5'

[saying to] her father, Anu:
'Father, [give me, please, the Bull of Heaven,]
  [so I] may slay [Gilgamesh.]'

*   *   *

Anu [heard] what she had to say,
  he placed in her [hands the nose-rope of the Bull of Heaven.]
. . . .
  in Uruk it did not . . . . . .
and a reed. It went [down to the river . . .]
  [the river] dropped [a full seven cubits.]   c ii 10'

The Megiddo tablet

The Megiddo tablet is a fragment found by chance in the 1950s at the
site of the ancient Palestinian town of Megiddo (Tell al-Mutasallim),
near the dump of the pre-war excavations. It is now in the Israel
Museum in Jerusalem (accession number 55-2). The piece dates to
about the fourteenth century BC and preserves two passages of text
similar to the latter part of Tablet VII of the standard version of the
epic. The obverse of the tablet deals with the doomed Enkidu's
second dream, in which he is taken captive by Death and led to the
Netherworld. The reverse describes his final decline and death, and
the grief of Gilgamesh.

Beginning missing

obverse

Enkidu [*lifted his head* . . . . . .]
[he was] speaking to [*Gilgamesh* . . . . . .]
'[I] cut down . . . . . .
you. When [we . . . . . . *to the Cedar Forest, we went up*]   5'
its mountains, and we [*destroyed Humbaba, who in*]
the Cedar Forest dwelt, [*we seized the Bull of Heaven and*]
[we] slew it. At the *shout* of . . . . . .
. . . this . . . . ' '[*The dream*]
was fine and *favourable* . . . . . .   10'

[it was] precious, it was fine and it was . . . . . .
. . . it was difficult.' 'In [my] dream [there was a man,]
short of stature, large of . . . [Like a roaring Thunderbird]
was the set of his face. [His hands were] a lion's [paws,]
[his claws] an eagle's talons . . . [*Grim was*]   15'
his face, all . . . .
[*of an*] *eagle*, [his] hand . . . . . .

    *   *   *

reverse

[He seized me by] my hair, [*he overpowered me* . . .]
to my friend . . . .
Take hold, Gilgamesh, ... [*My friend*]
had no [*fear*], he did not *desert me* . . .
You enabled me to roam . . .   5'
May [they offer] pure water [*to commemorate*] my name . . .
My friend, who rescued me . . . ' [Enkidu lay sick for one day and]
a second day. On his bed . . . . . . [a third]
and a fourth day on his bed. On him . . . . . .
the sickness worsened, his flesh . . . . . .   10'
Enkidu was lying on his bed . . . . . .
He called for Gilgamesh . . . . . .
with his cry he roused . . . [*Gilgamesh sobbed*]
like a dove. His . . . was *darkened* . . .
. . . in the night . . . .   15'
the foremost of *men* . . . . . . [*Gilgamesh sobbed*]
for his friend . . . .
'I will mourn . . . .
at his side I myself . . . .'

Remainder lost

The Ugarit tablet

A complete tablet of a Gilgamesh text, reportedly very fine, was
excavated in 1994 at Ras Shamra on the Syrian coast, the site of
ancient Ugarit, in a building identified as the House of Urtenu. It dates

to the twelfth century at latest and is likely to derive from the hand
of a student scribe or his teacher. The tablet is yet to be published
and no details of it are available beyond the fact that the text it holds
is an original composition utilizing selected episodes from the story
of Gilgamesh. That being so, it would appear not to be a primary
source for the Babylonian epic, but instead a derivative text of local,
Syrian origin.

5

The Sumerian Poems
of Gilgamesh

In the earliest texts from Mesopotamia Gilgamesh's name appears in a slightly different form, as Bilgames. The five Sumerian poems about Bilgames that were copied out, with varying degrees of popularity, by would-be scribes in eighteenth-century Babylonian schools are now much better known than formerly and of two in particular it is possible to give much fuller translations than ever before. They are collected here as individual compositions that can be enjoyed for their own sake, but also to facilitate comparison with the standard Babylonian epic and with the other material written in Akkadian that has been presented in the preceding chapters.

Like the Babylonian epic, the Sumerian poems of Gilgamesh are still in the process of reconstruction from hundreds of fragments of clay tablets stored in museums in many different countries. The more text that is recovered, the more one can observe the stark differences between the Sumerian poems and the Babylonian epic, and the more also one can appreciate how skilfully the Old Babylonian poet of the latter worked into a seamless whole the traditional themes and stories that were his raw material. This is not to say that the poet of the Babylonian epic must have had the Sumerian poems before him, but he knew them, or something very similar, at least in outline. We cannot yet determine whether this knowledge derived from his own experience of the written tradition in a scribal school, or from a knowledge of whatever Sumerian oral tradition (if any) was still current in his lifetime, or from a similar oral tradition in Akkadian. The obvious borrowings are the adaptation of the Sumerian story of Bilgames and Huwawa to furnish the much more elaborate narrative of the Expedition to the Forest of Cedar in Tablets III–V of the Babylonian epic, and the simple reworking of the Sumerian tale of Bilgames and the Bull of Heaven to yield the episode of Ishtar and

the Bull of Heaven in Tablet VI. The most recent discoveries of text
also reveal that the Akkadian narrative of Enkidu's funeral in Tablet
VIII is reminiscent of Bilgames's funeral in the Sumerian Death of
Bilgames, and that the tradition whereby Gilgamesh learnt the secrets
of the Flood Hero and thereby restored the cultic life of the land, long
disrupted by the Deluge, informs the Death of Bilgames as well as the
Babylonian epic.

The literary-historical background of these Sumerian poems has
been covered briefly in the main introduction at the beginning of this
book. They are written in poetry, that is clear, but we know even less
of Sumerian poetics than we do of Babylonian. Literary Sumerian is
a language that used more figurative expressions than Akkadian, and
these sometimes make the immediate sense of a line or passage opaque.
The present translation aims to be as faithful to the original as possible
but in order to produce a readable text small liberties have on occasion
been taken with phrasing.

Several of these five poems survive in different recensions, some
shorter, some longer. Where the text is repetitious, especially, some
tablets dispense with the repeated passages, while others might offer
an abbreviated version and yet others the full text. This is probably
because the written text is, to a degree, only an *aide-mémoire* and
some scribes expected the tablet's user to supply the full text of a
repetitious passage by recalling earlier parts of the poem. The policy
adopted here is to give a translation that reproduces the text in the
fullest possible form, even where no one manuscript provides it, since
only then do the poems emerge in the shape intended by the poets.
Where there is a traditional modern line-numbering that is based on
a shorter version of the text, lines and passages of interpolated text
that are not counted in that line-numbering are marked apart by
indentation.

As yet there exists no published scholarly edition that collects together the
Sumerian poems about Gilgamesh in the original language, and this is the first
occasion on which English translations of all five poems – as they are currently
extant – have been published in one place. All five tales together have recently
been translated into Italian by Giovanni Pettinato, 'Poemi sumerici su Gilgamesh',
in *La saga di Gilgamesh* (Milan: Rusconi, 1992), pp. 305–47, but the newest
discoveries of text have rendered even this out of date in places. Samuel Noah
Kramer's pioneering English translations of Bilgames and Akka, Bilgames and

Huwawa (known to him as Gilgamesh and the Land of the Living) and the Death of Bilgames, reproduced in James B. Pritchard's anthology of *Ancient Near Eastern Texts Relating to the Old Testament* and elsewhere, are now very largely superseded. Modern French translations of the three best-preserved poems, Bilgames and Akka, Bilgames and Huwawa and Bilgames and the Netherworld, can be found in Raymond Jacques Tournay and Aaron Shaffer, *L'Épopée de Gilgamesh* (Paris: Éditions du Cerf, 1994), pp. 248–74, 282–304. Other recent translations of individual poems are noted in the introductions below.

Bilgames and Akka: 'The envoys of Akka'

This poem was known in antiquity by its incipit, 'The envoys of Akka'. It is the shortest of the Sumerian tales of Bilgames and also the best preserved. It must have been a favourite copy-text in Old Babylonian schools. It differs from the other four Sumerian poems in having no obvious counterpart in the Akkadian material, though the consultation of the elders and the young men in assembly is a motif also found – in different context – in Tablet II of the standard version of the Babylonian epic.

The story tells how the city-state of Uruk achieved hegemony over the city-state of Kish. Akka, king of Kish, sends emissaries to Uruk, evidently to demand the submission of that city. Bilgames convenes the assembly and seeks the counsel of the elders, putting it to them that Uruk should not submit but should go to war. Prefaced to this proposal is the first of three occurrences of three enigmatic lines:

To empty the wells, to empty the wells of the land,
to empty the shallow wells of the land,
to empty the deep wells furnished with hoisting ropes.

These lines are usually taken to represent the literal demands of Akka, that the men of Uruk become drawers of water for Kish. I assume instead that in describing a menial task for which there can be no end, the poet conveys figuratively the endless and impossible toil that will follow a surrender of independence. However that may be, the elders counsel submission. Bilgames ignores their advice, and puts the same proposal to the young men of the city. They agree with Bilgames.

Their reiteration of his proposal is prefaced by a traditional saying, the gist of which is that to submit to the whims of a royal master is a painful and unpredictable experience, akin to standing behind a donkey. They laud Bilgames's prowess and predict the rout of Kish. Bilgames orders Enkidu, who in this tradition is his servant, to prepare for war.

Very soon Akka arrives and lays siege to Uruk. Bilgames asks for a volunteer to go to Akka and confound his plans. One of Bilgames's personal guard, the valiant Birhurturra (the reading of the name is uncertain), duly volunteers. As soon as he leaves the city he is captured, beaten and brought before Akka. At that moment the steward of Uruk is seen in the distance on the city wall and Akka asks Birhurturra if this is Bilgames. Birhurturra replies that it is not and that if it were battle would surely commence and, in an inevitable sequence of events, Akka would be defeated and captured. For his impudence he receives a second beating. Bilgames himself then climbs on to the city wall. As the weak cower under the spell of his glory, the young men prepare for battle and, led by Enkidu, go forth from the gate. Meanwhile, Akka has spotted Bilgames on the rampart and asks Birhurturra again whether it is his king who stands there. As Birhurturra replies in the affirmative the sequence of events takes place just as he had predicted on the previous occasion: battle commences and in due course Akka is defeated and captured. In the denouement Bilgames addresses Akka as his superior, recalling how Akka had once given him safe refuge. Akka asks Bilgames to repay his favour and Bilgames accordingly lets him go free to Kish.

The most recent scholarly edition of Bilgames and Akka is W. H. Ph. Römer, *Das sumerische Kurzepos 'Bilgameš und Akka'*. Alter Orient und Altes Testament 209, I (Kevelaer: Verlag Butzon & Bercker, Neukirchen-Vluyn: Neukirchener Verlag, 1980). Other modern translations are those of Jerrold S. Cooper, 'Gilgamesh and Akka: a review article', *Journal of Cuneiform Studies* 33 (Philadelphia: American Schools of Oriental Research, 1981), pp. 224–41; Thorkild Jacobsen, 'Gilgamesh and Aka', in idem, *The Harps that Once . . . : Sumerian Poetry in Translation* (New Haven and London: Yale University Press, 1987), pp. 345–55; and W. H. Ph. Römer, 'Bilgamesch und Akka', in Römer and Dietz Otto Edzard, *Mythen und Epen* 1. Texte aus der Umwelt des Alten Testaments 3, III (Gütersloh: Verlagshaus Gerd Mohn, 1993), pp. 549–59. Other modern studies are H. Vanstiphout, 'Towards a reading of "Gilgamesh and Agga"', *Aula Orientalis* 5 (Barcelona: Editorial AUSA, 1987), pp. 129–41; Dina Katz, *Gilgamesh and Akka*. Library of Oriental Texts 1 (Groningen: Styx Publications, 1993).

The envoys of Akka, Enmebaragesi's son,
came from Kish to Bilgames in Uruk.
Before his city's elders Bilgames
laid the matter, seeking a solution:
'"To empty the wells, to empty the wells of the land,   5
to empty the shallow wells of the land,
to empty the deep wells furnished with hoisting ropes:"
let us not submit to the house of Kish, let us wage war!'
The convened assembly of his city's elders
gave answer to Bilgames: 10
'"To empty the wells, to empty the wells of the land,
to empty the shallow wells of the land,
to empty the deep wells furnished with hoisting ropes:"
let us submit to the house of Kish, let us not wage war!'
Bilgames, the lord of Kullab,   15
placing his trust in the goddess Inanna,
took no notice of what his city's elders said.

Before his city's young men Bilgames
laid the matter a second time, seeking a solution:
'"To empty the wells, to empty the wells of the land,   20
to empty the shallow wells of the land,
to empty the deep wells furnished with hoisting ropes:"
let us not submit to the house of Kish, let us wage war!'
The convened assembly of his city's young men gave answer to
        Bilgames:
'To stand on duty, to sit in attendance,   25
to escort the king's son –
to hold a donkey by the hindquarters –
as they say, who is there has breath for that?
Let us not submit to the house of Kish, let us wage war!
Uruk, the smithy of the gods,   30
Eanna, house come down from heaven –
the great gods it was who gave them shape –
their great rampart, a cloudbank resting on the earth,

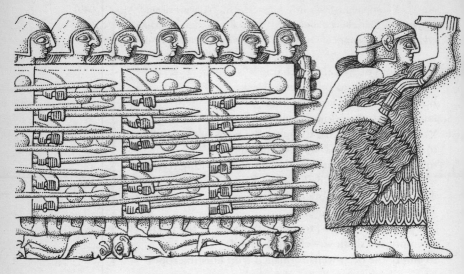

21 *'Let us wage war!'*

their lofty residence, founded by the god An:
they are given into your charge, you are their king and their
     warrior!   35
O *crusher of heads*, prince beloved of An,
when he arrives why be afraid?
That army is small and a rabble at the rear,
its men will not withstand us!'
Then Bilgames, the lord of Kullab,   40
his heart rejoiced in what his city's young men said, his mood
     turned bright,
he spoke to his servant, Enkidu:
'Now make ready the equipment and arms of battle,
let weapons of war return to your grasp!
Let them create terror and a dread aura,   45
so when he arrives fear of me overwhelms him,
so his good sense is confounded and his judgement undone!'

It was not five days, it was not ten days,
Enmebaragesi's son Akka laid siege to Uruk,
and Uruk's good sense was confounded.   50

Bilgames, the lord of Kullab,
addressed the city's warriors:
'O my warriors, whose eyes stare wide in alarm,
let one stout of heart volunteer, "I will go to Akka!"'
Birhurturra, his royal bodyguard,   55
did homage to his king:
'My lord, I will go to Akka,
so his good sense is confounded and his judgement undone!'
Birhurturra went forth from the city gate.
As Birhurturra passed through the city gate,   60
in the city's gateway he was taken captive,
they battered Birhurturra from head to toe.

He came into the presence of Akka,
he addressed Akka.
He had not finished speaking when the Steward of Uruk climbed up
            on the wall,   65
and raised his head on the rampart.
Akka caught sight of him,
and addressed Birhurturra:
'Slave, is that man your king?'
'That man is not my king!   70
Were that man my king,
were that his fearsome brow,
were those his bison eyes,
were that his beard of lapis lazuli,
were those his fingers fine,   75
would a myriad not fall, a myriad not rise,
would a myriad thereby not roll in the dust,
would all the nations thereby not be overwhelmed,
would the mouths of the land thereby not be filled with dust,
would he not cut down the horns of the boat,   80
would he not make Akka, king of Kish, a prisoner in the heart of
            his army?'
They hit him and they beat him,
they battered Birhurturra from head to toe.

After the Steward of Uruk, Bilgames climbed up on the wall,
(his) dread aura overwhelmed the old and the young of Kullab,   85

but [put] weapons of war in the hands of Uruk's young men.
At the door of the city gate he (*or* they) stood in the roadway,
Enkidu went forth *from* the city gate.
Bilgames raised his head on the rampart.
Looking up, Akka caught sight of him: 90
'Slave, is that man your king?'
'That man is indeed my king!'
And it was just as he had said,
a myriad did fall, a myriad did rise,
a myriad did thereby roll in the dust,   95
all the nations were thereby overwhelmed,
the mouths of the land were thereby filled with dust,
he cut down the horns of the boat,
in the midst of his army he took prisoner Akka, king of Kish.

        [The lord] of Uruk . . . that army.
Bilgames, the lord of Kullab,   100
addressed Akka:
'O Akka, my lieutenant, Akka, my captain, O Akka, my
        commander, Akka, my general,
O Akka, my field marshal!
O Akka, you gave me breath, Akka, you gave me life,
O Akka, you took to your bosom a man on the run,   105
O Akka, a runaway bird you sated with grain!'

Akka:

'Uruk, the smithy of the Gods,
its great rampart, a cloudbank resting on the earth,
its lofty residence, founded by the god An,
are given into your charge: [repay me] my favour!'   110

Bilgames:

'Before the Sun God I hereby repay you the favour of old!'
He let Akka go free to Kish.
O Bilgames, lord of Kullab,
sweet is your praise!

Bilgames and Huwawa:
'The lord to the Living One's Mountain'
and 'Ho, hurrah!'

The poem of Bilgames and Huwawa was another favourite copy-text in Old Babylonian schools. It tells the story of the expedition to the Forest of Cedar, the killing of Huwawa and the felling of the cedar, and it is thus a kind of precursor of Tablets III–V of the Babylonian epic, though the details of the story are very different. Most significantly, Huwawa is taken captive not by force of arms but by trickery, using a ruse divulged to Bilgames by the god Enki. The Sumerian poem exists as two distinct compositions, 'The lord to the Living One's Mountain', usually called Version A, and 'Ho, hurrah!', usually known as Version B (other translations are possible of both titles). The two poems are closely related and have many lines in common. To judge from the number of extant manuscripts, Version A was more popular than Version B and its text can be restored almost entirely. Version B is less complete.

In fear of death Bilgames turns his thoughts to deeds of glory and proposes an expedition to the fabled Cedar Mountain, where dwelt the Living One. This epithet apparently refers to its guardian spirit, the demigod Huwawa. In early tradition the Cedar Mountain was far in the east, where the sun rose. Bilgames's servant Enkidu tells him that he should seek the approval of the Sun God, Utu (the Sumerian Shamash). This Bilgames does, giving as the reason for the expedition that he has seen the impermanence of the human condition and wishes to establish his fame. Utu grants him the help of seven constellations, which will guide him on his journey. Bilgames mobilizes the young men of Uruk, arms them and sets out. The constellations guide him to the mountains where cedars grow. After crossing seven mountain ranges in search of a suitable tree, finally he finds one to his liking. Without further ado he fells the chosen cedar and his companions cut it into logs. Thereupon Huwawa, the cedars' guardian, awakes and launches at Bilgames one of his auras, the radiant numinous powers that protect him. Bilgames and Enkidu are stunned and fall unconscious. Enkidu wakes and eventually rouses Bilgames too. Bilgames swears to learn more of their assailant. Enkidu describes to him the

terrible being that is Huwawa but Bilgames is confident that the two
of them will succeed where one would fail.

As they approach Huwawa's dwelling Bilgames is stopped in his
tracks and the voice of Huwawa calls to him, telling him not to be
afraid but to kneel on the ground. Bilgames then pretends to wish to
form a marital alliance with Huwawa and offers him his sisters,
Enmebaragesi and Peshtur, to be his wives. He promises Huwawa
other pleasures of life that are evidently unknown in his remote
mountain lair: fine flour and water in leathern bottles, sandals large
and small, choice gemstones and other presents. For the betrothal of
the sisters and the promise of each further gift Huwawa surrenders
one of his protective auras. These are conceptualized as great cedars,
which Bilgames's men duly cut into logs for the journey home. When
Huwawa has no auras left and is helpless to attack, Bilgames shows
his true colours. He strikes him and takes him prisoner. Huwawa
then pleads for his life, complaining to Utu of Bilgames's treachery.
Bilgames shows him princely mercy but Enkidu warns that this is too
dangerous: if they let Huwawa go they will never see home again. As
Huwawa turns on Enkidu in anger, Enkidu cuts his throat. The heroes
take his head to the god Enlil. Enlil angrily asks them why they have
killed Huwawa and tells them they should instead have treated him
with every courtesy. In conclusion Enlil distributes Huwawa's auras.

Version A: 'The lord to the Living One's Mountain'

The most recent scholarly edition is Dietz Otto Edzard, 'Gilgameš und Huwawa
A. I. Teil', *Zeitschrift für Assyriologie und vorderasiatische Archäologie* 80
(Berlin and New York: Walter de Gruyter, 1990), pp. 165–203; idem, 'Gilgameš
und Huwawa A. II. Teil', *Zeitschrift für Assyriologie* . . . 81 (1991), pp. 165–
233. Edzard's translation is also given in W. H. Ph. Römer and Edzard, *Mythen
und Epen* 1. Texte aus der Umwelt des Alten Testaments 3, III (Gütersloh:
Verlagshaus Gerd Mohn, 1993), pp. 540–49, 'Gilgamesch und Huwawa'. See
also the study by Aaron Shaffer, 'Gilgamesh, the Cedar Forest and Mesopotamian
history', *Journal of the American Oriental Society* 103 (New Haven: American
Oriental Society, 1983), pp. 307–13.

The lord to the Living One's Mountain did turn his mind,
the lord Bilgames to the Living One's Mountain did turn his mind,

he called to his servant, Enkidu:
'O Enkidu, since no man can escape life's end,
I will enter the mountain and set up my name.   5
Where names are set up, I will set up my name,
where names are not yet set up, I will set up gods' names.'
Enkidu his servant answered him:
'My lord, if you are to enter the mountain, the god Utu should be
            informed,
Utu, Young Hero Utu should be informed!   10
Things to do with the mountain are Utu's concern,
things to do with Cut-Cedar Mountain are Young Hero Utu's
            concern, Utu should be informed!'

Bilgames took a white kid in hand,
as an animal offering he held a brown kid to his breast.
The pure staff in his hand he held at his nose,   15
he addressed Utu of Heaven:
'O Utu, I am to enter the mountain, be you my helper!
I am to enter Cut-Cedar Mountain, be you my helper!'
Utu answered him from heaven:
'Young man, in your own place you are a nobleman, but there in
            the mountain what would you be?'   20
'O Utu, let me speak a word to you, give ear to what I say!
Let me tell you something, may you give thought to it!
In my city a man dies, and the heart is stricken,
a man perishes, and the heart feels pain.
I raised my head on the rampart,   25
my gaze fell on a corpse drifting down the river, afloat on the
            water:
I too shall become like that, just so shall I be!
"No man can stretch to the sky, no matter how tall,
no man can compass a mountain, no matter how broad!"
Since no man can escape life's end,   30
I will enter the mountain and set up my name.
Where names are set up, I will set up my name,
where names are not yet set up, I will set up gods' names.'
Utu accepted his tears as he would a gift,
like a man of compassion he showed him pity.   35
Seven warriors they were, sons of one mother,

the first, their eldest, had paws of a lion, talons of an eagle,
the second was an [open]-mouthed *cobra* . . . ,
the third a Dragon Serpent hurling . . . ,
the fourth *spat* fire . . . ,   40
the fifth a serpent whose tongue . . . the uplands,
the sixth, a torrent in spate that batters the mountains,
the seventh blasted like lightning none could deflect:
these seven the warrior, Young Hero Utu, gave Bilgames:
> ' . . . the goddess Nissaba has given you in addition,   NiO
> [in the heavens] they shine, on earth they know the paths,
> [on earth] let them reveal the path [*to the east* . . . ,]
through the mountain passes let them lead you.'   45
Thus he put the Cedar Smiter in happy mood,
he put the lord Bilgames in happy mood.
In his city he sounded the horn like a man alone,
he blew it as one like two men together.
'He who has a family, to his family! He who has a mother, to his
            mother!   50
Let men who are unattached like me, fifty of them, be at my side!'
He who had a family, to his family. He who had a mother, to his
            mother.
Men who were unattached like him, fifty of them, were at his side.
He made his way to the forge,
he had them cast a *dirk* and battle-axe of bronze, his weapons of
            valour.   55
He made his way to the Dark Grove outside the city,
he had them fell ebony, willow, *apricot* and box,
[he set them] in the hands of the sons of his city who were going
            with him.

            [Seven] warriors [they were], sons of [one] mother,
the first, their eldest, had paws of a lion, talons of an eagle,
            [the second was an open-mouthed *cobra* . . . ,]
            [the third a Dragon Serpent hurling . . . ,]
            [the fourth *spat* fire . . . ,]
            [the fifth a serpent whose tongue . . . the uplands,]
            [the sixth, a torrent in spate that batters the mountains,]
            [the seventh blasted like lightning none could deflect:]
            [in the heavens they shone, on earth they knew the paths,]

[on earth] they revealed the path [*to the east*,]
through the mountain passes it did lead him.   60
He crossed the first mountain range, he did not find the cedar he
      wanted,
      he crossed the [second] mountain range, [he did not find] the
            cedar he [wanted,]   UrF
      he crossed the third mountain range, [he did not find] the
            cedar he wanted,
      he crossed the fourth mountain range, [he did not find] the
            cedar he wanted,
      he crossed the fifth mountain range, he did not [find] the
            cedar he wanted,
      he crossed the sixth mountain range, he did not find the
            cedar he wanted,
but crossing the seventh mountain range, he found the cedar he
      wanted.
He asked no question, he looked no further,
Bilgames smote the cedar.
Enkidu lopped off its branches . . . for Bilgames,   65
the sons of his city who had come with him stacked them in a pile.

      With all the commotion Bilgames disturbed Huwawa in his
         lair,
he launched against him his auras of terror.
Bilgames was overcome [with a stupor], as if in a sleep,
[Enkidu] was beset [with torpor], as if in a daze.
The sons of his city who had gone with him
like little puppies lay shivering at his feet.   70
Enkidu arose, it had been a dream, he shuddered, it had been a
      deep sleep.
He rubbed his eyes with his hands, there was desolate silence.

He touched him with his hand, but he could not rouse him,
he spoke to him, but he received no reply:
'You who lie, you who lie,   75
O Bilgames, young lord of Kullab, how long will you lie?
The mountain is dark, the shadows cast over it,
all the sunbeams of eventide are gone,

with head held high the Sun has gone to the bosom of Ningal, his
              mother:
O Bilgames, how long will you lie?   80
The sons of your city, who came with you,
do not keep them waiting for you at the foot of the mountain,
do not reduce the mothers who bore them to spinning yarn in the
              square of your city!'
[This message] he placed in his right ear,
his warrior's word covered him like a cloth.   85

He [Bilgames] took in his hands thirty shekels of oil and rubbed his
              chest,
he stood on the Great Earth like an ox [on all fours],
he bent his neck downwards and gave voice:
'By the life of the mother who bore me, the goddess Ninsun, and
              my father, the pure Lugalbanda!
Should I behave as if awestruck on the knees of Ninsun, the mother
              who bore me?'   90
And for a second time he said to him:
'By the life of the mother who bore me, the goddess Ninsun, and
              my father, the pure Lugalbanda!
Until I discover whether that fellow is a man or a god,
my mountain-bound feet I shall not turn home to the city!'
The servant – makes life pleasant, makes life sweet –   95
made answer to his master:
'My lord, you have not set eyes on that fellow, your heart is not
              stricken,
but I have set eyes on him, my heart is stricken:
a warrior he is, his teeth the teeth of a dragon,
his eye the eye of a lion!   100
His chest is a torrent in spate,
his brow devours the canebrake, none can go near him,
              like a man-eating lion, [on his tongue] the blood never *pales*.
My lord, you go on up the mountain, but let me go home to the
              city:
I will tell your mother you lived, so she laughs for joy,
should I then tell your mother you died, so she wails with grief?' 105
'Set to, O Enkidu! Two men together will not die: that lashed to a
              boat cannot sink,

no man can cut a three-ply rope,
a flood cannot sweep a man off a wall,
fire in a reed hut cannot be extinguished!
You join with me, I will join with you, what can anyone do to us
        then?   110
"After it sank, after it sank,
after the boat from Magan sank,
after the barge sank, the cargo-boat sank,
the boat under tow was the boat that gave life, it took (the
        survivors) *on board*."
Set to, let us go to him, let us set eyes on him!   115
Quick, let us go to him!
"Fright is countered with fright,
cunning with cunning!"
However you feel, set to, let us go to him!'

No man goes nearer than sixty pole-lengths,   120
and already Huwawa has occupied his house of cedar.
He turns his eye upon one, it is the eye of death,
he shakes his head at one, it is the gesture that pronounces one
        guilty.
When he addresses one, he does not mince words:
'Able fellow that you are, you will not go home to the city of the
        mother who bore you!'   125

Into his muscles, into his feet the terror flooded, his aura of terror
        flooded,
(Bilgames) could not *move* his foot from the ground.
His foot was *held fast by* his big toe,
in his flank, in his . . . it flooded.
'Ho, hallo! Tall-grown sapling,   130
noble one in whom the gods delight,
angry ox standing ready for combat,
well knew your mother how to make a child,
well knew your nurse how to suckle a baby!
Be not afraid, place both hands on the ground!'   135
He placed both hands on the ground, then he said to him:
'By the life of the mother who bore me, the goddess Ninsun, and
        my father, the pure Lugalbanda!

Where you dwell on the mountain, it is not known! Where you
       dwell on the mountain, it should be known:
let me send you my big sister Enmebaragesi, to be your wife on the
       mountain!'
And again he said: 140
'By the life of the mother who bore me, the goddess Ninsun, and
       my father, the pure Lugalbanda!
Where you dwell on the mountain, it is not known! Where you
       dwell on the mountain, it should be known:
let me send you my little sister Peshtur, to be your concubine on the
       mountain!
Give me one of your auras of terror, and I will become your
       kinsman!'
His first aura of terror he gave him.   145
The sons of his city who had come with him
lopped off its branches, lashed them together,
and laid it down at the foot of the mountain.

    [And a second time he said:]
    ['By the life of the mother who bore me, the goddess
       Ninsun, and my father, the pure Lugalbanda!]
    [Where you dwell on the mountain, it is not known! Where
       you dwell on the mountain, it should be known:]
    [let me bring you in the mountain . . .]
    [So may I not then join your family?]
    [Give me one of your auras of terror, and I will become
       your kinsman!']
    His second aura of terror he gave him.
    The sons of his city who had come with him   UnC
    lopped off its branches, lashed them together,
    and laid it down at the foot of the mountain.

    And a third time he said:
    'By the life of the mother who bore me, the goddess Ninsun,
       and my father, the pure Lugalbanda!
    Where you dwell on the mountain, it is not known! Where
       you dwell on the mountain, it should be known:
    let me bring you in the mountain

finest-quality flour, such as the great gods eat, and bottles of
     cool water.
So may I not then join your family?
Give me one of your auras of terror, and I will become your
     kinsman!'
His third aura of terror he gave him.
The sons of his city who had come with him
lopped off its branches, lashed them together,
and laid it down at the foot of the mountain.

And a fourth time he said:
'By the life of the mother who bore me, the goddess Ninsun,
     and my father, the pure Lugalbanda!
Where you dwell on the mountain, it is not known! Where
     you dwell on the mountain, it should be known:
let me bring you [in the mountain] big sandals for big feet.
So may I not then join your family?
Give me one of your auras of terror, and I will become your
     kinsman!'
His fourth aura of terror he gave him.
The sons of his city who had come with him
lopped off its branches, lashed them together,
and laid it down at the foot of the mountain.

And a fifth time he said:
'By the life of the mother who bore me, the goddess Ninsun,
     and my father, the pure Lugalbanda!
Where you dwell on the mountain, it is not known! Where
     you dwell on the mountain, it should be known:
let me bring you in the mountain little sandals for your little
     feet.
So may I not then join your family?
Give me one of your auras of terror, and I will become your
     kinsman!'
His fifth aura of terror he gave him.
The sons of his city who had come with him
lopped off its branches, lashed them together,
and laid it down at the foot of the mountain.

And a sixth time he said:
'By the life of the mother who bore me, the goddess Ninsun,
     and my father, the pure Lugalbanda!
Where you dwell on the mountain, it is not known! Where
     you dwell on the mountain, it should be known:
let me bring you in the mountain
rock crystal, chalcedony and lapis lazuli.
So may I not then join your family?
Give me one of your auras of terror, and I will become your
     kinsman!'
His sixth aura of terror he gave him.
The sons of his city who had come with him
lopped off its branches, lashed them together,
and laid it down at the foot of the mountain.

[And a seventh time he said:]
['By the life of the mother who bore me, the goddess
     Ninsun, and my father, the pure Lugalbanda!]
[Where you dwell on the mountain, it is not known! Where
     you dwell on the mountain, it should be known:]
[let me bring you in the mountain . . .]
[So may I not then join your family?]
[Give me one of your auras of terror, and I will become
     your kinsman!']
[His seventh aura of terror he gave him.]
[The sons of his city who had come with him]
[lopped off its branches, lashed them together,]
[and laid it down at the foot of the mountain.]

Having used up his seven auras of terror, he drew near to his lair.
Like a snake in the *wine harbour*, he followed behind him,   150
and making as if to kiss him, struck him on the cheek with his fist.
Huwawa bared bright his teeth, wrinkled his brow.
          Like a wild bull made captive he threw a rope on him,   SiA
          like a soldier taken prisoner he tied his arms.
          Huwawa spoke to Bilgames: UrG
'O deceitful warrior, [*you do me wrong!*]'
The two of them [fixed] a nose-rope . . . on him.

[*Dragging*] the warrior out of his lair, 'Sit down!' he [said]
    to him,
[*dragging*] Huwawa out of his lair, 'Sit down!' he [said] to
    him.
The warrior sat, racked by sobs he began to [weep],   UrA
Huwawa sat, racked by sobs he began to weep.
Huwawa [addressed] a plea to Bilgames:
'O Bilgames, set me free!
To the Sun God let me say a word!
O Utu, I never knew a mother to bear me, I never knew a father to
    rear me,   155
I was born in the mountains, it was you who reared me!
Bilgames swore by heaven, he swore by earth, he swore by the
    Netherworld!'
Seizing him by the hand, he threw himself prostrate.
Then the noble Bilgames, his heart took pity on him,
he spoke to his servant Enkidu: 160
'O Enkidu, let the captive bird go off to its place,
let the captive soldier go back to his mother's embrace!'

Enkidu gave answer to Bilgames:
'Ho, hurrah! Tall-grown sapling,
noble one in whom the gods delight,   165
angry ox standing ready for combat,
young lord Bilgames, honoured in Uruk,
well knew your mother how to make a child,
well knew your nurse how to suckle a baby!
Even the tallest, if lacking good counsel,   170
Namtar will devour and he will not know it!
If the captive bird goes off to its place,
the captive soldier goes back to his mother's embrace,
then you will not return to the city of the mother who bore you!
    A captive warrior given freedom, a captive priestess
        [returned] to the cloister,   UnB
    a captive priest returned to the wig, from days of old [who
        ever saw such a thing?]
    The mountain [road] he will [confound before you,]
    [the mountain path] he will [confuse before you.]'
    [The warrior gave] ear to what he had said,

Huwawa spoke to Enkidu: 175
'O Enkidu, you use evil words to him about me:
a hired man is hired for his keep, following behind his leader. Why
          use evil words to him?'
But as he said these words,
in rage and fury Enkidu severed his head at the neck.

22 *'In rage and fury Enkidu severed his head at the neck'.*

They put it in a leather bag,   180
and took it before the gods Enlil and Ninlil.
Having kissed the ground before Enlil,
he threw down the bag and tipped out the head.
They set it in front of Enlil.
When Enlil saw the head of Huwawa,   185
what Bilgames had done made him angry:
'Why have you done this thing?
Was it commanded that his name be wiped from the earth?
He should have sat before you,
he should have eaten the bread that you ate,   190
he should have drunk the water that you drank,
he should have been treated in the proper way.'
          From his throne Enlil distributed his heavenly auras: UnB
his first aura he gave to the field,   Ni
his second aura he gave to the river,
his third aura he gave to the canebrake,   195

his fourth aura he gave to the lion,
his fifth aura he gave to the woods,
his sixth aura he gave to the palace,
his seventh aura he gave to the goddess Nungal,
the remaining auras he took for himself.   200
Honour to the mighty Bilgames,
praise to the goddess Nissaba!

Version B: 'Ho, hurrah!'

The shorter, less popular poem of Bilgames and Huwawa is not yet
fully recovered. Apart from being obviously more concise than Version
A, Version B exhibits many minor variations. A major difference
between the two poems is one of plot. At the crucial point in the
story, when Bilgames awakes at last from the sleep induced by
Huwawa's auras, instead of encouraging the fearful Enkidu with a
show of bravado, here the hero doubts his own ability to match the
monster in strength and calls on his god, Enki, to 'emerge' in his
words. This phrase I understand to mean that the god of trickery is
to inspire him to overcome his opponent with cunning speech. Through
the medium of Enkidu, who apparently blurts out the words Bilgames
should use, Enki does exactly that and the plot moves directly on to
the meeting with Huwawa and Bilgames's ingratiating diplomacy.

   The only scholarly edition is Dietz Otto Edzard, 'Gilgameš und Huwawa'.
Zwei Versionen der sumerischen Zedernwaldepisode nebst einer Edition von
Version 'B', Philosophisch-historische Klasse, Sitzungsberichte 1993, IV (Munich:
Bayerische Akademie der Wissenschaften, 1993).

Ho, hurrah! Tall-grown sapling,
noble one in whom the gods delight,
angry ox standing ready for combat,
young lord Bilgames, honoured in Uruk!

Bilgames:

'In Uruk a man dies, and the mind is stricken,   5
a man perishes, and the heart feels pain.

I raised my head on the rampart,
I saw a corpse afloat on the water.
The mind despairs, the heart is stricken:
the end of life being inescapable –   10
the grave, the oppressive Netherworld, which spares no man:
"No man can reach across a mountain, no matter how lofty,
no man can compass a mountain, no matter how broad!" –
because no man can escape life's end,
by the life of the mother who bore me, the goddess Ninsun, my
          father, [the pure] Lugalbanda,   15
and my god Enki, the lord Nudimmud . . . '

                    *   *   *

'[I will enter the forest and bring] down [*a great cedar*,]
 . . . . I will finish,   20
to . . . I will have enter [*the timber I bring*] down!'
[His servant Enkidu] spoke to him:
'[My lord, if] you are to enter the [mountain,]
[the god Utu] should be informed!
If you would enter Cut-Cedar [Mountain,]   25
Utu should be informed!
Things to do with the mountain are Utu's concern,
things to do with Cut-Cedar Mountain are Young Hero Utu's
          concern.'
Heavenly Utu donned his lapis-lazuli lustre,
came forth with head held high.   30
Bilgames, the lord of Kullab, held the pure staff in his hand at his
          nose:
'O Utu, I am to enter the mountain, be you my helper!
I am to enter Cut-Cedar Mountain, be you my helper!'

                    *   *   *

[Seven warriors they were, sons of one mother,]
[these seven the warrior, Young Hero Utu, gave Bilgames:]
'[The first, their eldest, has lion's paws and eagle's talons,]
[the second is an open-mouthed *cobra* . . . ,]
[the third a Dragon Serpent hurling . . . ,]   40
[the fourth *spits* fire . . . ,]
[the fifth] . . . can seize . . . ,

[the sixth], a torrent in spate that batters the [mountains,]
the seventh blasts like lightning none can deflect:
in the heavens they shine, on earth they know the paths,   45
in the heavens they are stars blazing on high,
on earth [they know] the road to Aratta,
[like] merchants they know the pathways,
like pigeons they know the nooks and crannies of the mountains:
through the mountain passes let them lead you.'   50

In his city Bilgames held a levy,
in [*the midst*] of Kullab he sounded the horn:
'O city, he who has a wife, to his wife! He who has a child, to his
    child!
O warriors known, O warriors unknown,
who have not wives, who have not children,   55
let such men be at my side, with Bilgames!'
The king went out of the city,
Bilgames went out of Kullab.
Taking the road of Cut-Cedar Mountain,
he crossed the first mountain range, he did not find the cedar he
    wanted,   60
    [he crossed] the second mountain [range, he did not find the
      cedar he wanted,]   B
    [he crossed] the third mountain [range, he did not find the
      cedar he wanted,]
    [he crossed] the fourth mountain [range, he did not find the
      cedar he wanted,]
    [he crossed the fifth] mountain [range, he did not find the
      cedar he wanted,]
    [he crossed] the [sixth mountain range, he did not find the
      cedar he wanted,]
but crossing the seventh mountain range, he found the cedar he
    wanted.

Bilgames felled the cedar,
his servant Enkidu turned it into logs,
the sons of his city who had come with him
set them in a pile.   65

Then as the one warrior drew close to the other,
the aura [of Huwawa] was spread forth like a headcloth.
[Bilgames *was overcome, a stupor*] seized him like a sleep.

*   *   *

[Enkidu spoke to Bilgames:]   73
'[You] who sleep, [you] who sleep,
O young lord Bilgames, how long [will you] sleep?   75
The mountain has become [dark,] the shadows [cast over it,]
the [sunbeams of eventide have gone.]'
Bilgames* arose, it had been a dream,
he shuddered, it had been a deep sleep.
He rubbed his eyes with his hands, there was desolate silence.   80
'By the life of the mother who bore me, the goddess Ninsun, and
               my father, the pure Lugalbanda,
[may] my god [Enki, the lord Nudimmud,]
[*inspire* my words!]
I [have set eyes on him, I can] comprehend:
a warrior he is, his eyes are a lion's eyes,   85
his chest is a torrent in spate,
his brow devours the canebrake, there is none can go near him,
like a man-eating lion, on his tongue the blood never *pales*:
I have not the might to (match) the warrior, who has it indeed?'
His servant Enkidu spoke to him: 90

*   *   *

'By the life of the [mother who bore you, the goddess Ninsun], and
               your father, [the pure Lugalbanda,]   93
[may] your god Enki-[Nudimmud *inspire*] your words:
"O warrior, [where you dwell on] the mountain, it should be
               known: 95
[for] your little feet let [little] sandals be [made,]
[for your] big feet [let big sandals] be made!"'

---

*The tablet reads 'Enkidu', corruptly.

A few lines are lost, and the text resumes with Bilgames's address to Huwawa:

'[By the life of the] mother who bore me(!), the goddess Ninsun,
                and the father who sired me, the pure Lugalbanda,   103
[may] my* [god] Enki-Nudimmud *inspire* [my words!]
O warrior, where you dwell on the mountain, it should be
                known: 105
for your little feet [let] little sandals be made,
for your big [feet let] big sandals be made!'

            *   *   *

[The first aura]
[he gave to him.]   115
[The sons of his city who had come with him]
[set them in a pile.]
[The second aura,]
[the third aura,]
[the fourth aura,]   120
[the fifth aura,]
[the sixth aura,]
            they [heaped] in piles on the mountain.   A

Having used up his seven auras, he drew near to his lair,
he struck him on the ear with his fist.
Huwawa wrinkled his brow, bared his teeth at him.   125
Like a wild bull made captive he threw a rope on him,
like a warrior taken prisoner he bound his elbows (behind him).
Racked with sobs the warrior began to weep,
racked with sobs Huwawa began to weep:
'O warrior, you deceived me, you laid your hand on me, though
                you swore an oath to me.   130
By the life of [the mother who bore you], the goddess Ninsun, and
                your father, pure Lugalbanda,
[your] god [Enki]-Nudimmud, *inspired* your words!
[Like a wild bull made captive] you threw a rope on me,
[like a warrior taken prisoner you bound] my elbows (behind me)!'
[Then the] noble Bilgames, his heart [took] pity [on him,]   135

_____
*The tablet reads 'his', corruptly.

he spoke to his servant Enkidu:
'Come, I will set the warrior free,
    he shall be our guide, who will spy out the route for us, he
        shall be our guide,   W
    he shall be my [porter], he shall carry my pack.'
His servant Enkidu gave answer to Bilgames:
    'The tallest one can lack good counsel.'   W

    ❖   ❖   ❖

'A captive warrior given freedom,   140
a captive priestess returned to the cloister,
a captive priest returned to the wig,
from days of old who ever saw such a thing?
The mountain road he will confound before you,
the mountain path he will confuse before you,   145
we shall not [return to the city] of the mothers who bore us!'

    ❖   ❖   ❖

Huwawa gave [answer] to [Bilgames:]   151
'The mother who bore me was a cave in the mountains,
the father who sired me was a cave in the uplands!
O Utu, you made me dwell all alone on the mountain!'
Bilgames spoke to Huwawa: 155
'Come, . . .'

The remainder is missing.

Bilgames and the Bull of Heaven: 'Hero in battle'

The poem entitled 'Hero in battle' deals with the feud of Bilgames
and the goddess Inanna (the Sumerian Ishtar), and with Bilgames and
Enkidu's fight with the Bull of Heaven. As such it is a precursor of
Tablet VI of the Babylonian epic, though the beginnings of the two
stories are very different. To judge from the number of surviving
manuscripts this poem was less popular than the tales concerning
Akka and Huwawa, and its translation is beset by difficulties of
preservation and comprehension. Neither of the two most important
sources now extant comes from the schools of Nippur, which regularly

provide the most reliable copies. One is from Mê-Turan, a provincial town on the river Diyala (Tell Haddad, north-east of Baghdad), the other reportedly from Dilbat in western Babylonia (Dailem, south of Babylon). To make matters worse these two tablets sometimes differ in their redaction, often use unconventional spellings and are frequently corrupt, so that translation is often difficult and sometimes impossible. For this reason the rendering of the poem given below must be accepted as far from definitive. It is hoped that future discoveries of more and better manuscripts will correct those errors of understanding unwittingly perpetrated here.

Following a hymnic prologue, Bilgames begins to converse with his mother, the goddess Ninsun. Ninsun gives him instructions to carry out his duties, though what he has to do is for the moment difficult to understand. The passage is repeated as narrative. Soon afterwards Inanna appears on the scene and apparently tries to detain Bilgames so that he cannot fulfil his secular functions, here epitomized as sitting in judgement. The goddess of sexual love has other plans for him but the crucial line, which one would expect to read 'O Bilgames, be you my husband and I will be your wife!' (as in Tablet VI 9 of the Babylonian epic), does not quite bear this translation, at least as the present sources stand. Bilgames reports Inanna's overtures to his mother, adding that Inanna accosted him at the city gate in the lee of the wall. This was a place where prostitutes traditionally plied their trade (cf. Tablet VII 117 of the Babylonian epic). Ninsun forbids him to accept Inanna's gifts, apparently lest he fall into soft ways. The title given to Inanna at this point, 'divine Palace Lady' (Sumerian Ninegal), is one she bears in the ritual of the Sacred Marriage. In this ceremony, best known from a Sumerian hymn of the nineteenth-century king Iddin-Dagan, the king impersonated Inanna's consort, Dumuzi, and lay with her, thus ensuring that his reign enjoyed her favour. Thus the choice of title confirms that Inanna's intentions are the same in the Sumerian story as in the Babylonian.

Bilgames next encounters Inanna as he goes out to fulfil another of his lordly duties, to capture livestock to replenish the goddess's animal pens. He brusquely orders her out of his way. In the long lacuna that follows one may imagine that he poured scorn on her, perhaps also listing the fate of her former conquests as in the Babylonian epic. After this break, Inanna is found weeping in her chamber in heaven, if the text is correctly deciphered. Her father, An, enters and asks her why she is crying. She apparently answers that it is because she has not been able to give herself to the object of her affections. Her description of the rough Bilgames as a 'wild bull on the rampage' is reminiscent of the Babylonian epic at Tablet I 63–4. Inanna asks her father for the Bull of Heaven, so that she can kill Bilgames. He objects that the Bull of Heaven grazes in the sky (for it is the constellation Taurus) and would have no food on earth. Throwing a tantrum Inanna starts to scream, making a noise so infernal that An gives in. Inanna leads the Bull of Heaven down to Uruk, where it devours all the vegetation and drinks the river dry.

The following passage is broken. As reconstructed here, from what are evidently different redactions of the text, it appears that Bilgames's minstrel, Lugalgabangal, sees the Bull of Heaven amid the devastation and enters into his master's presence. Bilgames is in the midst of feasting and the news his minstrel brings in no way diverts him from his pleasure. Having finished his meal, however, Bilgames prepares for battle. He arms himself and instructs his mother and sister to make sacrifices in the temple of the god Enki. He vows to dismember the Bull of Heaven and give its meat to the poor. As Inanna looks on from the city wall, Bilgames and Enkidu tackle the Bull. Enkidu finds its weak spot and Bilgames duly dispatches the monstrous animal. He hurls a piece of its leg at Inanna. As she rushes out of its way, the limb demolishes the wall. Bilgames wishes he could treat her as he has the Bull of Heaven. And just as he had vowed earlier, the Bull is dismembered and its meat given to the poor. Its horns, however, are dedicated to Inanna in her temple, Eanna.

The significance of Bilgames's feud with Inanna has been variously debated. One view is that the conflict it relates symbolizes the political struggle by Sumer, represented by Uruk, to be free of the imperial yoke of Akkade, represented by the goddess Inanna. Now that it seems more probable that the story develops from King Bilgames's repudiation of his city's goddess in the specific rite of the Sacred Marriage, it appears less likely that Inanna can be other than the great goddess of Uruk and more likely that the composition bears a different ideological message. But perhaps it bears none at all. The purpose of court poetry such as the poems of Bilgames (and much other Sumerian literature) was probably simply to amuse and entertain the king and his guests, not to promote political ideology.

The most recent scholarly edition of this text, with important new manuscripts, is Antoine Cavigneaux and Farouk N. H. Al-Rawi, 'Gilgameš et Taureau de Ciel (Šul.mè-kam). Textes de Tell Haddad IV', *Revue d'assyriologie et d'archéologie orientale* 87 (Paris: Presses Universitaires de France, 1993), pp. 97–129. The sigla of manuscripts that appear here in the right margin follow the abbreviations used there.

Hero in battle, hero in battle, let me sing his song!
Lord Bilgames, hero in battle, let me sing his song!
Lord with beard of black, hero in battle, let me sing his song!
Fair of limb, hero in battle, let me sing his song!
> Young lord, mightiest of the mighty, hero in battle, let me
> > sing his song!   Nb obv. 4
> [Expert] in wrestling and trials of strength, [hero in battle,
> > let me sing his song!]   Nb obv. 6
Merry one, hero in battle, let me sing his song!   Ma 5
Rampaging against wrongdoers, hero in battle, let me sing his song!

The king, the lord, the mother who bore him addressed [him:] Nc 4'
'My king, go down to the river, [*take*] dust in hand, wash in the
> river!
My lord, to enter the juniper grove is a task *you know*,
. . . axe, the weapon . . .
in the Gipar house like a lordly sheep be shorn of hair,   Na 1'
be seated on the foremost . . .
That which is in the marsh,
my king, that which is in the marsh bend back with the oar,
my lord, let the oars dip in the water for you like a dense-growing
> reed-bed,
let its . . . dip in the water for you like . . . !'
> To the mother who bore him he gave . . .   Ma 14
In the wide courtyard of the house of Inanna
Bilgames [took his] *scythe* in hand,
the king, to enter the juniper grove is a task *he knows*,   Na 10'
in the Gipar house like a lordly sheep he was shorn of hair,
he was seated on the foremost . . .
In the marsh he . . .
in the marsh the king . . . , he bent it back with the oar,

for the king the oars dipped in the water like a dense-growing
      reed-bed,
its . . . dipped [in the water for him] like . . .
To . . . , the courtyard . . . . . .
in the Grand Court, without a fight, ...   Nedg c

At that time she [cast her] glance on the . . . ,
holy Inanna [cast her] glance on the . . . ,   Ma 20
from the palace of Abzu she cast her glance on the . . . :
'O wild bull, *you shall be* my man, I will not let you go,
O lord Bilgames, *you shall be* my man, I will not let you go,
in my temple Eanna I will not let you go to pass judgement,   A i 5'
in the holy Gipar I will not let you go to render verdicts,
in the god An's beloved Eanna I will not let you go to pass
      judgement!
O Bilgames, be you . . . , and I will be . . . !'
      The king [heard her] words,
      the king [spoke] to the mother who bore him,
      Bilgames [spoke to] the goddess Ninsun: Ma 30
      'O mother who bore me, like . . . . . .
      at the door of the city gate . . . . . .
      by the base of the city wall . . . . . .
      "O wild bull, my man, . . . I will not let you go,
      Bilgames, . . . I will not let you go,   Ma 35
      in my temple Eanna I will not let you go to pass judgement.
      in the holy Gipar I will not let you go to render verdicts,
      in the god An's beloved Eanna I will not let you go to pass
          judgement!
      O Bilgames, may you be . . . , and I will be . . . !"'
      After he had spoken like this to the mother who bore
        him,   Ma 40
      the mother who [bore him replied to Bilgames:]
'The gifts of Inanna must not enter your chamber,
the divine Palace Lady must not *weaken* (your) warrior's
      arm!'   A i 10'

Bilgames speaks to Inanna:

'O lady Inanna, you must not block my path!
Let me *catch* wild bulls in the mountains, let me fill your folds!
Let me *catch* sheep in the mountains, let me fill your pens!
Let me fill . . . with silver and carnelian!'
The queen spoke with a snort,   A i 15′
Inanna spoke with a snort . . .

Lacuna. When the text resumes, Inanna is in heaven requesting the Bull of Heaven
from her father, An:

Inanna was weeping, [she was *crying*.]
An to the one he loved . . . . . . ,
sitting there in the chamber, *An* [*spoke to her*:]
'O my child, why are you weeping, why are you *crying*?'
'It is the great bull on the rampage in Uruk,   A ii 10′
the great bull Bilgames on the rampage in Uruk!
Because *he would* not *let me* give my own self to him,
I am weeping, I am *crying*!
O my father, please give me the Bull of Heaven!
Let me kill the lord, let me kill the lord,   A ii 15′
the lord Bilgames, let me kill the lord!'
Great An answered holy Inanna:
'O my child, the Bull of Heaven would have no food, at the horizon
          is its food!
O maiden Inanna, it grazes where the sun rises!
I shall not give you the Bull of Heaven.'   A ii 20′
Holy Inanna answered him:
'Then I shall scream until sky draws nigh earth!'
It was terrifying, it was terrifying,
          [the scream of] Inanna was terrifying.   Np 15′
          [The maiden Inanna's] scream drew nigh heaven, the scream
                    drew nigh earth,
          [holy Inanna's] scream drew nigh heaven, the scream drew
                    nigh earth,
          [Heaven and earth] it covered like a [blanket], draped like a
                    cloth.
          Who was there could speak to [holy Inanna]?   Nk obv. 5′
Great An answered holy Inanna,   A ii 24′
he gave her the Bull of Heaven.   A iii 25′

Like an *ox*-driver the maiden Inanna took hold of the tether,
holy Inanna brought the Bull of Heaven down from the sky.
In Uruk the bull devoured the grass,
in the Engilua canal it drank the water,
one league it reached along the Engilua canal, its heart was not
              sated.   A iii 30′
It devoured the grass, it laid the earth bare,
it devoured the date-palms of Uruk, bending them to its mouth.
The bull, as it stood there, it filled (all of) Uruk,
the bull, on its own, it filled (all of) Kullab.

His minstrel, [Lugalgabangal] . . .   A iii 35′
as it lifted its eye . . . . . .
as it bent down . . .

Lacuna. The order of the next twenty lines is uncertain, but the text may probably
be reconstructed as given here:

               . . . he approached,   Ma 3′
      . . . [on the Bull of Heaven] he raised his glance.   Ni iii 2′
   [Lugalgabangal the minstrel,] he [came] into [the presence of
          Bilgames:]
   '[O lord,] you are drinking, O lord, [you are drinking,]
O lord Bilgames, you are drinking, [O lord, you are
              drinking!]   Nj iii 2′
Inanna [has brought] the Bull of Heaven [down from the
              sky.]   A iii 40′
In Uruk the bull [devours] the grass,
in the Engilua canal [it drinks] the water,   Nj iii 5′
one league [it reached] along the Engilua canal, [its heart was not
              sated.]
It devours the grass, it lays the earth [bare,]
it devours the date-palms of Uruk, [bending them] to its mouth.
The bull, as it stands there, it fills (all of) Uruk,
the bull, on its own, it fills (all of) Kullab.'   Nj iii 10′
Bilgames [answered] Lugalgabangal his minstrel:
'O my minstrel, sing your song, strum your strings!   Ma 86
I will drink beer, refill the tankard!'
The minstrel Lugalgabangal [answered] his master Bilgames:

'O my lord, may you eat, [may you] drink,
>   as for that matter is it not your concern?'   Nk rev. 5'
>   [Bilgames] answered his minstrel Lugalgabangal:
'Me! Why should that matter [frighten me?]'   Ma 90

To smite the bull [he took up his weapons,]
to smite the bull Bilgames [took up his weapons:]
with a *kilt* weighing fifty minas [he girt his loins,]
a dagger of seven talents and a half [he hung at his side,]
[his bronze] axe [for expeditions, he took up in his hand.]   Ma 95
His mother who bore him(!) . . . . . .
his sister . . . .
His mother [Ninsun] who bore him . . . . . .
[his] sister, Peshtur, ...
Bilgames . . . . . . [*spoke to them*:]   Ma 100
'O mother who bore me, [*go into*] the temple of Enki!
O little sister Peshtur, [*go into*] his temple . . .
at that . . . . . . [slaughter] oxen,
at that . . . . . . slaughter sheep,
>   at that . . . may . . . pour beer!'   Nn 7'
>   [Ninsun, the mother who bore him,] answered Bilgames:
'The Bull of Heaven and you, you . . . . . .   Ma 105
both you . . . .
and I . . . . '
>   Bilgames answered [Ninsun, the mother who bore
>   him:]   Nn 11'
'Forthwith *I shall smite* [the Bull of Heaven,]
may its corpse be [thrown down] in the narrow streets,
may its innards [be thrown down] in the broad streets,   Ma 110
may the orphans of [my city take shares] of its* meat [by] the
>   basket-load,
may its carcass [be handed over] to the tanner,
may Inanna in Eanna [pour sweet oil from] flasks made of its two
>   horns!'

Another version of the text has Bilgames speaking very similarly to the Bull of
Heaven itself:

*Emended text. The tablet reads 'your'.

'I will throw your corpse down in the narrow streets,
I will throw your innards down in the broad streets,
I will [hand over] your carcass to the tanner,
I will apportion your meat by the basket-load to the orphans of the
            city,
I will present your two horns to Inanna in Eanna to serve as flasks
            for sweet oil!'   A iv 10

Inanna looked on from the rampart,
the bull bellowed in the dust.
Bilgames . . . *its* head,   Ma 115
Enkidu *went up on its* . . .
The sons of his city who had come with him, like a calf untrained
            to the yoke it covered them with dust.
Enkidu went behind the bull, he seized its tail,
he shouted to his master Bilgames:
'Ho, hurrah! Tall-grown sapling,   Ma 120
noble one in whom the gods delight,
angry ox standing ready for combat,   A iv 20
O great lord Bilgames, honoured in Uruk,
well knew your mother how to make a child,
well knew your nurse how to suckle a baby!
        O noble lord Bilgames, ...   Nn 31'
have no fear, O warrior lacking strength (enough) *on his own*!
Where a sure path . . . . . .
O warrior, . . . your hand . . .
The people . . . .
the people . . . . '   Ma 125
Enkidu having spoken thus to Bilgames,
[Bilgames] with his axe of seven talents smote its crown.
Lifting its head aloft the bull collapsed from a height,
forming a shapeless mass like a lump of clay, lying flat like a
            harvested crop.
The king took a knife in his hand, no butcher being to hand,   Ma 130
he hacked off a haunch (to throw) at Inanna,
sent her flying off like a dove, and demolished the rampart.
The king stood at the head of the bull, he cried bitter tears:
'Just as I can demolish (the wall?), just so shall I do (with you?)!'
And it was just as he had said,

23 *'With his axe of seven talents he smote its crown'.*

its corpse he did throw down in the streets,	Ma 135

its corpse he did throw down in the streets,   Ma 135
its innards he did throw down in the broad streets,
its* meat he did apportion by the basket-load to the orphans of his*
    city,
its carcass he did hand over to the tanner,
from flasks made of its two horns Inanna in Eanna did pour sweet
    oil.
The Bull of Heaven being slain, O holy Inanna sweet is your
    praise!   Ma 140

Bilgames and the Netherworld:
'In those days, in those far-off days'

The poem known to the ancients as 'In those days, in those far-off
days' was also a favourite in the scribal schools of Old Babylonian
Nippur and Ur. Unlike the other Sumerian tales of Bilgames, this
composition begins with a mythological prologue: a long time ago,
shortly after the gods had divided the universe between them, there was
a huge storm. As the god Enki was sailing down to the Netherworld,

---

*Emended text. The tablet reads 'your'.

presumably to take up residence in his cosmic domain, the Ocean Below (*Abzu*), the hailstones piled up in the bottom of his boat and the waves churned around it. The storm blew down a willow tree on the bank of the river Euphrates. Out walking one day, the goddess Inanna picked up the willow and took it back to her house in Uruk, where she planted it and waited for it to grow. She looked forward to having furniture made from its timber. As the tree grew it was infested by creatures of evil and Inanna was sad. She told the whole story to the Sun God, her brother Utu, but he did not help her. Then she repeated the story to the hero Bilgames. Bilgames took up his weapons and rid the tree of its vile inhabitants. He felled the tree and gave Inanna the timber for the furniture she needed. With the remaining wood he made two playthings (there is no consensus among scholars as to what these playthings were: one possibility is that they were a ball and a mallet).

Bilgames and the young men of Uruk play with his new toys all day long. The men are worn out by their exertions and their women are kept busy bringing them food and water. The next day, as the game is about to restart, the woman complain, presumably to the gods (as in the Babylonian epic at Tablet I 73ff.), and the playthings fall through a hole deep into the Netherworld. Bilgames cannot reach them and weeps bitterly at his loss. His servant Enkidu volunteers to go and fetch them. Bilgames warns him about going to the Netherworld, the gloomy realm of the goddess Ereshkigal. If Enkidu is to avoid fatal consequences in the presence of the shades of the dead he must show the proper respect for them. He should behave as if at a funeral, acting with sensitivity and not drawing attention to himself. There in the Netherworld he will come upon the awful spectacle of Ereshkigal herself, who lies prostrate in perpetual mourning for her son Ninazu. The clothes torn from her body, she rakes her flesh with her nails and pulls out her hair.

Enkidu goes down to the Netherworld and blithely ignores Bilgames's warnings. He is duly taken captive there. Bilgames petitions the god Enlil in Nippur to help him but Enlil will not. He then petitions the god Enki in Eridu to help him. Enki instructs the Sun God, Utu, to bring up Enkidu's shade as he rises from the Netherworld at dawn. Temporarily reunited, Bilgames and Enkidu embrace. In a long session of question and answer that marks the climax of the poem Bilgames asks Enkidu about conditions in the Netherworld. The tone of brutal pessimism that informs this part of the text is relieved by a certain humour and sentimentality, and made topical, in one recension at least, by historical allusion. The principal message of the beginning of the heroes' dialogue is that the more sons a man has, the more his thirst in the afterlife will be relieved by the vital offerings of fresh water made periodically by his family. Those shades who are childless suffer worst, for nobody exists above on earth to make the necessary offerings to them.

The dialogue then turns to consider those who have it in common that they cannot be buried whole, either because they have been disfigured by leprosy or other diseases or because they have met violent ends. The revulsion of dying without a full complement of body parts persists in the Near East today. One recension perhaps adopts a moral tone, dealing also with those who have dishonoured their parents. Like these, most shades are in for a grim experience in the afterlife but, besides the fathers of many sons, there are others who suffer less. Those who are taken before their time, such as stillborn children, are compensated by an afterlife spent in luxury. However, those who are burnt to death disappear in smoke and do not go down to the Netherworld. An implication of this was that the ghosts of such people could not be appeased and thus they were feared most of all revenant spirits. Burning to death was hence the worst fate of all and a fittingly horrifying climax to Enkidu's report. The horror of death by burning endures to this day in Islam.

In one tradition of copying the text ends at this point, but tablets from the city of Ur provide a continuation which gives a more explicit lesson in how to care for the dead. The historical allusions it contains suggest that this continuation was probably a later addition which originated in the city-state of Girsu. Enkidu reports that the shades of the 'sons of Sumer and Akkad', and particularly of Girsu, have been overrun by Amorite tribesmen, who keep them away from the places in the Netherworld where the libations of fresh water are received from the world above and force them to make do with foul, polluted water. The passage clearly alludes to the situation that obtained in Sumer in the late third millennium BC, when the state ruled by the Third Dynasty of Ur collapsed under the pressure of Amorite incursions and Elamite invasion, and the settled people of the cities of lower Mesopotamia suddenly found themselves governed by Amorite dynasts of nomadic descent. Those who had possessed political and economic clout under the kings of Ur no doubt much resented the loss of it to newcomers. When Bilgames discovers that his own forebears in the Netherworld have suffered the same fate as the other 'sons of Sumer and Akkad' he is shamed into filial piety: in the poem's conclusion he is prompted to fashion statues of his ancestors, to institute mourning rites for them and to instruct the people of Girsu in the same rites. By this means the dead are appeased and do not threaten the living. One message of this meditation on a man's expectations in the afterlife was thus the encouragement of pious behaviour towards the dead and the prescription of the proper ritual. Bilgames's special association with such ritual is confirmed by early administrative documents which mention the 'Bank of Bilgames' as a place where the rulers of Girsu did indeed make offerings to the shades of their relatives.

A version of the second half of the text, from line 172 onwards, was rendered into Akkadian in antiquity and makes up Tablet XII of the Babylonian 'Series of Gilgamesh'. In that version Bilgames petitions the Moon God, as well as Enlil and Ea (Enki), for help in rescuing Enkidu. A translation of the Akkadian text follows the Sumerian poem.

This poem has been comprehensively edited by Aaron Shaffer, 'Sumerian Sources of Tablet XII of the Epic of Gilgameš', Ph.D. dissertation, University of Pennsylvania, 1963 (Ann Arbor: University Microfilms, 1963). Additional material is given by Claus Wilcke, *Kollationen zu den sumerischen literarischen Texten aus Nippur in der Hilprecht-Sammlung Jena* (Berlin: Akademie-Verlag, 1976), pp. 19–21; Antoine Cavigneaux and Farouk Al-Rawi, 'New Sumerian literary texts from Tell Haddad (ancient Meturan): a first survey', *Iraq* 55 (London: British School of Archaeology in Iraq, 1993), pp. 91–105; idem, 'Le Fin de Gilgameš, Enkidu et les enfers d'après deux manuscrits de Meturan' (unpublished paper); and Raymond Jacques Tournay and Aaron Shaffer, *L'Épopée de Gilgamesh* (Paris: Éditions du Cerf, 1994), pp. 270–74.

In those days, in those far-off days,
in those nights, in those distant nights,
in those years, in those far-off years,
in olden times, after what was needed had become manifest,
in olden times, after what was needed had been taken care of,   5
after bread had been swallowed in the sanctuaries of the land,

after the ovens of the land had been fired up with bellows,
after heaven had been parted from earth,
after earth had been separated from heaven,
after the name of mankind had been established –   10
then, after the god An had taken the heavens for himself,
after the god Enlil had taken the earth for himself,
and after he had presented the Netherworld to the goddess
      Ereshkigal as a dowry-gift,
after he had set sail, after he had set sail,
after the father had set sail for the Netherworld,   15
after the god Enki had set sail for the Netherworld,
on the lord the small ones poured down,
on Enki the big ones poured down –
the small ones were hailstones the size of a hand,
the big ones were hailstones that *made the reeds jump* –   20
into the lap of Enki's boat
they poured in a heap like a surging turtle.
At the lord the water at the front of the boat
snapped all around like a wolf,
at Enki the water at the back of the boat   25
flailed like a murderous lion.

At that time there was a solitary tree, a solitary willow, a solitary
      tree,
growing on the bank of the holy Euphrates,
drinking water from the river Euphrates.
The might of the south wind tore it out at the roots and snapped
      off its branches,   30
the water of the Euphrates washed over it.
The woman who respects the word of An,
who respects the word of Enlil,
picked up the tree in her hand and took it into Uruk,
took it into the pure garden of Inanna.   35
The woman did not plant the tree with her hand, she planted it
      with her foot,
the woman did not water the tree with her hand, she watered it
      with her foot.
She said, 'How long until I sit on a pure throne?'
She said, 'How long until I lie on a pure bed?'

After five years [had gone by, after ten years had gone by,]   40
the tree had grown stout, its bark had not split,
in its base a Snake-that-Knows-no-Charm had made its nest,
in its branches a Thunderbird had hatched its brood,
in its trunk a Demon-Maiden had built her home.
The maiden who laughs with happy heart,   45
holy Inanna was weeping.
Day was dawning, the horizon brightening,
birds were singing in chorus to the dawn,
as the Sun God came forth from his chamber,
and his sister, the holy Inanna,   50
spoke to Young Hero Utu:
'O brother, in those days, after destinies were determined,
when the land flowed with abundance,
when An had made off with the heavens,
Enlil had made off with the earth,   55
and he had given the Netherworld to Ereshkigal as a dowry-gift,
after he had set sail, after he had set sail,
after the father had set sail for the Netherworld,
after Enki had set sail for the Netherworld,
on the lord the small ones poured down,   60
on Enki the big ones poured down –
the small ones were hailstones the size of a hand,
the big ones [were] hailstones that *made the reeds jump* –
into the lap [of] Enki's boat
they [poured in a heap] like a surging turtle.   65
At the lord the water at the front [of] the boat
snapped all around like a wolf,
at Enki the water at the back [of] the boat
flailed like a murderous lion.

'At that time there was a solitary tree, a solitary willow, a solitary
        tree,   70
growing on the bank of the holy Euphrates,
drinking water from the river Euphrates.
The might of the south wind tore it out at the roots and snapped
        off its branches,
the water of the Euphrates washed over it.
I, the woman who respects the word of An,   75

I who respect the word of Enlil,
I picked up the tree in my hand and took it into Uruk,
took it into the pure garden of Inanna.
I, the woman, did not plant the tree with my hand, I planted it with
 my foot,
I, Inanna, did not water the tree with my hand, I watered it with
 my foot.   80
I said, "How long until I sit on a pure throne?"
I said, "How long until I lie on a pure bed?"

'After five years had gone by, after ten years had gone by,
the tree had grown stout, its [bark] had not split,
[in] its base [a Snake]-that-Knows-no-[Charm] had made its nest, 85
in its branches a Thunderbird had hatched its brood,
in its trunk a Demon-Maiden had built her home.'
The maiden who laughs with happy heart,
holy Inanna was weeping.
Her brother, Young Hero Utu, did not help her in this matter.   90

Day was dawning, the horizon brightening,
birds were singing in chorus to the dawn,
as the Sun God came forth from his chamber,
and his sister, the holy Inanna,
spoke to the warrior Bilgames: 95
'O brother, in those days, [after] destinies were determined,
when the land flowed [with abundance,]
[when An] had made off with [the heavens,]
[Enlil had] made off with [the earth,]
and he had given the Netherworld [to Ereshkigal] as a dowry-
 gift,   100
after he had set sail, after he had set sail,
after the father had set sail for the Netherworld,
after Enki had set sail for the Netherworld,
on the lord the small ones poured down,
on Enki the big ones poured down –   105
the small ones were hailstones the size of a hand,
the big ones were hailstones that *made the reeds jump* –
into the lap of Enki's boat
they poured in a heap like a surging turtle.

At the lord the water at the front of the boat   110
snapped all around like a wolf,
at Enki the water at the back of the boat
flailed like a murderous lion.

'At that time there was a solitary tree, a solitary willow, a solitary
    tree,
growing on the bank of the holy Euphrates,   115
drinking water from the river Euphrates.
The might of the south wind tore it out at the roots and snapped
    off its branches,
the water of the Euphrates washed over it.
I, the woman who respects the word of An,
I who respect the word of Enlil,   120
I picked up the tree in my hand and took it into Uruk,
took it into the pure garden of Inanna.
I, the woman, did not plant the tree with my hand, I planted it with
    my foot,
I, Inanna, did not water the tree with my hand, I watered it with
    my foot.
I said: "How long until I sit on a pure throne?"   125
I said: "How long until I lie on a pure bed?"

'After five years had gone by, after ten years had gone by,
the tree had grown stout, its bark had not split,
in its base a Snake-that-Knows-no-Charm had made its nest,
in its branches a Thunderbird had hatched its brood,   130
in its trunk a Demon-Maiden had built her home.'
The maiden who laughs with happy heart,
holy Inanna was weeping.
His sister having spoken thus to him,
her brother Bilgames helped her in this matter.   135

He girt his loins with a *kilt* of fifty minas,
treating fifty minas like thirty shekels.
His bronze axe for expeditions,
the one of seven talents and seven minas, he took up in his hand.
In its base the Snake-that-Knows-no-Charm he smote,   140

in its branches the Thunderbird gathered up its brood and went
      into the mountains,
in its trunk the Demon-Maiden abandoned her home,
and fled to the wastelands.
As for the tree, he tore it out at the roots and snapped off its
      branches.
The sons of his city who had come with him   145
lopped off its branches, lashed them together.
To his sister, holy Inanna, he gave wood for her throne,
he gave wood for her bed.
For himself its base he made into his *ball*,
its branch he made into his *mallet*.   150
Playing with the *ball* he took it out in the city square,
playing with the . . . he took it out in the city square.
The young men of his city began playing with the *ball*,
with him mounted piggy-back on a band of widows' sons.
'O my neck! O my hips!' they groaned.   155
The son who had a mother, she brought him bread,
the brother who had a sister, she poured him water.
When evening was approaching
he drew a mark where his *ball* had been placed,
he lifted it up before him and carried it off to his house.   160
At dawn, where he had made the mark, *he* mounted piggy-back,
but at the complaint of the widows
and the outcry of the young girls,
his *ball* and his *mallet* both fell down to the bottom of the
      Netherworld.
      With . . . he could not reach it,
he used his hand, but he could not reach it,   165
he used his foot, but he could not reach it.
At the Gate of Ganzir, the entrance to the Netherworld, he took a
      seat,
racked with sobs Bilgames began to weep:
'O my *ball*! O my *mallet*!
O my *ball*, which I have not enjoyed to the full!   170
O my . . . , with which I have not had my fill of play!
On this day, if only my *ball* had stayed for me in the carpenter's
      workshop!
O carpenter's wife, like a mother to me! If only it had stayed there!

O carpenter's daughter, like a little sister to me! If only it had
        stayed there!
My *ball* has fallen down to the Netherworld, who will bring it up
        for me?   175
My *mallet* has fallen down to Ganzir, who will bring it up for me?'
His servant Enkidu answered him:
'My lord, why are you weeping? Why are you sick at heart?
This day I myself will bring your *ball* up for you from the
        Netherworld,
I myself will [bring] your *mallet* up for you from Ganzir!'   180

Bilgames spoke to Enkidu:
'If this day you are going down to the Netherworld,
I will give you instructions, you should follow my instructions!
I will tell you a word, give ear to my word!
Do not dress in a clean garment,   185
they would surely take it as the sign of a stranger!
Do not anoint yourself in sweet oil from the flask,
at the scent of it they will surely surround you!
Do not hurl a throwstick in the Netherworld,
those struck by the throwstick will surely surround you!   190
Do not hold a cornel rod in your hand,
the shades will tremble before you!
Do not wear sandals on your feet,
it will surely make the Netherworld shake!
Do not kiss the wife you loved,   195
do not strike the wife you hated,
do not kiss the son you loved,
do not strike the son you hated,
the outcry of the Netherworld will seize you!
To the one who lies, the one who lies,   200
to the Mother of Ninazu who lies –
no garment covers her shining shoulders,
no linen is spread over her shining breast,
      her fingernails she wields like a *rake*,
      she wrenches [her hair] out like leeks.'   205

Enkidu paid no attention to the [word] of his master:
he dressed in a clean garment,

they took it as the sign of a stranger.
He anointed himself in sweet oil from the flask,
at the scent of it they surrounded him.   210
He hurled a throwstick in the Netherworld,
those struck by the throwstick surrounded him.
He held a cornel rod in his hand,
the shades did tremble before him.
He wore sandals on his feet,   215
it made the Netherworld shake.
He kissed the wife he loved,
he struck the wife he hated,
he kissed the son he loved,
he struck the son he hated,   220
the outcry of the Netherworld seized him.
　　　　　[To the one who lies, the one who lies,]   (XII)
　　　　　[to the Mother of Ninazu who lies −]
　　　　　[no garment covered her shining shoulders,]
　　　　　[no linen was spread over her shining breast,]
　　　　　[her fingernails she wielded like a *rake*,]
　　　　　[she was wrenching her hair out like leeks.]

From that wicked day to the seventh day thence,   Mt₁ 10
from the Netherworld his servant Enkidu came not forth.
The king uttered a wail and wept bitter tears:
'My favourite servant, [my] steadfast companion, the one
　　　who counselled me − the Netherworld [seized him!]
Namtar did not seize him, Azag did not seize him, the
　　　Netherworld [seized him!]
Nergal's *pitiless* sheriff did not seize him, the Netherworld
　　　seized him!   Mt₁ 15
He did not fall in battle, the field of *men*, the Netherworld
　　　seized him!'

24 *'He did not fall in battle, the field of men'*.

The warrior Bilgames, son of the goddess Ninsun,
made his way alone to Ekur, the house of Enlil,
before the god Enlil he [wept:]
'[O Father] Enlil, my *ball* fell into the Netherworld, my *mallet* fell
      into Ganzir,   225
Enkidu went to bring it up and the Netherworld [seized him!]
     My favourite [servant,] my steadfast companion, the one
       who counselled me – [the Netherworld] seized
       him!   Mt₁ 22
[Namtar did not] seize him, Azag did not seize him, the
      Netherworld seized him!
Nergal's *pitiless* sheriff did not seize him, the Netherworld seized
      him!
He did not fall in battle, the field of men, the Netherworld seized
      him!'
Father Enlil did not help him in this matter. [He went to Ur.]   230

    [He made his way alone to Ur, the house of Nanna,]   (XII)
    [before the god Nanna he wept:]
    ['O Father Nanna, my *ball* fell into the Netherworld, my
      mallet fell into Ganzir,]
    [Enkidu went to bring it up and the Netherworld seized
      him!]
    [Namtar did not seize him, Azag did not seize him, the
      Netherworld seized him!]
    [Nergal's *pitiless* sheriff did not seize him, the Netherworld
      seized him!]
    [He did not fall in battle, the field of men, the Netherworld
      seized him!']
    [Father Nanna did not help him in this matter.] He went to
      Eridu.

He made his way alone to Eridu, the house of Enki,
before the god Enki he wept:
'O Father Enki, my *ball* fell into the Netherworld, my *mallet* fell
      into Ganzir,
Enkidu went to bring it up and the Netherworld seized him!
    [My favourite servant, my steadfast companion, the one
      who counselled me – the Netherworld seized him!]   [Mt]

Namtar did not seize him, Azag did not seize him, the Netherworld
        seized him!   235
Nergal's *pitiless* sheriff did not seize him, the Netherworld seized
        him!
He did not fall in battle, the field of men, the Netherworld seized
        him!'
Father Enki helped him in this matter,
he spoke to Young Hero Utu, the son born of Ningal:
'Now, when (as the Sun God) you make an opening in the
        Netherworld,   240
bring his servant up to him from the Netherworld!'
He made an opening in the Netherworld,
by means of his phantom he brought his servant up to him from the
        Netherworld.

He hugged him tight and kissed him,
in asking and answering they made themselves weary: 245
'Did you see the way things are ordered in the Netherworld?
If only you could tell me, my friend, if only [you could tell] me!'
'If I am to [tell] you the way things are ordered in the Netherworld,
O sit you down and weep!' 'Then let me sit down and weep!'
'[The *one*] whom you touched with joy in your heart,   250
he says, "I am going to [*ruin*.]"
Like an [old garment] he is infested with lice,
like a crack [in the floor] he is filled with dust.'
'Ah, woe!' cried the lord, and he sat down in the dust.

'Did you see the man with one son?' 'I saw him.' 'How does he
        fare?'   255
'For the peg built into his wall bitterly he laments.'
'Did you see the man with two sons?' 'I saw him.' 'How does he
        fare?'
'Seated on two bricks he eats a bread-loaf.'
'Did you see the man with three sons?' 'I saw him.' 'How does he
        fare?'
'He drinks water from the waterskin slung on the saddle.'   260
'Did you see the man with four sons?' 'I saw him.' 'How does he
        fare?'
'Like a man with a team of four donkeys his heart rejoices.'

'Did you see the man with five sons?' 'I saw him.' 'How does he
         fare?'
'Like a fine scribe with a *nimble* hand he enters the palace with
         ease.'
'Did you see the man with six sons?' 'I saw him.' 'How does he
         fare?'   265
'Like a man with ploughs in harness his heart rejoices.'
'Did you see the man with seven sons?' 'I saw him.' 'How does he
         fare?'
'Among the junior deities he sits on a throne and listens to the
         proceedings.'
'Did you see the man with no heir?' 'I saw him.' '[How does] he
         fare?'
'He eats a bread-loaf like a *kiln-fired* brick.'   270
'Did you see the palace *eunuch*?' 'I saw him.' 'How does he fare?'
'Like a useless *alala*-stick he is propped in a corner.'
'Did you see the woman who had not given birth?' 'I saw her.'
         'How does she fare?'
'Like a *defective* pot she is cast aside, no man takes pleasure in her.'
'Did you see the young man who had not bared the lap of his wife?'
         'I saw him.' 'How does he fare?'   275
'You have him finish a hand-worked rope, he weeps over it.'
'Did you see the young woman who had not bared the lap of her
         husband?' 'I saw her.' 'How does she fare?'
'You have her finish a hand-worked reed mat, she weeps over it.' 278

                    *   *   *

'Did you see the leper?' 'I saw him.' 'How does he fare?'   287
'His food is set apart, his drink is set apart, he eats uprooted grass,
         he roots for water (in the ground), he lives outside the
         city.'
'Did you see the man afflicted by *pellagra*?' 'I saw him.' 'How does
         he fare?'
'He twitches like an ox as the maggots consume him.'   290
         'Did you see the man eaten by a lion?' 'I saw him.' 'How
               does he fare?'   V
         'Bitterly he cries, "O my hand! O my foot!"'
         'Did you see the person who fell from a roof?' 'I saw him.'
               'How does he fare?'

'They cannot repair his bones.

He twitches like an ox as the maggots consume him.'

'Did you see the man whom the Storm God [drowned] in a
        flood?' 'I saw him.' 'How does he fare?'

'He twitches like an ox as the maggots consume him.'

'Did you see the man who did not respect the word of his
        mother and father?' 'I saw him.' 'How does he fare?'

'He drinks water *weighed out* in a scale, he never gets
        enough.'

'Did you see the man accursed by his mother and father?' 'I
        saw him.' 'How does he fare?'

'He is deprived of an heir, his ghost still roams.'

'Did [you see] the man fallen in battle?' ['I saw him.' 'How does he
        fare?']

'His father* and mother cradle his head, his wife weeps.'

'Did you see the shade of him who has no one to make funerary
        offerings?' 'I saw him.' 'How does he fare?'

'He eats scrapings from the pot and crusts of bread thrown away in
        the street.'

'Did you see the man struck by a mooring-pole?' ['I saw him.']
        'How does he fare?'   295

'Let a man only say, "O my mother!", and with *rib* torn-out . . .

The top part . . . his daily bread.'

'Did you see the little stillborn babies, who knew not names of their
        own?' 'I saw them.' 'How do they fare?'

'They play amid syrup and ghee at tables of silver and gold.'

'Did you see the man who died [*a premature*] death?' 'I saw him.'
        'How does he fare?'   300

'He lies on the bed of the gods.'

'Did you see the man who was burnt to death?' 'I did not see him.

His ghost was not there, his smoke went up to the heavens.'

The version of the poem known at Nippur ends abruptly here. A second version,
known from the provincial centre of Mê-Turan, adds three lines that link the
text with the beginning of the poem of Bilgames and Huwawa:

---

*Emended text.

The heart was stricken, his mind despaired.
The king searched for life,
the lord to the Living One's Mountain did turn [his] mind.

A third recension, known from tablets from Ur, continues the dialogue:

> 'Did you see the one who cheated a god and swore an oath?'
>   'I saw him.' 'How does he fare?'   UET VI 58
> 'He cannot get near the places in the Netherworld where the
>   libations of water are made, he drinks in thirst.'
> 'Did you see the citizen of Girsu *at the place of sighs* of his
>   father and mother?' 'I saw him.' 'How does he
>   fare?'   rev. 9–10
> 'Facing each man there are a thousand Amorites, his shade
>   cannot push them off with his hands, he cannot charge
>   them down with his chest.
> At the places in the Netherworld where the libations of
>   water are made, the Amorite takes *precedence*.'
> 'Did you see the sons of Sumer and Akkad?' 'I saw them.'
>   'How do they fare?'
> 'They drink water from the place of a massacre, dirty
>   water.'
> 'Did you see where my father and mother dwell?' 'I saw
>   them.' '[How do they fare?]'   rev. 15
> '[The two] of them drink water from the place of a
>   massacre, [dirty water.]'

*   *   *

> He sent them back to [Uruk,]   UET VI 60
> he sent them back to his city.
> Gear and equipment, hatchet and spear he put [away] in the
>   *store*,
> he made merry in his palace.
> The young men and women of Uruk, the worthies and
>   matrons of Kullab,   rev. 5
> looked upon those statues and their hearts rejoiced.
> He lifted his head to the Sun God coming forth from his
>   chamber,
> he issued instructions:

'O my father and my mother, I will have you drink clear
    water!'
The day was not half gone, . . .   rev. 10
Bilgames performed the mourning rites.
For nine days he performed the mourning rites,
the young men and women of Uruk, the worthies and
    matrons of Kullab wept.
And it was just as he had said,
the citizens of Girsu *matched his actions*:   rev. 15
'O my father and my mother, I will have you drink clear
    water!'
O warrior Bilgames, son of the goddess Ninsun, sweet is
    your praise!

Tablet XII of the Babylonian epic preserves a slightly different version of ll. 172–301 in an Akkadian translation:

'Today, had I only left my *ball* in the carpenter's workshop!
[O carpenter's wife who is like a mother] to me! Had I only [left it!]
O [carpenter's daughter who is like a] little sister [to me!] Had [I
    only left it!]
Today [my] *ball* fell down to the Netherworld,
my *mallet* fell [down] to the Netherworld!'   XII 5
Enkidu [answered] Gilgamesh:
'O master, why did you weep [sick] at heart?
Today I myself shall [bring you] the *ball* up from the Netherworld,
I myself shall [bring you] the *mallet* up from the Netherworld!'

Gilgamesh [answered] Enkidu: XII 10
'If [you are going down] to the Netherworld,
[you must pay heed to] my instructions!
[You must not dress in] a clean garment,
[you] will be revealed as a stranger!
You must not anoint yourself in sweet oil from the flask,   XII 15
at the scent of it they will gather around you!
You must not hurl a throwstick in the Netherworld,
those struck by the throwstick will surround you!
You must not carry a staff in your hand,
the shades will tremble before you!   XII 20

You must not wear sandals on your feet,
you must not make a noise in the Netherworld!
You must not kiss the wife you loved,
you must not strike the wife you hated,
you must not kiss the son you loved,   XII 25
you must not strike the son you hated,
the outcry of the Netherworld will seize you!
The one who lies, the one who lies, the Mother of Ninazu who
          lies,
her gleaming shoulders are not draped in a garment,
her breasts are bare like flasks of stone.'   XII 30

[As Enkidu] went down [to the Netherworld,]
he paid no heed [to the instructions of Gilgamesh:]
he dressed himself in [a clean garment,]
[he] was revealed [to be a] stranger.
He anointed himself in sweet oil from the flask,   XII 35
at the scent [of it] they gathered around him.
He hurled a throwstick in the [Netherworld,]
          [the shades] did tremble,
those [struck] by the throwstick surrounded him.
He carried a staff in [his] hand,
[the shades did] tremble.   XII 40
[He wore] sandals on [his feet,]
[he made] a noise [in the Netherworld.]
[He kissed] the wife [he loved,]
[he struck the] wife he hated,
he [kissed the] son he loved,   XII 45
he [struck the] son he hated,
the outcry of the Netherworld seized him.
The one who lies, [the one who] lies, the Mother of Ninazu who
          lies,
[her] gleaming shoulders were not draped in a garment,
her breasts were bare like flasks of stone.   XII 50
From the Netherworld Enkidu wailed [out] to the world above:
Namtar [had not] seized him, Asakku had not seized him, the
          Netherworld [had seized] him!
[Nergal's] pitiless sheriff had not seized him, the Netherworld [had
          seized] him!

He had not fallen where men do battle, the Netherworld had seized
    him!
Then the goddess Ninsun's son [went] weeping for his servant,
    Enkidu,   XII 55
he went off alone to Ekur, the house of Enlil:
'O Father [Enlil], today my *ball* fell into the Netherworld,
my *mallet* fell into the Netherworld!
Enkidu, who [went down] to bring [them up, the Netherworld
    seized him!]
Namtar did not seize him, Asakku did not seize him, the
    Netherworld seized him!   XII 60
Nergal's pitiless sheriff did not seize him, the Netherworld seized
    him!
He did not fall where men do [battle], the Netherworld seized him!'
Father Enlil answered him not a word.

He went off [alone to Ur, the house of Sîn:]
'O Father Sîn, today my *ball* fell into the Netherworld,   XII 65
my *mallet* fell [into the Netherworld!]
Enkidu, who [went] down to bring [them up], the Netherworld
    seized him!
Namtar did not seize him, Asakku did not seize him, the
    Netherworld seized him!
Nergal's pitiless sheriff [did not seize] him, the Netherworld seized
    him!
He did not fall where [men do battle], the Netherworld seized
    him!'   XII 70
Father [Sîn answered him not a word.]

[He went off alone] to [Eridu, the house of Enki:]
'O [Father Enki, today my *ball* fell into the Netherworld,]
my *mallet* [fell into the Netherworld,]
Enkidu, [who went down to bring them up, the Netherworld seized
    him!]   XII 75
Namtar did not [seize him, Asakku did not seize him, the
    Netherworld seized him!]
Nergal's pitiless sheriff [did not seize him, the Netherworld seized
    him!]

[He did not fall] where men do battle, [the Netherworld seized
      him!]'
Father Enki [helped him] in [this matter,]
[he spoke] to Young Hero [Shamash:]   XII 80
'O Young Hero Shamash, [*as you rise into the sky*,]
be it [that you make] an opening [in the Netherworld,]
[that you bring up] the shade of Enkidu [from the Netherworld as a
      phantom!]'
To [his] word . . . .
the Young Hero Shamash . . . . . .   XII 85
He made an opening in the Netherworld,
he brought up the shade of Enkidu from the Netherworld as a
      phantom.
They hugged each other and they kissed each other,
exchanging their thoughts and questions:
'O tell me, my friend! Tell me, my friend!   XII 90
Tell me what you saw of the ways of the Netherworld!'
'I cannot tell you, my friend, I cannot tell you!
If I tell you what I saw of the ways of the Netherworld,
O sit you down and weep!'
'Then I will sit me down and weep!'   XII 95
'[I, the] *friend* whom you touched so your heart rejoiced,
[*my body* like an] old *garment* the lice devour.
[Enkidu, the *friend* whom you] touched so your heart rejoiced,
[like a crack in the ground] is filled with dust.'
['Ah woe!'] cried he, and threw himself [on the] ground,   XII 100
['Ah woe!'] cried [Gilgamesh], and threw himself [on the ground.]

'Did [you see the man with one son?]' 'I saw him.
[A peg is] fixed [in his wall] and he weeps over [it bitterly.]'
'[Did you see the man with two sons?' 'I] saw him.
[Seated on two bricks] he eats a bread-loaf.'   XII 105
'[Did you see the man with three sons?]' 'I saw him.
He drinks water [from the waterskin slung on the saddle.]'
'Did [you see the man with four sons?]' 'I saw him.
[Like a man with a donkey]-team his heart rejoices.'
'Did you see [the man with five sons?]' 'I saw him.   XII 110
[Like a] fine [scribe] his hand is *nimble*,
he enters the palace [with ease.]'

'Did you see [the man with six sons?]' 'I saw him.
[Like a ploughman his heart rejoices.]'
'[Did you see the man with seven sons?' 'I saw him.]   XII 115
[Among the junior deities he sits on a throne and listens to the
    proceedings.']
['Did you see the one with no heir?' 'I saw him.]
He eats a bread-loaf like a *kiln-fired* brick.']
['Did you see the palace eunuch?' 'I saw him.]
Like a fine standard *he is propped in* the corner,
 like . . . . '   XII 119

           *   *   *

'Did you see the one who was struck by a mooring-pole?' 'I [saw
    him.]
Alas for his mother [and father!] When pegs are pulled out [he]
    wanders about.'   XII 145
'Did you see the one who [*died a*] *premature* death?' '[I saw him.]
He lies on a bed drinking clean water.'
'Did you see the one who was killed in battle?' 'I [saw him.]
His father and mother honour his memory and his wife [weeps]
    over [him.]'
'Did you see the one whose corpse was left lying on the plain?' 'I
    saw him.   XII 150
His shade is not at rest in the Netherworld.'
'Did you see the one whose shade has no one to make funerary
    offerings?' 'I saw him.
He eats scrapings from the pot and crusts of bread thrown away in
    the street.'

The Death of Bilgames:
'The great wild bull is lying down'

Thanks to the recent discovery at Mé-Turan (Tell Haddad) of several
new manuscripts this poem is now much better known than formerly,
but it is still very difficult in places. The remarks about the provisional
nature of the translation prefaced to 'Bilgames and the Bull of Heaven'
apply here too.

    The poem begins with a lament for the stricken Bilgames. He has been seized by Namtar, the emissary of Death, and lies sick and delirious on his death-bed. In his guise as Nudimmud the god Enki shows Bilgames a vision, in which he finds himself at a meeting of the gods' assembly. The business in hand is his own destiny. The gods review his heroic career, his exploits in the Forest of Cedar, his journey to the end of the world, and the ancient knowledge he learned from Ziusudra, the survivor of the Deluge. Their predicament is that Bilgames, though a man, is the son of a goddess: should he be mortal or immortal? The final judgement seems to be voiced by Enki, and this is appropriate, for it is this god's role to solve problems. The only mortal, he says, to achieve immortality is that self-same Ziusudra, but in special circumstances (as described in Tablet XI of the Babylonian epic). Despite his divine birth Bilgames must descend to the Netherworld like other men. But there he will have a special position as the chief of the shades, sitting in judgement over the dead like Ningishzida and Dumuzi, two divine residents of the Netherworld. Not only this, but after his death Bilgames will be commemorated among the living during an annual Festival of Lights, when young men will wrestle with each other (as Gilgamesh did with Enkidu in the Babylonian epic). Elsewhere this festival, in the fifth month of the Babylonian year (roughly August), is known for the ceremonial lighting of torches and braziers, and as 'the month of Gilgamesh: on the ninth day the young men fight in their doorways in wrestling matches and trials of strength'. Then Enlil appears, and explains in simpler terms the message of the dream thus far: Bilgames was born to be a king but he cannot escape the inevitable fate of mortal man. Even so, he is not to despair. In the Netherworld he will be reunited with his family and with his beloved Enkidu, and he will be numbered among the lesser deities.

Bilgames awakes, stunned by what he has seen. The text is damaged at this point but it seems that the hero seeks counsel. At all events, the poem launches into a wholesale repetition of the dream, and the simplest explanation of this is that Bilgames is retelling the dream to those whose advice he seeks regarding its import (even if this verbatim repetition fails to make the expected change from third person in the narrative to first in the reportage). The reply of Bilgames's interlocutors is that he should not be sad. Death is inevitable, even for a king, and he should be pleased with the exalted status that he will enjoy after death.

A break in the text intervenes at this point, after which, prompted by Enki, Bilgames sets to work on building his tomb. The break prevents us from knowing exactly how Enki communicated with Bilgames, but the agent was apparently a dog rather than a man. The message so conveyed evidently answered the question of where to site Bilgames's tomb so that it would be inviolable. As a result of Enki's wisdom Bilgames has his labour force divert the river Euphrates, and the tomb is built of stone in the river bed. The royal harem and entourage take their places in the tomb and prepare to accompany their king in the afterlife. This long-known passage famously evokes the mass interment of whole households discovered in the 1920s by Sir Leonard Woolley in the early third-millennium 'Royal Cemetery' at Ur. To ensure that he and his retinue receive a favourable reception in the Netherworld Bilgames presents gifts to the deities of Ereshkigal's court (just as he does on Enkidu's behalf in Tablet VIII of the Babylonian epic), and lays himself down. The doorway is sealed with the great stone fashioned for the purpose and the river is returned to its bed so that the site of the tomb cannot be discovered. The people of Uruk mourn for their king. Two different endings survive. One, less well preserved, simply voices the praise of Bilgames, the greatest of kings. The other, more didactic, explains that men past and present live on after death in the memories of those alive. First, the practice of placing votive statues in temples ensures the continued invocation of the name of the dead individual, providing as it does a focus for his funerary cult. Second, the gods have so arranged matters that men beget families, whose function is to continue their line.

The scholarly edition is by Antoine Cavigneaux and Farouk N. H. Al-Rawi, 'Gilgameš et la Mort. Textes de Tell Haddad VI' (Groningen: Styx Publications, in press 1997).

The great wild bull is lying down, never to rise again,
the lord Bilgames is lying down, never to rise again,
he who was perfect *in combat* is lying down, never to rise again,
the warrior girt with a shoulder-belt is lying down, never to rise
     again,
he who was perfect in strength is lying down, never to rise
     again,   M 5
he who diminished the wicked is lying down, never to rise again,

he who spoke wisdom is lying down, never to rise again,
the wakeful one of the land is lying down, never to rise again,
he who climbed the mountains is lying down, never to rise again,
the lord of Kullab is lying down, never to rise again,   M 10
he is lying on his death-bed, never to rise again,
he is lying on a bed of woe, never to rise again.
He is not capable of standing, he is not capable of sitting, he can
      only groan,
he is not capable of eating, he is not capable of drinking, he can
      only groan,
the lock of Namtar holds him fast, he is not capable of rising.   M 15
Like a . . . fish . . . in a pond, he is hoisted in a [*net*,]
like a gazelle caught in a snare, he is [*held fast*] where he lies.
Namtar, who has no hands, who has no feet, who [*snatches*] a man
      by night,
Namtar, who gores [. . . *has hold of the lord Bilgames* . . .]   M 19

        *   *   *

For six days [he lay] sick, ...
[the sweat rolled] from his body like (melting) fat.   N₂ obv. 5
The lord Bilgames [lay] sick, ...
Uruk and Kullab . . . . . .
the land's spoken word . . . . . .
Then the young lord [Bilgames] . . . . . .   M 45
[as he lay] on the bed of Namtar . . .   N₂ obv. 10
. . . in sleep . . . [*he had a dream.*]
In that dream, the god [Nudimmud opened his eyes: −]

In the assembly, the place of [the gods'] ceremonial,
[the lord] Bilgames [having] drawn [nigh,]   M 50
they said to him, the lord [Bilgames, on his account:]
'Your matter − having travelled each and every road,
having fetched that unique cedar down from its mountain,
having smitten Huwawa in his forest,
having set up monuments for future days,   M 55
having founded temples of the gods,
you reached Ziusudra in his abode!
The rites of Sumer, forgotten there since distant days of old,
the rituals and customs − *it was you* brought them down to the land.

The rites of hand-washing and mouth-washing you put in good
    order,   M 60
[*after* the] Deluge *it was you* made known all the *tasks* of the
    land . . .

      *   *   *

'[Now, Bilgames,] you are brought here for . . . '   M 66
[The will of Enlil to Enki] they *spoke*,
[to An and Enlil Enki] responded:
'[In those days,] in those far-off days,
[in those nights,] in those far-off nights,   M 70
[in those years,] in those far-off years,
after [the assembly] had made the Deluge sweep over,
so we could destroy the seed of mankind,
in our midst a single man still lived,
Ziusudra, one of mankind, still lived!   M 75
From that time we swore by the life of heaven and the life of earth,
from that time we swore that mankind should not have life eternal.
And now we look on Bilgames:
despite his mother we cannot show him mercy!
Bilgames, in the form of his ghost, dead in the underworld,   M 80
shall be the governor of the Netherworld, chief of the shades!
He will pass judgement, he will render verdicts,
what he says will be as weighty as the word of Ningishzida and
    Dumuzi.
Then the young lord, the lord Bilgames . . . '   M 84

The text of M falls into disorder, and breaks off after a few more lines. A slightly
different version of this passage (or, strictly, of its repetition at ll. 174ff.) appears
on tablets from Nippur and can be restored here:

'[The Dream God Sissig, son of Utu,]
[shall provide light for him in the Netherworld, the place of
    darkness.]
[Men, as many as are given names,]
[when their (funerary) statues are fashioned in future days,]
[the warrior-youths and the onlookers shall make a semicircle
    around a doorway,]

[and in front of it wrestling matches and trials of strength will be
     conducted.]
[In the Month of Torches, the festival of ghosts,]
[without him being present light will not be provided before them.]'

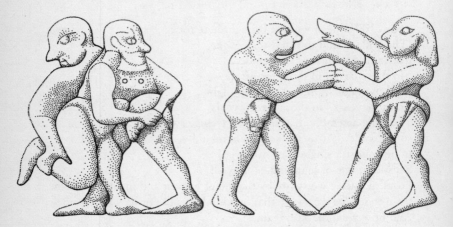

25 *'Wrestling matches and trials of strength will be conducted'*.

[Great Mountain Enlil, the father of the gods,]
[conversed in the dream with the lord Bilgames:]
['O Bilgames, I made your destiny a destiny of kingship, but I did
     not make it a destiny of eternal life.]
[For mankind, *whatever life it has*, be not sick at heart,]
[be not in despair, be not heart-stricken!]
[The bane of mankind is *thus come*, I have told you,]
[what (was fixed) when your navel-cord was cut is *thus come*, I
     have told you.]
[The darkest day of mortal man has caught up with you,]
[the solitary place of mortal man has caught up with you,]
[the flood-wave that cannot be breasted has caught up with you,]
[the battle that cannot be fled has caught up with you,]
[the combat that cannot be matched has caught up with you,]
[the fight that shows no pity has caught up with you!]
[But do not go down to the Great City with heart knotted (in
     anger),]
[let it be undone before Utu,]

[let it be unravelled like palm-fibre and peeled like an onion!]
Go ahead, [when the great] Anunna [gods sit down] to the funerary
        banquet,   M 103
to the place where the *en*-priests lie, where the [*lagar*-priests lie,]
to where the *lumah*-priests and *nindingir*-priestesses lie,   M 105
to where the *nindingir*-priestesses lie, where the 'true one' lies,
to where the *guda*-priests lie, where the linen-clad priests lie,
the place where your father is, and your grandfathers,
your mother, your sisters, your *siblings*,
your precious friend, your little brother,   M 110
your friend Enkidu, the young man your companion!
[(There) in the Great City, dwell] governors and kings,
there chiefs of armies [lie,]
[there captains of troops lie.]
[When in the Great City Aralli a man . . . ,]
[the man . . . . . . will not . . .]
[From the sister's house the sister will come to you,]
[from the *sibling's*] house [the *sibling* will come to you,]
your own [will come to you, your precious one will come to you,]
the elders of your city will come to you!
Be not in despair, be not heart-stricken,   M 120
for now you will number among the Anunna gods,
you will be accounted one of the lesser gods,
you will act as the governor of the Netherworld,
you will pass judgement, you will render verdicts,
what [you say] will be as weighty [as the word of Ningishzida and]
        Dumuzi.'   M 125
Then the young [lord,] the lord Bilgames,
arose, it had been a [dream,] he shuddered, [it had been a deep
        sleep.]
[He rubbed] his eyes with his hands, there was desolate [silence.]
The dream . . . .
The dream . . . .   M 130
. . . .
      [The lord Bilgames, lord of] Kullab,
      . . . . . . the hero of the Shining Mountain,   N₄ obv. 10'
      [*lord* of Uruk,] smithy of the great gods,
[took] counsel with . . . . . . :   M 132
'By the life [of the mother who bore me,] the goddess Ninsun,

[my father, the pure] Lugalbanda,
[and my god Enki, the lord] Nudimmud!
Should I behave as if [awe]-struck on the knees of [Ninsun,] the
      mother who bore me?   M 135
. . . . . . a great mountain . . . ,
Namtar, who has no hands, who has no feet, who [knows not how]
      to spare a man,
my having . . . . . . [*I had a dream.*]
In that dream, the god Nudimmud opened *my* eyes: –

'In the assembly, the place of the gods' ceremonial,   M 140
the lord Bilgames having drawn nigh,
they said to him, lord Bilgames, on his account:
"Your [matter] – having travelled each and every road,
having fetched that unique cedar down from its mountain,
having smitten Huwawa in his forest,   M 145
having set up [monuments] for future days,
having founded [temples of the gods,]
you reached [Ziusudra in his abode!]
[The rites of Sumer,] forgotten since distant days of old,
[the rituals and customs – you] brought them down to the
      [land.]   M 150
The rites of hand-washing and mouth-washing you put in good
      order,
[*after* the] Deluge *it was you* made known all the *tasks* of the
      land . . .

       *   *   *

' "[Now,] Bilgames, [you are brought here for . . .]"   M 156
The will of Enlil to Enki [they *spoke*,]
to An and Enlil Enki [responded:]
"In those days, [in those far]-off days,
in those nights, [in those far]-off nights,   M 160
in those years, [in those far]-off years,
[after] the assembly had made the Deluge sweep over,
so we could destroy the seed of mankind,
in our midst a single man still lived,
Ziusudra, one of mankind, still lived!   M 165
From that time we swore by the life of heaven and the life of
      earth,

from that time we swore that mankind should not have life
      eternal.
And now we look on Bilgames:
despite his mother we cannot show him mercy!
Bilgames, in the form of his ghost, dead in the underworld,   M 170
shall be [the governor of the Netherworld,] chief of the shades!
[He will pass judgement,] he will render verdicts,
[what he says will be as weighty as the word of] Ningishzida and
      Dumuzi.
[Then the young lord, the lord] Bilgames . . . "   M 174

    *   *   *

' "The Dream God Sissig, son of Utu,   (M 180)
shall provide light for him in the Netherworld, the place of
      darkness.   N₁ v 5
Men, as many as are given names,
when their (funerary) statues are fashioned in future days,
the warrior-youths and onlookers shall make a semicircle around a
      doorway,
and in front of it wrestling matches and trials of strength will be
      conducted.
In the Month of Torches, the festival of ghosts,   N₁ v 10
without him being present light will not be provided before them."

'Great Mountain Enlil, the father of the gods,
conversed in the dream with the lord Bilgames:
"O Bilgames, I made your destiny a destiny of kingship, but I did
      not make it [a destiny] of eternal life.
For mankind, *whatever life it has*, be not sick at heart,   N₁ v 15
be not in despair, be not heart-stricken!
The bane of mankind is *thus come*, I have told you,
what (was fixed) when your navel-cord was cut is *thus come*, I have
      told you.
The darkest day of mortal man has caught up with you,
the solitary place of mortal man has caught up with you,   N₁ v 20
the flood-wave that cannot be breasted has caught up with you,
the battle that cannot be fled has caught up with you,
the combat that cannot be matched has caught up with you,
the fight that shows no pity has caught up with you!

But do not go down to the Great City with heart knotted (in
        anger),   M 190
let it be undone before Utu,
let it be unravelled like palm-fibre and *peeled* like an onion!
Go ahead, when the great Anunna gods sit down to the funerary
        banquet,   N$_1$ v 28
to the place where the *en*-priests lie, where the *lagar*-priests lie,
to where the *lumaḫ*-priests and *nindingir*-priestesses lie,   M 195
to where the *guda*-priests lie, where the linen-clad priests lie,
to where the *nindingir*-priestesses lie, where the 'true one' lies,
the place where your father is, and your grandfathers,
your mother, your sisters, your *siblings*,
your precious friend, your little brother,   M 200
your friend Enkidu, the young man your [companion!]   N$_4$ rev. 2′
(There) in the Great City, dwell governors and kings,
there chiefs of armies lie all alone,
there captains of troops lie all alone.
When in the Great City Aralli a man . . . ,   M 205
the man . . . . . . will not . . .
From the sister's house the sister will come to you,
from the *sibling*'s house the *sibling* will come to you,
your own will come to you, your precious one will come
        to you.   N$_4$ rev. 10′
The elders of your city will come to you,   M 210
      . . . . . . will come to you,
      . . . . . . will come to you,
      . . . . . . will come to you!
Be not in despair, be not heart-stricken,
for now [you will number] among the Anunna gods,
[you will be accounted] one of the lesser gods,
[you will act as the governor of the Netherworld,]
[you will pass judgement, you will render verdicts,]   M 215
[what you say] will be as weighty [as the word of Ningishzida and
        Dumuzi."]'   N$_1$ vi 1

After [the young lord, the lord] Bilgames,
[the lord of Kullab] had related that [dream,]
[the *counsellors*] to whom he related it
[to Bilgames] gave answer: N$_1$ vi 5

'[O lord Bilgames, what] is the cause of your tears?
For what reason is made . . . ?
[*The man death did not*] seize, the Mother Goddess has yet to bear
           him!
[*Since the seed of man first*] . . . came forth,
. . . . does not exist.   N₁ vi 10
Even . . . the wrestler can be caught in a *throw*-net!
A bird of the sky, once *fenced in* by the net, does not escape one's
           hand!
A fish of the deep sees the . . . *rushes* no more,
when the young fisherman casts his net, it is trapped within!
No man, whoever he may be, can ascend . . . from the midst of the
           Netherworld,   N₁ vi 15
from days of old whoever saw (such a thing)?
Another king there will never be, whose destiny is the same as
           yours.
Men, as many as are given names –
where is he, the man . . . whose destiny [is the same] as yours?
The governorship of the Netherworld [*is to be yours*,]
you, your ghost, [*will number among the Anunna gods*,]   N₁ vi 20
you will pass judgement, [you will render verdicts,]
[what you say will be as weighty as the word of Ningishzida and
           Dumuzi.]'

                    *   *   *

Like . . . his architect designed his tomb.   M 235
His head in a spin, his god, Enki,
showed him the place where the dream could be solved.
That vision, the king's dog solved it, no man solved it!

The lord levied a workforce in his city,
the herald sounded his horn in the lands: M 240
'O Uruk, arise! Breach open the river Euphrates!
O Kullab, arise! Empty the Euphrates of water!'
The levy of Uruk was a Deluge,
the levy of Kullab was a thick-settled fog!
Not even the middle of a single month had passed,   M 245
it was not five days, it was not ten days,
they breached the Euphrates, they emptied it of water,

its pebbles gazed on the Sun God in wonder.
Then in the bed of the Euphrates the earth cracked dry.
He built his tomb of stone,   M 250
he built its walls of stone,
he made the stone doors of its entrance.
The bar and threshold were hardest diorite,
the bolts were hardest diorite,
the beams were cast in gold,   M 255
into its . . . he moved a heavy block of stone,
        . . . he moved a heavy block of stone,
. . . he laid out . . . of every sort,
[so that] . . . . in future days,
. . . . [would not] discover,
. . . who searched would never discover its emplacement.   M 260
        [Thus the young lord, the lord] Bilgames
established in the midst of Uruk a secure *chamber*.

His beloved wife, his beloved child,   N₃ 1
his beloved senior wife and junior wife,
his beloved minstrel, steward and . . . ,
his beloved barber, [his beloved] . . . ,   (M 265)
[his beloved] attendants and servants,   N₃ 5
[his] beloved goods . . . ,
were laid down in their places, as if [attending] a palace-review in
        the midst of Uruk.
Bilgames, the son of the goddess Ninsun,
set out their audience-gifts for Ereshkigal,
set out their presents for Namtar,   N₃ 10
set out their surprises for Dimpikug,   (M 270)
set out their gifts for Bitti,
set out their gifts for Ningishzida and Dumuzi,
for Enki and Ninki, Enmul and Ninmul,
for Endukuga and Nindukuga,   N₃ 15
for Endashurimma and Nindashurimma   (M 275)
for Enutila and Enmesharra,
the mothers and fathers of Enlil,
for Shulpae, the lord of the table,
for Shakkan and Ninhursanga,   N₃ 20
for the Anunna gods of the Holy Mound,   (M 280)

for the Igigi gods of the Holy Mound,
for the dead [*en*-priests, for the] dead *lagar*-priests,
[for the dead] *lumah*-priests and *nindingir*-priestesses,
[for the dead] *guda*-priests, linen-clad priests and . . .   N₃ 25
The audience-gifts he . . . . . . ,   (M 285)
the fine . . . he . . . . . . ,
he set [out] their presents for . . .
He lay himself down on . . . overlaid with . . .
Bilgames, the son of the goddess Ninsun,   N₃ 30
where . . . . . . he poured (an offering of) water.

   *   *   *

. . . They took . . . inside (the tomb), they [sealed] its doorway.
They opened the Euphrates,   N₁ viii 3
its waters swept over.
his [*resting place*] the waters removed (from view).   N₁ viii 5
[Then for the] young [lord,] the lord Bilgames,
[*the people*] gnashed their teeth . . . ,
. . . they tore out [their hair.]
The people . . . of his city,
not putting their own . . . . . . ,
smeared their . . . with dirt.   M 295
Then for the young [lord], the lord Bilgames,
the mood despaired, the heart was stricken.

Men, as many as are given names,
their (funerary) statues have been fashioned since days of old,
and stationed in chapels in the temples of the gods: M 300
how their names are pronounced will never be forgotten!
The goddess Aruru, the older sister of Enlil,
for the sake of his name gave (men) offspring:
their statues have been fashioned since days of old, and (their
                names still) spoken in the land.
O Ereshkigal, mother of Ninazu, sweet is your praise!   M 305

Another manuscript concludes differently:

The . . . of his . . . , ceaseless in the care of Enlil,
O Bilgames, son of the goddess Ninsun,
. . . offshoot . . . , a king who matched him . . . was never born, N₃ 40
. . . cannot be found, . . . does not exist,
O Bilgames, lord of Kullab, sweet is your praise!

Appendix:
From Tablet to Translation

As with any work of ancient Mesopotamian literature, the translation of the Gilgamesh epic from the original manuscripts is a more complex task than most translating. For one thing, for most literary compositions in Sumerian and Akkadian there is no ready-made established text such as the series of Oxford Classical Texts provides for Greek and Latin literature. The translator must make his own. This he can do in one of two ways: either by accepting as definitive the work of those previous editors who have read the original clay tablets and published pen-and-ink drawings of them, or by reading all the tablets for himself. In this book the vast majority of the Akkadian material – everything in Chapters 1–3 and much of Chapter 4 – has been translated from tablets read at first hand. The translations of the Sumerian poems in Chapter 5 rely for the most part on the eyes of others.

Second, whether the translator works from the tablets or from the drawings of others, such is the complexity of the cuneiform writing system that before he can translate he must decipher. Most of the hundreds of cuneiform signs commonly used by the scribes of ancient Mesopotamia can convey more than one sound – syllables or half-syllables – and many of them can also stand on their own for whole words or even several different words. Some signs express neither sounds nor words but act as silent guides to reading, for example determining the class or number of a noun. So the would-be reader of any clay tablet must first decide how any given sign is to be read, whether as a word (and if so, which word), or as a syllable or half-syllable (and if so, which syllable or half-syllable), or as a silent determinative. In practice this is easier than it sounds, because years of experience in reading languages written in cuneiform script teach the Assyriologist which spellings are likely and which are not.

Also standing in the way of the translator is the intrinsic difficulty of how one interprets languages that are so long dead. With Sumerian there are still many, many difficulties that hinder our comprehension. Akkadian is more easily grasped and better understood, but even so there are some words whose meaning is still unknown.

A fourth problem is the nature of the material on which the ancient texts are written. Unlike other ancient writing materials, such as papyrus, parchment, wax and wood, clay is very durable. However, there are very few clay tablets that are not broken or damaged in some way. Even a tablet of fired clay will disintegrate if treated roughly enough. We know that some legal tablets, especially deeds of sale, were baked hard to act as permanent records and that such documents had to be forcibly smashed if they became invalid or outdated. The destruction of a fired tablet would take considerable force. Less violence is needed to destroy the writing on the surface of an unbaked tablet. Time itself was one enemy. Old tablets still in use were sometimes slightly damaged, so that a scribe who recopied the text inscribed on one might be obliged to annotate the new tablet in places with the words 'break' or '*x* lines destroyed'. Accidents could speed up the decay wrought by time. The collapse of a roof or wall might have serious consequences for tablets kept in the building if it brought down the shelves of a library or smashed the large pots in which business archives were commonly stored. An invading army could wreak similar destruction when sacking a city and pillaging its buildings. It was not only the Crusaders who destroyed libraries. Many tablets were thrown away intentionally in antiquity, or used as a kind of hardcore in making new floors or mud-brick benches. Naturally these tablets are among the worst preserved.

Even while buried beneath the surface of ruin mounds in collapsed buildings or in rubbish dumps, unbaked tablets are susceptible to damage of a different kind. Many is the text that bears the scar of an earthworm passing by – or, on occasion, even through. And, of course, the excavation of tablets, licit or illicit, brings further problems. Clay tablets can be difficult to distinguish from the surrounding matrix of crumbled mud brick, mud plaster and other debris, so that many bear the scars of pick and trowel. Even a perfectly excavated tablet can become a sorry mess if it has absorbed the salts that are present in the high ground-water of lower Mesopotamia. Unless the work of conservation is timely and well done, the salts in the drying tablet can destroy a tablet's surface and body most effectively. One or several of these kinds of damage can severely reduce the legibility of a tablet.

This particular problem, of broken tablets and damaged texts, is often alleviated by the existence of multiple manuscripts, that is, copies of the same text on different tablets. Where one manuscript is broken or illegible, another sometimes comes to the rescue.

A problem of a different order that besets the translator – one already signalled in the introduction – is that there are many gaps in these ancient poems that are yet to be filled, and more places where what text we do have is in an incomplete state of preservation. The translation of fragmentary passages is often necessarily uncertain, so that the discovery of a new tablet can sometimes radically alter our understanding of the episode in question.

Leaving aside the difficulties raised by holes in the text, the purpose of this appendix is to show how the Assyriologist attempts to overcome the first four obstacles outlined above, how despite the problems of legibility, decipherment, lexicon and textual pioneering that beset him he goes about recovering the text and making a translation. As examples of the procedures involved I have taken three passages of the Babylonian epic: five lines from Tablet III which describe Ninsun's adoption of Enkidu (a), seven lines from Tablet X which relate Shiduri's apprehensive reaction on sighting the wandering Gilgamesh (b), and six lines of Tablet XI which recount the onset of the storm that brought the Deluge (c).

Ideally, the first step in making a translation is the examination of the original manuscripts at first hand. Two tablets are witness to passage (a), to which I give the sigla MSS M and aa. MS M comes from the royal libraries assembled at Nineveh in Assyria by King Ashurbanipal and thus dates to the middle of the seventh century BC (Fig. 26). It is now in the British Museum. The piece which supplies text for passage (a) is made up of three separate pieces glued together, which form the right-hand half of a typical first-millennium Gilgamesh tablet, broader than it is high and divided on each side into three columns of text, making six in all. Probably the tablet was already smashed in antiquity, for the three pieces that make up its right-hand part were excavated separately, one by Austen Henry Layard and Hormuzd Rassam in 1850 or 1853, one by George Smith in 1874 and one by Rassam on his return to Nineveh early in 1878. The first and last were joined to each other by Reginald Campbell Thompson

of six columns. The three pieces were excavated as seven different fragments, found variously by Layard and Rassam in 1850 and 1853, Smith in 1874 and Rassam in 1878. Though George Smith was responsible for joining two of the seven fragments in the early 1870s the piece he himself brought back from Assyria remained unidentified until quite recently: it was joined to the assemblage by W. G. Lambert in 1963. MS f, which supplies the ends of lines missing from MS K, is made up of three joining fragments from near the top left-hand corner of a broad tablet written at Babylon early in the third century BC (Fig. 11 on page 87). The fragments were excavated by local people in the late 1870s and were purchased by Rassam and other agents of the British Museum between 1877 and 1880 as parts of three separate consignments totalling about 2,700 pieces. These Babylonian tablets, whose number was soon swollen by the acquisition of many tens of thousands of further fragments, received far less attention in the Museum than the Assyrian libraries of Ashurbanipal, and it was not until the 1950s and 1960s that the pieces of MS f were identified, joined and published.

Three tablets are extant for passage (c), MSS C, J and T. They are all from Ashurbanipal's libraries and are kept in the British Museum, where MS J is exhibited in the Mesopotamian gallery.* All are parts of broad tablets of six columns. Two of the three were already known to George Smith in the early 1870s (MSS C and J). MS C was rebuilt by him from some seventeen small fragments. Sixteen of these had been found by Layard and Rassam, but Smith's own excavations at Nineveh later added a further fragment. Much of the surface of the obverse is still missing. MS J is a large fragment comprising the right-hand part of a similar tablet. The bottom edge of this tablet was

---

*For reasons of economy the manuscripts of passage (c), which are much better known than those of passages (a) and (b), are not illustrated here. A photograph of the reverse of MS C (British Museum tablet WA K 2252+2602+3321+4486+Sm 1881) is reproduced in the British Museum booklet, *The Babylonian Story of the Deluge and the Epic of Gilgamesh*, ed. C. J. Gadd (London: British Museum, 1929), p. 32. Photographs of the famous right-hand fragment of MS J (WA K 3375) have been much reproduced; for the obverse consult Henrietta McCall, *Mesopotamian Myths* (London: British Museum Publications, 1990), p. 20, for the reverse see Dominique Collon, *Ancient Near Eastern Art* (London: British Museum Publications, 1995), p. 30. A photograph of the part of MS T that is witness to passage (c) (WA Sm 2131+2196+Rm II 383+390+82-5-22, 316) can be found in John Gardner and John Maier, *Gilgamesh* (New York: Vintage Books, 1985), obverse and reverse on pp. 276–7 (top right) respectively.

vitrified by the intense heat generated when the citadel of Nineveh burned in 612 BC. The fragment was found by Layard and Rassam. A smaller piece also badly vitrified, that probably represents the same tablet's top left-hand corner, was recovered by Rassam more than twenty-five years later, in 1878. MS T was pieced together later from nine different pieces, most of which were excavated in the 1870s and early 1880s by Smith and Rassam and identified in the late 1880s by T. G. Pinches, George Smith's successor at the British Museum, and Paul Haupt. In the absence of further fragments this manuscript is still in two disconnected parts.

Photographs of tablets have limitations that make them less than perfect for reading. The tablet and the writing inscribed on it are three-dimensional. A single photograph cannot supply the reader with the different angles of shadow that are needed to read cuneiform, and also cannot usually show clearly any text that runs over on to the edge of the tablet. To overcome these limitations it is conventional in Assyriology to make scale drawings, or 'copies', of tablets in pen and ink, such as the ones that have been used to illustrate some of the texts in this book. My copies of the sources for passages (a) and (b) are given on Figs. 27 and 28. These can be compared with the highlighted parts of the photographs on Fig. 26.

Passage (a) comes from the right-hand column of the reverse of both manuscripts, from near the top of the column on MS aa and near the bottom on MS M. The different distribution of the lines in question is because the division of lines into columns in tablets of the epic was not standardized, so that while tablets begin and end at fixed points in the poem, columns do not. So also passage (c) is found near the bottom of the middle column of the obverse on MSS C and J, but appears slightly higher up on MS T, nearer the middle of this column. Coming as it does from near the beginning of Tablet X, passage (b) is preserved towards the top of the first column on both manuscripts that are witness to it.

The first step towards translation is to decipher each line as it appears on the extant manuscripts by choosing the correct values of the preserved signs of cuneiform writing and rendering them one by one into roman script. This is called transliteration. Signs deciphered as syllabic are transliterated in lower-case type. Signs that are employed as word signs, or logograms (i.e. Sumerian words that stand for the equivalent words in Akkadian), are given in small capitals. Signs that

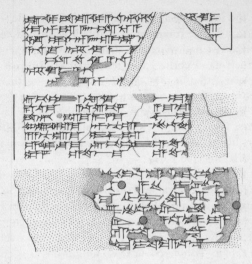

28 *Details from drawings of MSS M (top), K (middle) and*
f (bottom), illustrating passages (a) and (b).

act as determinatives are rendered in lower-case raised above the line.
Signs that are entirely lost through damage are placed within full
square brackets, as too are lost beginnings and ends of signs. Signs
otherwise damaged are enclosed in half square brackets, while those
that were erroneously omitted by the ancient scribe are restored
between angle brackets.

(a)   124   M   in-di it-ta-di a-na ti-ik-k[i ᵈ]en-ki-dù
      aa   [. . . . .] ana ti-ik-ki ᵈen-ki-d[ù]
      125   M   NIN.DINGIR.RAᵐᵉˢ il-qa-a [. . . . . -t]a
      aa   [. . . . . .i]l-ˈqa-a liˀ-qu-ˈtuˀ
      126   M   ù DUMU.MUNUS-DINGIRᵐᵉˢ ú-rab-b[a-a. . . . . . -t]a
      aa   [. . . . .] ú-r[ab-b]a-a tar-bu-ˈtaˀ
      127   M   a-na-ku ᵈen-ki-dù š[a . . .] / il-te-qé a-na [. . . . . .]
      aa   [. . . . . e]l-[q]a-a ana DUMU-ú-tu
      128   M   ᵈen-ki-dù ˈa-naˀ[. . .] / ᵈ[giš-g]ím-maš l[i- . . . . . .]
      aa   [. . . . -da]m-me-eq-ˈšuˀ

(b) 10 K   sa-bi-tum ana ru-qí ina-aṭ-ṭ[a- . . . .]

     f   [. . . . . -q]u i-na-ˈaṭ-ṭa-al'-šum-ˈma'

     11 K   uš-tam-ma-a <a>-na lìb-bi-šá a-ma-t[a . . . . .]

     f   [. . . . .]-šú a-mat i-qab-b[i]

     12 K   it-ti ra-ma-ni-šá-ma ši-i [. . . . .]

     f   [. . . . . -š]ú-ma ši-i im-ˈtal'-l[ik]

     13 K   mi-in-de-e-ma an-nu-ú mu-na-'-[. . . . .]

     f   [. . . . .]-ˈú' mu-na-ˈ''-ir AMᵐᵉ[ˢ]

     14 K   a-a-nu-um-ma i-ši-ra ina [. . . .]

     f   [. . . . . -i]r a-na KÁ-ia

     15 K   e-mur-šu-ma sa-bi-tum e-te-d[il . . . .]

     f   [. . . . . -b]it ˈi'-te-dil KÁ-š[ú]

     16 K   KÁ-šá e-te-dil-ma e-te-l[a-a . . . .]

     f   [. . . . . . . -di]l-ma i-te-la-<a> a-na ú-ˈrù'

(c) 101 C   ˈtar'-kul-li ᵈèr-ra-kal ú-n[a- . . .]

     J   [. . . . . -g]al i-na-as-saḫ

     T   [(absent, written in one line with 100)]

     102 C   il-lak ᵈnin-ˈurta' mi-iḫ-ra [. . . . .]

     J   [. . . . . -i]ḫ-ri ú-šar-di

     T   il-l[ak . . . .]

     103 C   ᵈa-nun-na-ki iš-šu-ú di-pa-[. . .]

     J   [. . . . .]-ˈú' di-pa-ra-a-ti

     T   [(absent, written in one line with 102)]

     104 C   ina nam-ri-ir-ri-šú-nu ú-ḫa-am-ma-ṭu m[a- . . .]

     J   [. . . . . -a]m-ma-ṭu ma-a-tum

     T   ina n[am- . . . .]

     105 C   ša ᵈIŠKUR šu-ḫar-ra-as-ˈsu' i-ba-'-ˈu'[. . .]

     J   [. . . . -b]a-'-ú AN-e

     106 C   [mi]m-ma nam-ru ana ˈda'-[ˈ-u]m-[mat] ut-te[r- .]

     J   [. . . .] ut-ter-ru

The sources for each line can then be combined to yield a composite
transliteration, with the alternative and inferior spellings, or variants,
that dissent from the composite transliteration collected at the end:

(a) Maa 124 in-di it-ta-di a-na ti-ik-ki ᵈen-ki-dù

     Maa 125 NIN.DINGIR.RAᵐᵉˢ il-qa-a ˈli'-qu-ˈtu'

     Maa 126 ù DUMU.MUNUS-DINGIRᵐᵉˢ ú-rab-ba-a tar-bu-ˈta'

Maa   127   a-na-ku ᵈen-ki-dù š[a . . . e]l-[q]a-a ana DUMU-ú-tu
Maa   128   ᵈen-ki-dù ⌈a-na⌉[. . .] ᵈ[giš-g]ím-maš l[i-da]m-me-
                eq-⌈ršu⌉

Variants. 125 M: [li-qu-t]a 127 M: il-te-qé

(b) Kf   10   sa-bi-tum ana ru-qí ina-aṭ-⌈ṭa-al⌉-šum-⌈ma⌉
     Kf   11   uš-tam-ma-a <a>-na lìb-bi-šá a-ma-t[a] i-qab-b[i]
     Kf   12   it-ti ra-ma-ni-šá-ma ši-i im-⌈tal⌉-l[ik]
     Kf   13   mi-in-de-e-ma an-nu-ú mu-na-'-ir AMᵐᵉ[š]
     Kf   14   a-a-nu-um-ma i-ši-ra a-na KÁ-ia
     Kf   15   e-mur-šu-ma sa-bi-tum e-te-dil KÁ-š[ú]
     Kf   16   KÁ-šá e-te-dil-ma e-te-l[a-a] a-na ú-⌈rù⌉

Variants. 10 f: ru-q]u i-na- 11 f:]-šú a-mat 12 f: ra-ma-ni-š]ú-ma 14 K: ina
f: i-ši-i]r 15 f: sa-b]it 'i'-te-dil 16 f: i-te-la-<a>

(c) CJ   101   ⌈tar⌉-kul-li ᵈèr-ra-kal i-na-as-saḫ
     CJT   102   il-lak ᵈnin-⌈urta⌉ mi-iḫ-ri ú-šar-di
     CJ   103   ᵈa-nun-na-ki iš-šu-ú di-pa-ra-a-ti
     CJT   104   ina nam-ri-ir-ri-šú-nu ú-ḫa-am-ma-ṭu ma-a-tum
     CJ   105   šá ᵈIŠKUR šu-ḫar-ra-as-⌈su⌉ i-ba-'-ú AN-e
     CJ   106   [mi]m-ma nam-ru ana ⌈da⌉-['-u]m-[mat] ut-ter-ru

Variants. 101 J: [ᵈèr-ra-g]al C: ú-n[a-as-saḫ] 102 C: mi-iḫ-ra 105 C: i-ba-'-u

Next, the syllable signs that render each word are joined up and
the Sumerian logograms are rendered into the equivalent words in
Akkadian. What emerges from the succession of signs is a text of
words. This procedure is conventionally known as transcription and
the result as normalized text. At this point any words still missing
can be suggested:

(a) III 124   *indī ittadi ana tikki Enkīdu*
         125   *ugbakkāti ilqâ liqûtu*
         126   *u mārāt-ilī urabbâ tarbûta*
         127   *anāku Enkīdu sh[a arammu(?) e]lqâ ana mārūtu*
         128   *Enkīdu ana [aḫḫūti(?) Gilg]āmesh l[ida]mmeqshu*

(b) X 10   *sābītum ana rūqi inaṭṭalshumma*
        11   *ushtammâ ana libbīsha amāta iqabbi*
        12   *itti ramānīshāma shī imtallik*

13   *mindēma annû muna"ir rīmī*
14   *ayyānumma īshira ana bābīya*
15   *ēmurshūma sābītum ētedil bābsha*
16   *bābsha ētedilma ētelâ ana ūru*

(c) XI 101   *tarkullī Errakal inassaḫ*
102   *illak Ninurta miḫrī ushardi*
103   *Anunnakkī isshû dipārāti*
104   *ina namrirrīshunu uḫammaṭū mātu*
105   *sha Adad shuḫarrassu ibā'u shamê*
106   *mimma namru ana da'ummati utterru*

Since the passages are poetry one must ask at this point, where are
the pauses and accents that mark the rhythm in such text? First, it is
possible to identify pairs of lines, or couplets, and punctuate accord-
ingly. Each line of poetry, or verse, can then be divided into three or
four smaller units, which comprise essentially a word or a word and
its adjunct or adjuncts. Sometimes in later compositions longer lines
can occur, of five or six units. In Babylonian poetry it seems that each
such unit is defined by a heavy beat, which falls on the syllable that
carries the principal stress. Verses of four units fall into two equal
halves either side of a caesura (|||). In this way we have a text that can
be recited in a manner that one hopes a Babylonian would recognize
(stressed syllables are underlined):

(a) III 124   *indī | ittadi || ana tikki | Enkīdu.*
125   *ugbakkāti | ilqâ | liqûtu,*
126   *u mārāt-ilī | urabbâ | tarbûta.*
127   *anāku | Enkīdu | sh[a arammu(?) || e]lqâ || ana mārūtu,*
128   *Enkidu || ana [aḫḫūti(?) || Gilg]āmesh |*
            l[ida]mmeqshu.

(b) X 10   *sābītum | ana rūqi | inaṭṭalshumma,*
11   *ushtammâ | ana libbīsha || amāta | iqabbi,*
12   *itti ramānīshāma | shī | imtallik:*
13   *mindēma | annû | muna"ir rīmī,*
14   *ayyānumma | īshira | ana bābīya.*
15   *ēmurshūma | sābītum || ētedil | bābsha,*
16   *bābsha | ētedilma || ētelâ | ana ūru.*

(c) XI 101   *tarkullī | Errakal | inassah̠,*
     102   *illak | Ninurta || mih̠rī | ushardi.*
     103   *Anunnakkī | ishshû | dipārāti,*
     104   *ina namrirrīshunu | uh̠ammaṭū | mātu.*
     105   *sha Adad | shuh̠arrassu || ibā'u | shamê* (or perhaps
                       trisyllabic *shamē'ē*),
     106   *mimma | namru || ana da'ummati | utterru.*

Notice in passing other poetic effects: in passage (a) the repeated
dental plosive consonants (*d, t*) in l. 124 contrast with the emphasis
on velar plosives (*g, k, q*) in l. 125. In passage (b) the slower rhythms
that mark Shiduri's pondering in ll. 12–14 give way in the following
couplet to a faster beat that suits her sudden haste. In (c) one observes
the repetition in l. 101 of the sequence of consonants *r-k-l*, the chiastic
construction of l. 102 (verb, noun; noun, verb), and the heavy allitera-
tion of the consonant *m* in ll. 104 and 106, a device which evokes the
thunder rumbling on the horizon and also heightens the tension like
a slow drum-roll.

   The texts thus established are now ready for translation into Eng-
lish:

(a)   She placed the symbols on Enkidu's neck.
        'The priestesses took in the foundling,   III 125
          and the Divine Daughters brought up the foster-child.
        Enkidu, whom [I *love*,] I take for my son,
          Enkidu in [*brotherhood*,] Gilgamesh shall favour him!'

(b)   As the tavern-keeper watched him in the distance,   X 10
        talking to herself she spoke a word,
          taking counsel in her own mind:
        'For sure this man is a hunter of wild bulls,
          but where does he come from, making straight for my gate?'
        Thus the tavern-keeper saw him, and barred her gate,   X 15
          barred her gate and went up on the roof.

(c)   The god Errakal was uprooting the mooring-poles,
          Ninurta, passing by, made the weirs overflow.
        The Anunnaki gods carried torches of fire,

scorching the country with brilliant flashes.
The stillness of the Storm God passed over the sky,   XI 105
and all that was bright then turned into darkness.

Glossary of Proper Nouns

ADAD The storm god, venerated as a supreme power especially in Syria and Lebanon, where in the epic he has a particular association with the Forest of Cedar.

AKKA King of Kish, possibly Gilgamesh's nephew.

AN 'Sky': the name of heaven in Sumerian, equals Anu in Babylonian.

ANSHAN An area of south-western Iran.

ANTU The wife of Anu, and at Uruk the mother of Ishtar.

ANU The father of the gods, the god of the sky, but also resident in Uruk, where he is Ishtar's father.

ANUNNA See Anunnaki.

ANUNNAKI A traditional name for one of the two divisions of the pantheon, in the later periods assigned to the gods of the Netherworld; see Igigi.

ARALLI A name of the Netherworld.

ARATTA A city-state far away in the highlands of Iran, traditionally a rival of Uruk.

ARURU Another name for Belet-ili, the Mother Goddess.

ASAKKU See Azag.

ATRA-HASIS 'Surpassing Wise': an epithet of Uta-napishti.

AYA Goddess of dawn, the bride of Shamash.

AZAG A demon.

BELET-ILI 'Lady of the Gods': the Mother Goddess, who created mankind with Ea, also known as Aruru. As Mother Earth she once enjoyed the attentions of Anu, the sky.

BELET-ṢERI 'Lady of the Desert': the scribe of the Netherworld, who keeps tally for Ereshkigal.

BIBBU Ereshkigal's butcher and cook.

BILGAMES 'The Ancestor is a Hero': an older form of the name Gilgamesh.

BIRHURTURRA One of Bilgames's personal guard. The reading and meaning of the name are uncertain.

BITTI Or Bidu, 'He opens!'. The gate-keeper of the Netherworld.

DIMPIKUG A Netherworld deity.

DUMUZI 'Steadfast Child': the Babylonian Tammuz, lover and husband of Ishtar, punished with annual death and descent to the Netherworld.

EA The god of the freshwater Ocean Below (*Apsû*). The wisest of the gods, he is adept in every skill and finds a solution to every problem. His expertise enabled the Mother Goddess to create mankind, whom he civilized and saved from the wrath of Enlil.

EANNA 'House of Heaven': the temple of the goddess Ishtar and the god Anu in the city of Uruk.

EBABBARA 'Shining House': the temple of Shamash at Larsa.

EKUR 'Mountain House': the temple of Enlil at Nippur.

ENGILUA Or Idengilua, a waterway of Uruk. Perhaps a variant form of Idurungal, the principal eastern branch of the river Euphrates.

ENKI The name of Ea in Sumerian.

ENKIDU 'Lord of the Pleasant Place': in the Babylonian tradition a wild man created by the gods as Gilgamesh's equal, in the Sumerian his favoured servant.

ENLIL 'Lord Wind': the divine ruler of Earth and its human inhabitants. Aided by Anu, Ea and the Mother Goddess he governs the cosmos. His cult-centre was Nippur. His ancestors counted as 'dead' gods, and dwelt in the Netherworld.

ENMEBARAGESI Apparently the elder sister of Gilgamesh, but in history an early ruler of Kish, and assumed to be male.

ERESHKIGAL 'Mistress of the Great Earth': the queen of the Netherworld.

ERIDU An ancient city in the far south of Babylonia, the cult-centre of Enki-Ea. Now Tell Abu Shahrein, south-west of Nasiriyah.

ERRAKAL A manifestation of Nergal as a god of wanton devastation.

ETANA A legendary king of Kish, who rode an eagle to heaven, but remained a mortal. In the afterlife he was, like Gilgamesh, an officer in the court of the Netherworld.

GANZIR The first of seven gates of the Netherworld.

GILGAMESH A legendary king of Uruk, son of a goddess but doomed to die. In the afterlife he became a judge in the Netherworld.

GIPAR The private chambers of Inanna in her temple Eanna.

GIRSU A city-state of eastern Babylonia, now Telloh, north of Nasiriyah.

HUMBABA The monstrous guardian of the Forest of Cedar, appointed by Enlil to protect its timber.

HUSHBISHA 'Its Fury is Fine': a member of Ereshkigal's court.

HUWAWA An old form of the name Humbaba.

IGIGI A traditional name for one of the two divisions of the pantheon, in the later periods assigned to the great gods of heaven; see Anunnaki.

INANNA 'Queen of Heaven': in Sumerian texts the name of Ishtar.

IRKALLA 'Great City': a name of the Netherworld, and also of its queen, the goddess Ereshkigal.

IRNINA A name given to the goddess Ishtar, but also a deity of the Netherworld.

ISHTAR Deity of the city of Uruk, the goddess of sexual love and war, daughter of Anu. Sometimes she is a mature woman, sometimes an impetuous young virgin. In heaven she is Venus, daughter of the Moon God.

ISHULLANU 'Shorty': a cultivator of dates, one of Ishtar's former lovers.

Publication of the Sources of the
Babylonian Epic

COMPREHENSIVE EDITIONS

i. George Smith, *The Chaldean Account of Genesis* (London: Sampson Low, Marston, Searle and Rivington, 1876), pp. 167–295. Translation

ii. Paul Haupt, *Das babylonische Nimrodepos* (Leipzig: J. C. Hinrichs, 1884 and 1891). Cuneiform text

iii. P. Jensen, *Assyrisch-babylonische Mythen und Epen* (Berlin: Keilinschriftliche Bibliothek 6/1; Reuther and Reichard, 1900; reprinted Amsterdam: Celibus, 1970), pp. 116—265. Edition and translation

iv. R. Campbell Thompson, *The Epic of Gilgamish* (Oxford: Clarendon Press, 1930; reprinted New York: AMS Press, 1995). Cuneiform text and edition

v. A. R. George: *The Babylonian Gilgameš Epic* (Oxford: Oxford University Press, in preparation). Cuneiform text, edition, translation and commentary

STUDENT READER

vi. Simo Parpola: *The Standard Babylonian Epic of Gilgamesh* (State Archives of Assyria Cuneiform Texts 1; Helsinki: Neo-Assyrian Text Corpus Project, 1997). Standardized composite cuneiform text, transliteration, glossary

The following is a list of publications of tablets and fragments that have been identified since 1930 as sources for the Babylonian epic – in other words, pieces that were not included when the sources for the epic were last collected in one book. Except where otherwise identified, all are manuscripts of the standard version. References are in chronological order, and usually to places of first publication only.

1. Erich Ebeling, *Keilschrifttexte aus Assur religiösen Inhalts* 2 (Wissenschaftliche Veröffentlichungen der Deutschen Orient-Gesellschaft 34; Leipzig: J. C. Hinrichs, 1923), nos. 319–20

2. Adam Falkenstein, *Literarische Keilschrifttexte aus Uruk* (Berlin: Staatlichen Museen Vorderasiatische Abteilung, 1931), nos. 39–40

3. Ernst F. Weidner, 'Ein neues Bruchstück der XII. Tafel des Gilgameš-Epos',

Archiv für Orientforschung 10 (Graz: Selbstverlag Weidner, 1936), pp. 363–65

4. Alexander Heidel, 'A Neo-Babylonian Gilgamesh fragment', *Journal of Near Eastern Studies* 11 (Chicago: University of Chicago Press, 1952), pp. 140–43

5. O. R. Gurney, 'Two fragments of the Epic of Gilgamesh from Sultantepe', *Journal of Cuneiform Studies* 8 (New Haven, Conn.: American Schools of Oriental Research, 1954), pp. 87–95; also in idem and J. J. Finkelstein, *The Sultantepe Tablets* 1 (London: British Institute of Archaeology at Ankara, 1957), nos. 14–15

6. Theo Bauer, 'Ein viertes altbabylonisches Fragment des Gilgamesch-Epos', *Journal of Near Eastern Studies* 16 (Chicago: University of Chicago Press, 1957), pp. 254–72; recopied by Samuel Greengus, *Old Babylonian Tablets from Ishchali and Vicinity* (Istanbul: Nederlands Historisch-Archaeologisch Instituut, 1979), no. 277. The Ishchali tablet

7. J. J. A. van Dijk: 'Textes divers du musée de Baghdad, II', *Sumer* 13 (Baghdad: Directorate-General of Antiquities, 1957), Pl. 12; also in idem, *Cuneiform Texts of Varying Content* (Texts in the Iraq Museum 9; Leiden: Brill, 1976), no. 43. Tell Harmal tablet Ha[1]

8. J. J. A. van Dijk: 'Textes divers du musée de Bagdad III', *Sumer* 15 (Baghdad, 1959), Pls. 3–4, 13–15; also in idfem, *Cuneiform Texts of Varying Content* (TIM 9), no. 45. Tell Harmal tablet Ha[2]

9. A. Goetze and S. Levy, 'Fragment of the Gilgamesh epic from Megiddo', *'Atiqot* 2 (Jerusalem: Department of Antiquities, 1959), pp. 121–28. The Megiddo tablet

10. R. Frankena, 'Nouveaux fragments de la sixième tablette de l'Épopée de Gilgameš', in P. Garelli (ed.), *Gilgameš et sa légende* (Paris: Klincksieck, 1960), pp. 113–22

11. W. G. Lambert, 'Gilgameš in religious, historical and omen texts and the historicity of Gilgameš. Appendix', in Garelli, *Gilgameš et sa légende*. pp. 52–55

12. D. J. Wiseman, 'Additional Neo-Babylonian Gilgamesh fragments', in Garelli, *Gilgameš et sa légende*, pp. 123–35

13. A. R. Millard, 'Gilgamesh X: a new fragment', *Iraq* 26 (London: British School of Archaeology in Iraq, 1964), pp. 99–105. Part of the Old Babylonian tablet reportedly from Sippar

14. W. G. Lambert and A. R. Millard, *Babylonian Literary Texts* (Cuneiform Texts from Babylonian Tablets 46; London: British Museum, 1965), nos. 16–35

15. C. J. Gadd and S. N. Kramer, *Literary and Religious Texts, Second Part* (Ur Excavations Texts 6/2; London: British Museum, Philadelphia: University Museum, 1966), no. 394; also Gadd, 'Some contributions to the Gilgamesh epic', *Iraq* 28 (London: British School of Archaeology in Iraq, 1966), pp. 105–21. The Ur tablet

16. Benno Landsberger, 'Zur vierten und siebenten Tafel des Gilgamesch-Epos', *Revue d'assyriologie et d'archéologie orientale* 62 (Paris: Presses Universitaires

228 Publication of the Sources of the Babylonian Epic

de France, 1968), pp. 128–30. Transliteration of British Museum tablet WAK
9196 (standard version)

17. Egbert von Weiher, 'Ein Fragment des Gilgameš-Epos aus Uruk', *Zeitschrift
für Assyriologie und vorderasiatische Archaëologie* 62 (Berlin and New York:
Walter de Gruyter, 1972), pp. 222–29; also in idem, *Spätbabylonische Texte aus
Uruk* 2 (Ausgrabungen der Deutschen Forschungsgemeinschaft in Uruk-Warka
10; Berlin: Gebr. Mann, 1983), no. 30

18. D. J. Wiseman, 'A Gilgamesh epic fragment from Nimrud', *Iraq* 37 (London:
British School of Archaeology in Iraq, 1975), pp. 157–61; also in idem and
J. A. Black, *Literary Texts from the Temple of Nabû* (Cuneiform Texts from
Nimrud 4; London: British School of Archaeology in Iraq, 1996), no. 199

19. J. van Dijk, *Cuneiform Texts of Varying Content* (Texts in the Iraq Museum
9; Leiden: Brill, 1976), no. 46. A tablet in Baghdad, of unknown provenance

20. Egbert von Weiher, 'Ein Fragment der 5. Tafel des Gilgameš-Epos aus Uruk',
Baghdader Mitteilungen 11 (Berlin: Gebr. Mann, 1980), pp. 90–105; also in
idem, *Spätbabylonische Texte aus Uruk* 3 (ADFU 12; Berlin: Gebr. Mann,
1988), no. 59

21. Jeffrey H. Tigay, *The Evolution of the Gilgamesh Epic* (Philadelphia: Univer-
sity of Pennsylvania Press, 1982), pp. 266–67, 297. The Nippur exercise tablet

22. Irving L. Finkel, 'Necromancy in ancient Mesopotamia. Appendix', *Archiv
für Orientforschung* 29–30 (Horn: Ferdinand Berger, 1984), pp. 16–17

23. R. Borger, 'Einige Texte religiösen Inhalts IV. Ein neues Gilgameš-Fragment',
Orientalia 54 (Rome: Pontificium Institutum Biblicum, 1985), pp. 25–26

24. Daniel Arnaud, *Recherches au pays d'Aštata. Emar* VI.1–4 (Paris: Éditions
Recherche sur les Civilisations, 1985–87), Nos. 781–82. The fragments from
Emar

25. Jan van Dijk, *Literarische Texte aus Babylon* (Vorderasiatische Schriftdenk-
mäler der Staatlichen Museen 24; Berlin: Akademie-Verlag, 1987), nos. 95–96

26. Gernot Wilhelm, 'Neue akkadische Gilgameš-Fragmente aus Hattusa',
Zeitschrift für Assyriologie ... 78 (Berlin: Walter de Gruyter, 1988), pp. 99–
121; also in Heinrich Otten and Christel Rüster, *Die hurritisch-hethitische
Bilingue und weitere Texte aus der Oberstadt* (Keilschrifttexte aus Boghazköi
32; Berlin: Gebr. Mann, 1990), nos. 128–33. The fragments from Hattusa, Bo[1]

27. Egbert von Weiher, *Uruk. Spätbabylonische Texte aus dem Planquadrat U
18* (Ausgrabungen in Uruk-Warka Endberichte 12; Mainz: Philipp von Zabern,
1993), nos. 122–24

28. D. J. Wiseman and J. A. Black, *Literary Texts from the Temple of Nabû*
(Cuneiform Texts from Nimrud 4; London: British School of Archaeology in
Iraq, 1996), no. 153

29. T. Kwasman, 'A new join to the Epic of Gilgameš Tablet I', *Nouvelles
Assyriologiques Brèves et Utilitaires* 1998 (Paris: Société pour l'Étude du
Proche-Orient Ancien), no. 99

30. A. Cavigneaux and J. Renger, 'Ein altbabylonischer Gilgameš-Text aus
Nippur', forthcoming 1999. Translations in French and German are already
published. The Nippur school tablet

READ MORE IN PENGUIN

In every corner of the world, on every subject under the sun, Penguin represents quality and variety – the very best in publishing today.

For complete information about books available from Penguin – including Puffins, Penguin Classics and Arkana – and how to order them, write to us at the appropriate address below. Please note that for copyright reasons the selection of books varies from country to country.

In the United Kingdom: Please write to *Dept. EP, Penguin Books Ltd, Bath Road, Harmondsworth, West Drayton, Middlesex UB7 ODA*

In the United States: Please write to *Consumer Sales, Penguin Putnam Inc., P.O. Box 12289 Dept. B, Newark, New Jersey 07101-5289*. VISA and MasterCard holders call 1-800-788-6262 to order Penguin titles

In Canada: Please write to *Penguin Books Canada Ltd, 10 Alcorn Avenue, Suite 300, Toronto, Ontario M4V 3B2*

In Australia: Please write to *Penguin Books Australia Ltd, P.O. Box 257, Ringwood, Victoria 3134*

In New Zealand: Please write to *Penguin Books (NZ) Ltd, Private Bag 102902, North Shore Mail Centre, Auckland 10*

In India: Please write to *Penguin Books India Pvt Ltd, 11 Community Centre, Panchsheel Park, New Delhi 110017*

In the Netherlands: Please write to *Penguin Books Netherlands bv, Postbus 3507, NL-1001 AH Amsterdam*

In Germany: Please write to *Penguin Books Deutschland GmbH, Metzlerstrasse 26, 60594 Frankfurt am Main*

In Spain: Please write to *Penguin Books S. A., Bravo Murillo 19, 1° B, 28015 Madrid*

In Italy: Please write to *Penguin Italia s.r.l., Via Benedetto Croce 2, 20094 Corsico, Milano*

In France: Please write to *Penguin France, Le Carré Wilson, 62 rue Benjamin Baillaud, 31500 Toulouse*

In Japan: Please write to *Penguin Books Japan Ltd, Kaneko Building, 2-3-25 Koraku, Bunkyo-Ku, Tokyo 112*

In South Africa: Please write to *Penguin Books South Africa (Pty) Ltd, Private Bag X14, Parkview, 2122 Johannesburg*

READ MORE IN PENGUIN

A CHOICE OF CLASSICS

Matthew Arnold	**Selected Prose**
Jane Austen	**Emma**
	Lady Susan/The Watsons/Sanditon
	Mansfield Park
	Northanger Abbey
	Persuasion
	Pride and Prejudice
	Sense and Sensibility
William Barnes	**Selected Poems**
Mary Braddon	**Lady Audley's Secret**
Anne Brontë	**Agnes Grey**
	The Tenant of Wildfell Hall
Charlotte Brontë	**Jane Eyre**
	Juvenilia: 1829–35
	The Professor
	Shirley
	Villette
Emily Brontë	**Complete Poems**
	Wuthering Heights
Samuel Butler	**Erewhon**
	The Way of All Flesh
Lord Byron	**Don Juan** .
	Selected Poems
Lewis Carroll	**Alice's Adventures in Wonderland**
	The Hunting of the Snark
Thomas Carlyle	**Selected Writings**
Arthur Hugh Clough	**Selected Poems**
Wilkie Collins	**Armadale**
	The Law and the Lady
	The Moonstone
	No Name
	The Woman in White
Charles Darwin	**The Origin of Species**
	Voyage of the Beagle
Benjamin Disraeli	**Coningsby**
	Sybil

READ MORE IN PENGUIN

A CHOICE OF CLASSICS

Charles Dickens	**American Notes for General Circulation**
	Barnaby Rudge
	Bleak House
	The Christmas Books (in two volumes)
	David Copperfield
	Dombey and Son
	Great Expectations
	Hard Times
	Little Dorrit
	Martin Chuzzlewit
	The Mystery of Edwin Drood
	Nicholas Nickleby
	The Old Curiosity Shop
	Oliver Twist
	Our Mutual Friend
	The Pickwick Papers
	Pictures from Italy
	Selected Journalism 1850–1870
	Selected Short Fiction
	Sketches by Boz
	A Tale of Two Cities
George Eliot	**Adam Bede**
	Daniel Deronda
	Felix Holt
	Middlemarch
	The Mill on the Floss
	Romola
	Scenes of Clerical Life
	Silas Marner
Fanny Fern	**Ruth Hall**
Elizabeth Gaskell	**Cranford/Cousin Phillis**
	The Life of Charlotte Brontë
	Mary Barton
	North and South
	Ruth
	Sylvia's Lovers
	Wives and Daughters

READ MORE IN PENGUIN

A CHOICE OF CLASSICS

Edward Gibbon	**The Decline and Fall of the Roman Empire** (in three volumes)
	Memoirs of My Life
George Gissing	**New Grub Street**
	The Odd Women
William Godwin	**Caleb Williams**
	Concerning Political Justice
Thomas Hardy	**Desperate Remedies**
	The Distracted Preacher and Other Tales
	Far from the Madding Crowd
	Jude the Obscure
	The Hand of Ethelberta
	A Laodicean
	The Mayor of Casterbridge
	A Pair of Blue Eyes
	The Return of the Native
	Selected Poems
	Tess of the d'Urbervilles
	The Trumpet-Major
	Two on a Tower
	Under the Greenwood Tree
	The Well-Beloved
	The Woodlanders
George Lyell	**Principles of Geology**
Lord Macaulay	**The History of England**
Henry Mayhew	**London Labour and the London Poor**
George Meredith	**The Egoist**
	The Ordeal of Richard Feverel
John Stuart Mill	**The Autobiography**
	On Liberty
	Principles of Political Economy
William Morris	**News from Nowhere and Other Writings**
John Henry Newman	**Apologia Pro Vita Sua**
Margaret Oliphant	**Miss Marjoribanks**
Robert Owen	**A New View of Society and Other Writings**
Walter Pater	**Marius the Epicurean**
John Ruskin	**Unto This Last and Other Writings**

READ MORE IN PENGUIN

A CHOICE OF CLASSICS

Walter Scott	**The Antiquary**
	Heart of Mid-Lothian
	Ivanhoe
	Kenilworth
	The Tale of Old Mortality
	Rob Roy
	Waverley
Robert Louis Stevenson	**Kidnapped**
	Dr Jekyll and Mr Hyde and Other Stories
	In the South Seas
	The Master of Ballantrae
	Selected Poems
	Weir of Hermiston
William Makepeace Thackeray	**The History of Henry Esmond**
	The History of Pendennis
	The Newcomes
	Vanity Fair
Anthony Trollope	**Barchester Towers**
	Can You Forgive Her?
	Doctor Thorne
	The Eustace Diamonds
	Framley Parsonage
	He Knew He Was Right
	The Last Chronicle of Barset
	Phineas Finn
	The Prime Minister
	The Small House at Allington
	The Warden
	The Way We Live Now
Oscar Wilde	**Complete Short Fiction**
Mary Wollstonecraft	**A Vindication of the Rights of Woman**
	Mary and Maria (includes Mary Shelley's Matilda)
Dorothy and William Wordsworth	**Home at Grasmere**

READ MORE IN PENGUIN

A CHOICE OF CLASSICS

Aeschylus	**The Oresteian Trilogy**
	Prometheus Bound/The Suppliants/Seven against Thebes/The Persians
Aesop	**The Complete Fables**
Ammianus Marcellinus	**The Later Roman Empire (AD 354–378)**
Apollonius of Rhodes	**The Voyage of Argo**
Apuleius	**The Golden Ass**
Aristophanes	**The Knights/Peace/The Birds/The Assemblywomen/Wealth**
	Lysistrata/The Acharnians/The Clouds
	The Wasps/The Poet and the Women/ The Frogs
Aristotle	**The Art of Rhetoric**
	The Athenian Constitution
	Classic Literary Criticism
	De Anima
	The Metaphysics
	Ethics
	Poetics
	The Politics
Arrian	**The Campaigns of Alexander**
Marcus Aurelius	**Meditations**
Boethius	**The Consolation of Philosophy**
Caesar	**The Civil War**
	The Conquest of Gaul
Cicero	**Murder Trials**
	The Nature of the Gods
	On the Good Life
	On Government
	Selected Letters
	Selected Political Speeches
	Selected Works
Euripides	**Alcestis/Iphigenia in Tauris/Hippolytus**
	The Bacchae/Ion/The Women of Troy/ Helen
	Medea/Hecabe/Electra/Heracles
	Orestes and Other Plays

READ MORE IN PENGUIN

A CHOICE OF CLASSICS

Hesiod/Theognis	**Theogony/Works and Days/Elegies**
Hippocrates	**Hippocratic Writings**
Homer	**The Iliad**
	The Odyssey
Horace	**Complete Odes and Epodes**
Horace/Persius	**Satires and Epistles**
Juvenal	**The Sixteen Satires**
Livy	**The Early History of Rome**
	Rome and Italy
	Rome and the Mediterranean
	The War with Hannibal
Lucretius	**On the Nature of the Universe**
Martial	**Epigrams**
	Martial in English
Ovid	**The Erotic Poems**
	Heroides
	Metamorphoses
	The Poems of Exile
Pausanias	**Guide to Greece (in two volumes)**
Petronius/Seneca	**The Satyricon/The Apocolocyntosis**
Pindar	**The Odes**
Plato	**Early Socratic Dialogues**
	Gorgias
	The Last Days of Socrates (Euthyphro/ The Apology/Crito/Phaedo)
	The Laws
	Phaedrus and Letters VII and VIII
	Philebus
	Protagoras/Meno
	The Republic
	The Symposium
	Theaetetus
	Timaeus/Critias
Plautus	**The Pot of Gold and Other Plays**
	The Rope and Other Plays

READ MORE IN PENGUIN

A CHOICE OF CLASSICS

Pliny	**The Letters of the Younger Pliny**
Pliny the Elder	**Natural History**
Plotinus	**The Enneads**
Plutarch	**The Age of Alexander (Nine Greek Lives)**
	Essays
	The Fall of the Roman Republic (Six Lives)
	The Makers of Rome (Nine Lives)
	Plutarch on Sparta
	The Rise and Fall of Athens (Nine Greek Lives)
Polybius	**The Rise of the Roman Empire**
Procopius	**The Secret History**
Propertius	**The Poems**
Quintus Curtius Rufus	**The History of Alexander**
Sallust	**The Jugurthine War/The Conspiracy of Cataline**
Seneca	**Dialogues and Letters**
	Four Tragedies/Octavia
	Letters from a Stoic
	Seneca in English
Sophocles	**Electra/Women of Trachis/Philoctetes/Ajax**
	The Theban Plays
Suetonius	**The Twelve Caesars**
Tacitus	**The Agricola/The Germania**
	The Annals of Imperial Rome
	The Histories
Terence	**The Comedies (The Girl from Andros/The Self-Tormentor/The Eunuch/Phormio/The Mother-in-Law/The Brothers)**
Thucydides	**History of the Peloponnesian War**
Virgil	**The Aeneid**
	The Eclogues
	The Georgics
Xenophon	**Conversations of Socrates**
	Hiero the Tyrant
	A History of My Times
	The Persian Expedition

READ MORE IN PENGUIN

A CHOICE OF CLASSICS

Basho	**The Narrow Road to the Deep North** **On Love and Barley**
Cao Xueqin	**The Story of the Stone** also known as **The Dream of The Red Chamber** (in five volumes)
Confucius	**The Analects**
Khayyam	**The Ruba'iyat of Omar Khayyam**
Lao Tzu	**Tao Te Ching**
Li Po/Tu Fu	**Poems**
Shikibu Murasaki	**The Tale of Genji**
Sarma	**The Pañćatantra**
Sei Shonagon	**The Pillow Book of Sei Shonagon**
Somadeva	**Tales from the Kathasaritsagara**
Wu Ch'Eng-En	**Monkey**

ANTHOLOGIES AND ANONYMOUS WORKS

The Bhagavad Gita
Buddhist Scriptures
Chinese Love Poetry
The Dhammapada
Hindu Myths
Japanese No Dramas
The Koran
The Laws of Manu
Poems from the Sanskrit
Poems of the Late T'Ang
The Rig Veda
Speaking of Siva
Tales from the Thousand and One Nights
The Upanishads

READ MORE IN PENGUIN

A CHOICE OF CLASSICS